THE EVERYTHING
Learning Russian Book

Dear Reader,

I clearly remember my very first encounter with the English language: it was in my elementary school in Moscow, where fifteen classmates and I learned the ABCs and practiced pronunciation of English words for colors, animals, and plants. How amazing it was to realize that the world, and even its most familiar objects and notions, could feel so surprisingly different when put in the milieu of another language! As my enchantment with English grew, so did my sense of appreciation for Russian, my first language. Through the study of English, I became more attuned to the beautiful melody, intricate grammatical structures, and cultural imagery of the Russian language. It is my hope that you, too, will experience a sense of wonder and discovery as you begin learning Russian.

Writing this book was not an easy task. It took hours of research and writing, and many a night was spent sleepless at my laptop. What kept me going was my desire to share with you the language and culture that mean so much to me. My goal for this book was to ignite an interest in all things Russian and to provide you with the basic communicative tools so that you can begin your own personal exploration of Russian culture. Reading about Russia in English might be a good starting point, but it is only through the study of the language that you will be able to establish an intimate connection to Russian culture and gain a deep understanding and appreciation of what it is that binds it together.

Thank you for considering this book, but more importantly, thank you for your interest in the language and culture that I dearly love and will always call my spiritual home. I hope that your journey into to the world of the Russian language will be both educational and fun and that this book will be your first step in a life-long engagement with Russian culture.

Всего самого хорошего (All the best),

Julia Stakhnevich

Welcome to the EVERYTHING® Series!

These handy, accessible books give you all you need to tackle a difficult project, gain a new hobby, comprehend a fascinating topic, prepare for an exam, or even brush up on something you learned back in school but have since forgotten.

You can choose to read an *Everything®* book from cover to cover or just pick out the information you want from our four useful boxes: e-questions, e-facts, e-alerts, and e-ssentials.

We give you everything you need to know on the subject, but throw in a lot of fun stuff along the way, too.

We now have more than 400 *Everything®* books in print, spanning such wide-ranging categories as weddings, pregnancy, cooking, music instruction, foreign language, crafts, pets, New Age, and so much more. When you're done reading them all, you can finally say you know *Everything®*!

QUESTIONS?
Answers to
common questions

FACTS
Important snippets
of information

ALERTS!
Urgent
warnings

ESSENTIALS
Quick
handy tips

PUBLISHER Karen Cooper

DIRECTOR OF ACQUISITIONS AND INNOVATION Paula Munier

MANAGING EDITOR, EVERYTHING SERIES Lisa Laing

COPY CHIEF Casey Ebert

ACQUISITIONS EDITOR Lisa Laing

DEVELOPMENT EDITOR Elizabeth Kassab

EDITORIAL ASSISTANT Hillary Thompson

Visit the entire Everything® series at *www.everything.com*

THE
EVERYTHING®
LEARNING RUSSIAN BOOK

Speak, write, and understand basic Russian in no time!

Julia Stakhnevich, Ph.D.

Avon, Massachusetts

With love for Dan, Henry, Jozhik, and Kickapoo.

An Everything® Series Book.
Everything® and everything.com® are registered trademarks of F+W Media, Inc.

Published by Adams Media, a division of F+W Media, Inc.
57 Littlefield Street, Avon, MA 02322 U.S.A.
www.adamsmedia.com

ISBN 10: 1-59869-387-5
ISBN 13: 978-1-59869-387-4

Printed in the United States of America.

10   9   8   7   6   5   4

Library of Congress Cataloging-in-Publication Data

Stakhnevich, Julia.
The everything learning Russian book with CD /
Julia Stakhnevich.
p. cm. — (Everything series book)
ISBN-13: 978-1-59869-387-4 (pbk. with cd)
ISBN-10: 1-59869-387-5 (pbk. with cd)
1. Russian language—Textbooks for foreign
speakers—English. 2. Russian language—Self-instruction.
I. Title.
PG2129.E5S73 2007
491.782'421—dc22   2007030953

This book is available at quantity discounts for bulk purchases.
For information, please call 1-800-289-0963.

Contents

Acknowledgments

My thanks go to everyone who assisted me with research and writing of this book. I am especially grateful to my husband Dan Johnson for his unwavering support and encouragement in all stages of the writing process. I would like to acknowledge Dan for his generous help with the sections of this book on Russian culture, art, and literature.

Top Ten Reasons to Learn Russian

1. Read maps, train schedules, and road signs when you travel in Russia.

2. Order in Russian with confidence at an authentic Russian restaurant.

3. Get and give directions in Russian when you visit the Hermitage.

4. Converse with your fellow passengers on the Trans-Siberian Railway.

5. Be able to correct your music teacher when she (again) mispronounces the names of famous Russian musicians.

6. Read Tolstoy and Dostoyevsky in the original language.

7. Stop relying on subtitles when watching Russian-language movies.

8. Converse with your Russian-speaking relatives and friends.

9. Research your family roots and interpret old documents.

10. Read about the history of the Russian Empire in Russian.

Introduction

▶ WHEN YOU LEARN A NEW LANGUAGE, you learn its pronunciation, vocabulary, and grammar. At the same time, you become more knowledgeable about the people who speak this language, about their values, traditions, and lifestyles. You gain a deeper appreciation for their cuisine, literature, music, and fine arts. You begin to understand preferred communication styles, family dynamics, and culturally acceptable ways of dealing with everyday problems. Moreover, you become more aware of the specifics of your own cultural norms and linguistic behavior. In this sense, language learning is not about rote memorization of conjugation patterns and declensions. It is about discovering new ways of looking at the world by shifting the way you think and using a different linguistic lens.

With this in mind, the goal of this book is to offer English-speaking readers an introduction to the Russian language and its culture. Learning Russian will open a door to the worldview of more than 250 million people who speak Russian as their mother tongue. The majority of them live in Russia, but there are large communities of Russian speakers in other European countries and in the United States, Canada, and Israel. Regardless of where they live, what unites them is their cultural identity, which is firmly rooted in the language and an amazing literary and artistic legacy.

As you learn Russian, you will develop an understanding of the important cultural reference points that guide Russians in their everyday lives, points that are critical for successful cross-cultural interactions and key for the effective interpretation of Russian literature, history, politics, and art. Because of the intimate and strong connection between culture and language, there is no adequate substitution to language study for anyone who is genuinely interested in learning about Russia and its people. Yes, you can read someone else's opinion in English about what it is that makes Russians Russian, but the only way to form your own opinion is to become familiar with the language. Language study allows you to dismiss secondary interpretations and go directly to the source of a culture: its language.

No matter what specific motivations you have for studying Russian, be it family roots, a desire to travel to Russia and communicate with the locals, or an interest in Russian literature, history, music, film, politics, and/or cuisine, you will be proud of your accomplishments. As a language learner you will uncover the expressive nature of the Russian language, become familiar with its creativity, and learn about the differences and similarities between the Russian and English sound systems and grammars. Last but not least, prior teaching experience shows that learning how to read and write in the Cyrillic alphabet, though a challenge at first, will eventually give you a palpable sense of achievement derived from the ability to read any and all texts in Russian.

The Everything® Learning Russian Book with CD can serve as a one-stop study resource for the acquisition of basic skills in speaking, listening, reading, and writing or as a steppingstone for further study. It includes recommendations for other reference materials, CDs, films, and Web sites. You can also use it as a handy travel guidebook as you prepare for your trip to Russia or as reference material for a language course. No matter how you use it, remember that language learning is about gaining direct access to a new culture, new ways of seeing the world, new ways of being yourself. Be brave, be open, be consistent, be creative! But most of all, enjoy it! **Доброго пути!**

Chapter 1

Presenting the Russian Language

Russian is a Slavic language, and it also happens to be one of the most commonly spoken languages in the world. It is a language of great political importance and is famous all over the world for its extraordinary literary legacy. This chapter explores the origins of this remarkable language and the evolution of modern literary Russian. By the end of this chapter, you will have even more reasons for learning Russian. The rest of this book will give you the tools to accomplish your goal.

Why Learn Russian?

Maybe you have dreamed of reading Dostoyevsky's *Crime and Punishment* in its original language and then strolling down Nevsky Prospekt, exploring the same streets Raskolnikov frequented. Or perhaps you want to visit Moscow to see for yourself what makes this city the heart and soul of Mother Russia. Maybe the alluring Trans-Siberian Railway beckons you. You may be a descendant of Russian immigrants who would like to trace your family history. You might be an aspiring musician who loves Russian classical music and wants to be able to appreciate Tchaikovsky's operas in their original language. Or you might be motivated by business; possibly your company is opening a branch in Russia and you will have to travel there frequently to work with new colleagues.

Whatever the reason, be it cultural curiosity, family roots, or professional development, learning Russian is a decision you won't regret. In fact, mastering this language will bring about a sense of accomplishment and pride. As you begin to unravel the intricacies of the Russian language, you will learn how Russians perceive themselves and the world around them. As you discover new culturally specific ways of being and thinking, you will be able to articulate your own views with more precision. Last but not least, Russian is still among the least commonly taught languages in the United States, making this language a great choice if you are looking for a road less traveled. Congratulate yourself on your adventurous spirit, and prepare to embark on a new and exciting journey!

The Origins of the Russian Language

Russian belongs to the large and diverse Indo-European language family, a diverse group that includes English, French, German, Hindi, and many others. Specifically, Russian belongs to the Slavic branch of the Indo-European family. Other Slavic languages include Czech, Slovak, Polish, Serbian, Slovenian, Bulgarian, Macedonian, Belorussian, and Ukrainian. Russian, Ukrainian, and Belorussian are considered sister languages because all three of them were developed from the same linguistic stock and have retained many similarities in their sound systems, grammars, and vocabularies.

Russian is the most commonly spoken Slavic language in the world; it is the mother tongue of at least 145 million people.

FACT

Linguists classify languages into families based on their demonstrated similarities and differences in basic vocabulary and grammar. The assumption is that languages from the same family are modern-day descendants of a common ancestor: an ancient proto-language. Within each family, there are separate groups or branches comprised of languages that share closer ties.

Although Russia's political influence diminished after the fall of the Soviet Union, the Russian language is still widely spoken in Eastern Europe and in the former Soviet republics. The United States, Canada, Israel, and Australia each have sizeable Russian-speaking immigrant communities. Although not all of the immigrants are ethnically Russian, many choose to preserve Russian as the community language. In addition, approximately 100 million people worldwide use Russian as their second language.

Russian is the official language of the Russian Federation and is one of the six working languages of the United Nations. It is written in a script known as the Cyrillic alphabet. The vocabulary of the Russian language consists of native words of Slavic origin and borrowings from Greek, Latin, French, English, and other languages.

The Beginning

Although it is impossible to identify the exact date when a language is born, most scholars agree that Russian became a distinctive language in the fourteenth or fifteenth century. At that time, various dialects of Russian co-existed with Old Church Slavonic, an archaic language used for religious and educational purposes.

With the development of Russian secular literate traditions, regional dialects became more acceptable, not only in oral communication but also in writing. After the unification of Russia under the leadership of Moscow in the seventeenth century, Russian became the country's national language.

Further Development

The eighteenth century played a significant role both in the history of Russia and in the development of its language. The country transformed itself from a backwater state on the outskirts of Europe to a powerful empire with strategic access to the Baltic and Black Seas. Simultaneously, many foreign words (especially French) entered the Russian vocabulary. In fact, French became the unofficial first language among Russian nobility, setting a clear linguistic divide between the masses, who spoke several regional varieties of Russian, and the upper classes, who were often more comfortable in French. French continued to play an important role in the lives of the Russian elite well into the twentieth century.

Alexander Pushkin and the Russian Language

Inspired by the beauty of Russian dialects spoken by commoners, a poet of incredible talent was able to successfully synthesize common vernacular and existing literary language into what is now universally known as Modern Literary Russian. Enriched by the expressiveness of everyday folk language, literary Russian has become standard both in writing and in speech, culturally unifying Russian society under its umbrella and marginalizing other varieties of Russian. Although today dialectal differences still exist, they are less divergent than in many other languages. Regional dialects of Russian are often grouped in Northern and Southern clusters, with Moscow being within the transitional zone between the two. Due to its political, cultural, and historic importance, the Moscow accent is considered to be the standard and is widely used in mass media, education, and politics.

The name of the poet who is universally credited with the creation of modern literary Russian is Alexander Sergeyevich Pushkin. Born in 1799,

Pushkin is still by far the most revered literary figure in Russia. (And that's in the country that gave the world Tolstoy, Dostoyevsky, and Chekov!) Often referred to as the national poet, Pushkin's impact on Russian language and culture is hard to overestimate. It will suffice to say that Pushkin's poetry and prose is as widely read today as it was in the nineteenth century. In fact, Pushkin's works are so popular that it will be hard to find a Russian who can't recite several of his poems by heart. Most Russians still feel a twinge when they speak of his untimely death at the age of thirty-seven. Pushkin's birthday, the 6th of June, is widely celebrated through literary events, festivals, and concerts all over Russia.

FACT

In the nineteenth century, Vladimir Dahl, a famous Russian lexicographer and ethnographer, studied dialects of the Russian language. Based on his work, the critically acclaimed *Explanatory Dictionary of the Great Living Russian Language* was published. It was the first dictionary to include regional terminology from various Russian dialects.

At the core of the nation's spiritual and intellectual identity, Pushkin's legacy is evident in the mundane minutia of everyday life in the countless streets, metro stations, and monuments that bear his name. Pushkin remains alive in the twenty-first century in popular biographies, hip theatre productions, and television shows. On a lighter note, Pushkin, the man who did so much for his country, is immortalized in a popular rhetorical question, as in "Who do you think will change the light bulb? Pushkin?"

Modern Russia

The October Revolution of 1917 was a turning point in the development of the Russian language. Many words that used to be exclusive to the educated elite entered the everyday lexicon, while words that dealt with concepts rooted in the political, legal, and military spheres of pre-revolutionary life instantly became obsolete. In addition to numerous lexical changes, many cities, towns, and streets were renamed in dedication to new heroes of the state.

For example, St. Petersburg was renamed Leningrad, Yekaterinburg became Sverdlovsk, and Volgograd became Stalingrad. With the beginning of *perestroika* in 1985, many pre-revolutionary names were eventually restored.

Although the great majority of Russians welcomed this change in an effort to demonstrate historical continuity, for some it was an emotional process. This became especially clear during the renaming of St. Petersburg. The objections came from the people who associated the city's Soviet name, Leningrad, with the 900-day siege that caused unimaginable suffering during World War II. In the 1991 referendum, 44 percent of the city's inhabitants voted against the change. With the majority's approval, the city's historical name was restored, but to honor the memory of those who perished during the blockade, the city's metropolitan area still bears the name of Leningradskaya Region.

FACT

Pushkin is also remembered as a romantic figure whose life ended tragically in a duel with George d'Anthès in 1837. Pushkin's wife, Natalya Goncharova, was one of the most beautiful women of her time, and Pushkin was madly in love with her. He initiated the duel to protect her honor after rumors of her alleged affair with d'Anthès began to spread. Pushkin was mortally wounded and died two days later.

The beginning of *perestroika* in 1985 marks another important date both in Russian history and in the development of the Russian language. As a result of the policy of *glasnost*, or openness, censorship was lifted, allowing citizens to engage in discussions without fear. Mass media was no longer an obedient tool of Communist propaganda; it openly questioned previously taboo subjects and criticized the Soviet regime and its leaders. Initiated as a policy of liberalization, *perestroika* exposed the deficiencies of the Communist rule leading up to the collapse of the Soviet Union in 1991.

For the first time in more than seventy years, Russian people had the opportunity to exercise their freedom of speech, travel abroad, and engage in free enterprise. The language, too, underwent a transformation, especially evident in its lexicon. For example, you no longer were expected to address your fellow citizens with "comrade," an address that bears distinct communist overtones. Instead, pre-revolutionary forms of address and semantically neutral gender salutations became popular.

FACT

Russians often refer to World War II as the Great Patriotic War. The war has left a tremendous impact on the Russian psyche, and even today its impact is hard to overestimate. Since 1945, May 9 has been celebrated as the Victory Day of the Great Patriotic War and is a Soviet holiday that survived into the 21st century.

The last decade of the twentieth century also saw an extraordinary influx of foreign words and phrases, especially in the fields of business, entertainment, fashion, and technology. This continuous onslaught of non-Russian words and phrases did not go unnoticed by the literati and those concerned with the "purity" of the Russian language, and a backlash resulted via the establishment of laws designed to discourage the use of foreign terminology in place of Russian words. Language purists such as Alexander Solzhenitsyn advocated language reforms that would ensure the use of native words and prefixes to create Russian equivalents instead of borrowing from other languages. Ninety-nine percent of current borrowings in the Russian language come from American English, which will help facilitate your understanding of Russian as you begin reading Russian newspapers and exploring Russian Web sites.

As a way to introduce you to several words that are identical in modern Russian and English, take a look at the following examples:

Similar Vocabulary in Russian and English

TRACK 1

Russian	English
бизнес	business
Интернет	Internet
си ди	CD
ксерокс	xerox
баскетбол	basketball

Russian	English
хип-х**о**п	hip-hop
ш**о**у	show
пр**а**йс-лист	price list
метр**о**	metro

Tips for Learning Russian

As you begin working on your Russian skills, remember that learning a new language is an exciting and challenging activity that requires dedication, commitment, and intellectual curiosity. The mere fact that you are reading this book shows that you are on the right track and are ready to accept the challenge. The following are several tips that will help you achieve the best results as a learner of Russian.

Develop a Schedule

Research shows that planning is an important component of learning. Look at your calendar and decide how much time you can realistically dedicate to studying. Think in terms of your week. Where can you fit in the time to study, and how much time can you set aside?

ESSENTIAL

Repetition and consistency are key in studying a foreign language. Doing tasks over and over will allow you to remember them more easily. If you set aside a consistent amount of time every week to practice your language skills, you will be able to see yourself progress.

What's important here is to set a schedule and stick to it. Sure, there might be distractions, and on some days you might have to cancel your study session. But having a specific time set aside for language study will help you maintain the consistency and focus that learning a foreign language requires. Also, try to schedule your study sessions at the times when you are feeling refreshed and energized. Language learning requires cognitive flexibility, so try to study when your brain is the most receptive.

Remember the Four Language Skills

Learning a language involves the development of at least four skills: speaking, listening comprehension, writing, and reading. When you plan your study sessions, try to do a little bit of all four. It will be helpful to have a separate notebook to make notes, write down questions, and practice writing. Remember to listen to the CD that comes with this book to practice your listening comprehension and speaking skills.

Review, Practice, and Be Creative!

Factor review time into your learning sessions. Try to find additional opportunities to practice your language skills—explore the Russian Internet, see if your public library has books in Russian, watch Russian movies, and get involved with local community organizations that might have connections with similar groups in Russia. The key here is to search for opportunities to be immersed in the Russian language and culture!

Stay Positive!

In order to maximize your learning experience, keep a positive outlook. Studying Russian might not be easy, but think about exciting opportunities that knowledge of Russian will bring into your life. Think about the sense of accomplishment associated with being able to function in another language.

Moreover, remember that language study is an incremental process that starts slowly and then accelerates. Don't be too modest: every little thing you learn about the Russian language and culture sets you apart from others who are not in the know. Recognize your accomplishments, big and small, and continue the good work!

Chapter Quiz

Choose the best possible answer and check your answers in Appendix A.

1. How many people speak Russian as their mother tongue?

a. more than 250 million
b. at least 145 million
c. less than 90 million
d. approximately 180 million

3. Who is considered the father of modern literary Russian?

a. Pushkin
b. Dahl
c. Dostoyevsky
d. Solzhenitsyn

2. Which of the following languages became a surrogate first language for Russian nobility in the 18th century?

a. German
b. Polish
c. Ukrainian
d. French

4. Which of the following historic events did not made a significant impact on the development of the Russian language?

a. The Great Patriotic War
b. The October Revolution
c. Perestroika
d. World War II

Chapter 2

The Cyrillic Alphabet

Learning Russian involves learning to read the Cyrillic alphabet. You might think this would make learning the language more challenging, but it doesn't have to. In fact, you are already familiar with some of the letters and their pronunciations. In this chapter, you will apply your analytical skills to learn the Cyrillic alphabet efficiently without getting overwhelmed. Once you learn the alphabet, you will be able to sound out words and read Russian in no time.

The Roots of the Cyrillic Alphabet

You already know that Russian is not written in the Latin alphabet. Instead, it uses Cyrillic. The history of the Cyrillic alphabet spans more than a thousand years. Throughout the ages, it has been modified several times, and what we use now in Russian differs from its earlier forms. The Russian Cyrillic alphabet contains thirty-three letters, including ten letters for vowel sounds, twenty-one letters for consonant sounds, and two silent signs.

Cyrillic originated directly from the Greek alphabet without any direct impact from the Latin alphabet. However, scholars agree that the roots of the Latin alphabet also lie with the Greeks, so the Cyrillic and Latin alphabets are related by proxy. This explains why Cyrillic contains letters that are similar to Greek (e.g. Ф, П, Г) and letters that are similar to those found in Latin languages (e.g. B, K, H).

The Cyrillic alphabet is named after St. Cyril, a monk from Byzantium. St. Cyril and St. Methodius are credited with spreading Christianity among the Slavs in southern Europe in the ninth century A.D. Everyone agrees on that much, but some scholars argue that St. Cyril didn't actually create the alphabet that bears his name.

St. Cyril himself may have developed the alphabet during his missionary trip to Bulgaria and Moravia where he and his brother worked on translating the Bible for newly converted Slavs. Other researchers suggest the alphabet was invented later in the tenth century, probably by other missionaries who followed in the footsteps of St. Cyril and St. Methodius. Another theory suggests that Slavs educated in the Greek tradition created the alphabet to share the word of God with the rest of their people.

FACT

In the Soviet Union, several languages which had previously used the Arabic (Kazakh and Azerbaijani) or Latin scripts (Moldovan) were forcefully switched over to the Cyrillic alphabet. After the breakup of the Soviet empire, many of these languages returned to their previous scripts or, in the case of Azerbaijani, have switched over to Latin script.

What is clear is that the alphabet was created in order to facilitate the translation of the Bible into Old Church Slavonic, the language spoken at that time by the Slavic people of southern Europe. The creation of an original alphabet made it possible to develop a writing system that can effectively express all of the sounds of the Slavic phonetic system without relying on approximations and diacritic marks. Since then, Cyrillic has been successfully used to write Slavic languages such as Russian, Belorussian, Ukrainian, Bulgarian, Serbian, and Macedonian. Due to Russian imperial expansion, the Cyrillic alphabet was adopted in the native languages of the Russian North and Siberia.

Although the territory where Cyrillic is used today has diminished since the deconstruction of the Soviet Union, it is still used in several non-Slavic languages, including the languages of Uzbekistan and Turkmenistan. Before we begin looking closely at specific Cyrillic letters, consult Table 2-1 to get a general idea of the alphabet and see the approximations of the sound of its letters in English.

TRACK 2

Table 2-1

Русский алфавит	Russian Alphabet	
Russian Capital Letter	**Lower Case**	**English Approximation**
А	а	**fa**ther
Б	б	**B**en
В	в	**V**ictor
Г	г	**g**row
Д	д	**d**inner
Е	е	**ye**sterday
Ё	ё	**Yo**rk
Ж	ж	plea**s**ure
З	з	**z**ero
И	и	s**ee**m
Й	й	to**y**
К	к	**c**o**c**o
Л	л	**l**amp
М	м	**m**other

Russian Capital Letter	Lower Case	English Approximation
Н	н	**N**ick
О	о	**or**
П	п	**P**eter
Р	р	p**er**o (Spanish)
С	с	**S**andra
Т	т	s**t**omp
У	у	l**oo**n
Ф	ф	**f**reckles
Х	х	the composer Ba**ch**
Ц	ц	ma**ts**
Ч	ч	**ch**eers
Ш	ш	**sh**eep
Щ	щ	fre**sh sh**ed
Ъ	ъ	hard sign – no sound
Ы	ы	s**ea**
Ь	ь	soft sign – no sound
Э	э	S**e**ptember
Ю	ю	**u**nion
Я	я	**ya**hoo

Letter approximation, or transliteration, is an important technique of letter-by-letter transcription of a text or a word from one script into another. You will learn more about the placement of vowels and consonants and the function of silent signs in later chapters. For now, just focus on matching the visual letter with its pronunciation.

The Letters You Already Know

Identifying the letters that are shaped and pronounced similarly in both Russian and English will help make learning Russian easier.

Table 2-2

Similar Letters and Sounds

Russian Letter	English Approximation
А а	A a
К к	K k

Russian Letter	English Approximation
М м	M m
О о	O o
Т т	T t

Note the slight difference in the graphic forms of the lower case letters K, M, and T.

Below are several Russian words that utilize these letters. Some of these words are new to you, but some are close to similar words in English. As you begin learning new words in Russian, remember to utilize what you already know.

Table 2-3

Words Spelled with Letters that You Know

TRACK 3

Russian Words	English Translation
ма́ма	mama
кот	cat
мак	poppy seed
так	so
как	how
там	over there
том	tome
ата́ка	attack
а́том	atom

Stress Patterns in Russian

When we say a word in either English or Russian, there is always a syllable that is pronounced with more strength, with more emphasis, or, in other words, with stress. For example, in English we stress the first syllable in the word "treasure," as in "trEAsure." In Russian, in the word "атака" we stress the second "a," as in "атАка," but in the word "атом" we stress the first "a," as in "Атом." As you can see from the examples above, in both English and Russian, vowel sounds change their pronunciation depending on whether they are in a stressed or unstressed position. Compare the pronunciation of "a" in English in such words as "r̲ather" and "a̲ttuned." Similarly, the very same process, known as vowel reduction, occurs in Russian. You will learn more about vowel reduction as you continue learning about pronunciation in Russian in Chapter 3.

FACT

In English, many words can have two stresses, as in "translation" or "rEvolUtion." In Russian, only one stress is allowed per word.

Be aware that in regular Russian publications stress is rarely indicated. However, to facilitate your learning of Russian, this book will denote stress in boldface, as in the word "**ма**ма" where the first syllable is stressed. We will not mark the stress in one-syllable words, as in "кто."

Russian children learn their ABCs or "**a**zbuka" from books which have clear indications of stress marks. ("**A**zbuka" comes from the old names of the first two letters in the Cyrillic alphabet: А and Б.) As children become more proficient in reading, stress marks become redundant. The same applies to you: as you increase your proficiency in Russian, you will develop a better sense of stress patterns, making stress marks unnecessary. Until then, it is recommended that you, too, write down words with stress indicators.

Looks Are Not Everything!

Now that you've eased into the Cyrillic alphabet by studying letters that have similar pronunciations in Russian and English, go back to Table 2-1 and identify six letters that look familiar to you but have a different pronunciation in Russian. Compare your answer with the following list of letters from the Russian Cyrillic alphabet that are visually similar to the letters from the Latin alphabet but represent different sounds. These letters are often more difficult to remember for English speaking learners of Russian. Don't feel bad if it takes you a little while to remember them, but make it a point to keep studying them. Repetition is the key to learning a new language.

Table 2-4

Similar Letters with Different Pronunciation in Russian

Russian Letter	English Approximation
В в	v
Е е	ye, as in yesterday
Н н	n
Р р	r, as in the Scottish dialect of English
С с	s
Х х	kh, as in loch

The following are several Russian words that utilize some of the letters that look familiar to you and the letters that were covered in Table 2-2.

Table 2-5

Russian Words with Letters You Know

Russian Word	English Translation
вор	thief
хвост	tail
рост	height
вера	faith
нора	burrow
марка	stamp
стена	wall
тема	topic
хохот	laughter
автомат	machine

TRACK 4

Similar Sounds, Different Letters

Several letters from the Russian Cyrillic alphabet represent sounds similar to those in English but are written with different symbols. This is a good example of the arbitrary nature of the relationship between form and meaning in any language; similar sounds can be represented by different symbols in various languages, just as identical concepts are rendered differently. Following is a list of Russian letters that fall within this category.

Table 2-6

Similar Sounds, Different Letters

Russian Letter	English Approximation
Б б	b
Г г	g, as in get
Д д	d
З з	z
Л л	l
П п	p
У у	oo, as in goose

Table 2-7

Russian Words with Letters You Know

Russian Word	English Translation
бор	forest
город	town
дорога	road
зуб	tooth
лодка	boat
продукт	product
ура	hooray

TRACK 5

Additional Consonants

The letters in this group represent the remaining Cyrillic letters for consonant sounds. Some of these sounds are rarely heard in English or they are not used at all.

Table 2-8

Several Unusual Consonants

Russian Words	English Approximation
Ж ж	zh, as in treasure
Ц ц	ts, as in darts
Ч ч	ch, as in chair
Ш ш	sh, as in shop
Щ щ	shch, as in fresh cheese

The sounds represented by the Cyrillic letters Ц and Щ are nearly non-existent in the English sound system. The examples of their pronunciation provided above are rough approximations. The best way to imitate these sounds is to listen to the soundtrack and practice.

Table 2-9

Russian Words with Unusual Consonants

TRACK 6

Russian Words	English Translation
жук	beetle
цирк	circus
чемодан	suitcase
шум	noise
борщ	Russian beet soup, borsch

Additional Vowels

This is the group of the Cyrillic letters that represent the remaining vowel sounds.

Table 2-10

Several Vowel Sounds to Remember

TRACK 7

Russian Words	English Approximation
Ё ё	yo, as in yoyo toy
Э э	e, as in let
Ю ю	yu, as in universe

Russian Words	English Approximation
Я я	ya, as in yard
Й й	y, as in boy
Ы ы	similar to the vowel sound in hill

In this group, there are three letters that have two segments in their graphic form: Ё, Й and Ы.

The letter "Ё" is always in the stressed position. It it thus redundant to mark the stress in the words where it occurs. However, "Ё" is often written as "Е" in Russian newspapers and other print media. Please remember this as you continue working with this textbook.

The letters "Й" and "Ы" usually occur at the end of words. The letter "Й" is an obligatory last letter in the endings of masculine forms of Russian adjectives, as in "краси**вый**" - beautiful and "**до**бр**ый**" - kind. The letter "Ы" occurs in adjectives and as the last letter in plural forms of nouns, as in "**у**мн**ый**" - clever and "**к**омнат**ы**" - rooms. Neither letter ever occurs at the beginning of words, with the exception the use of Й when it is used to transliterate foreign geographic names that start with the sound combination of "yo," as in York.

Don't forget to write the cap in the letter "Й." Otherwise, you will end up with an absolutely different letter, "И."

The letter "Э" is often used at the beginning of words, especially to approximate foreign names that start with the Latin letter "E" as in **Э**рик - Eric, **Э**мили - Emily, **Э**лизабет –Elizabeth, and **Э**мори - Emory.

Table 2-11

More Russian Words to Read

TRACK 8

Russian Words	English Translation
Эрик	Erick
юр**и**ст	lawyer
ясно	clear
р**у**сский	Russian
р**ы**ба	fish

Writing Your Own Name in Cyrillic

Now that you know all of the letters of the Cyrillic alphabet and their Russian pronunciations, you are probably wondering how to write your own name in Cyrillic. Here are a few important points to remember:

- Russians spell foreign names in the way they are pronounced in Russian.
- In Russian, there is no letter to represent the "J" sound. English names that begin with J in their Russian version begin with "Дж", as in Джон – John.
- English names that begin with the "H" sound are usually rendered with the Russian Г sound, as in Генри – Henry and Ганнибал - Hannibal, but sometimes, especially in last names, the same H sound is transferred with the Russian "Х" sound, as in Холмс – Holmes.
- There is no corresponding sound in Russian for either of the sounds represented in English by "th," as in there and thick. English names that begin or contain these two sounds are transliterated with the Russian letter "Т," as in Теодор – Theodor.
- English names beginning with the letters "Ch" and "Sh" are written in Russian respectively with the Russian letters "Ч" and "Ш."
- Russian does not contain a sound similar to the English "W," as in Weston. English names that begin with this letter can be transliterated either with the Cyrillic letter "В" or a letter combination of "Уа," as in Ватсон or Уатсон for Watson.
- The English sound "E," as in Mel, and "A," as in Sam and Stanley, are transliterated using the Russian letter "Е" or "Э" or "А," as in Мел, Сэм, and Станли. Some names might have several possible transliterations. For example, the name Stanley can be transliterated as Стэнли, Станли, and Стенли.

The following are some examples of American and English names written in Russian. Transliterate them into English.

Names	in English
Мишель Браун	
Дороти Блэйн	
Майкл Джонсон	
Эрик Родман	
Николас Винстон	
Эдди Мерфи	
Ричард Спаркс	

Chapter Review

Review the material covered in this chapter and complete the following exercises.

Chapter Quiz

Answer the following questions and check your answers in Appendix A.

1. How many letters are in the Cyrillic alphabet used in the Russian languages? _____

2. Why is it called Cyrillic?

   _____

3. What was the initial motivation for the creation of the Cyrillic alphabet?

   _____

4. What is the synonym for "letter approximation?"

   _____

5. How many Cyrillic letters represent consonant sounds?

   _____

6. What is the largest number of stresses allowable in Russian words?

   _____

7. What is the Russian word for "alphabet book?"

   _____

8. What is the basic rule of transferring foreign names into Russian letters?

   _____

Reading Practice

Read the following Russian words describing weather. Check your pronunciation by listening to Track 9. Practice your pronunciation by imitating the speaker on the CD.

TRACK 9

Russian Weather Vocabulary

Russian Word	English Translation
пог**о**да	weather
х**о**лодно	cold
тепл**о**	warm
ж**а**рко	hot
светл**о**	light
темн**о**	dark
д**у**шно	stuffy
вл**а**жно	humid
температ**у**ра	temperature
мор**о**з	frost
снег	snow
с**о**лнце	sun
прогн**о**з	forecast
прогн**о**з пог**о**ды	weather forecast

Writing Practice

These Americans are famous in Russia. Translate their names back into their original English form. Check your answers in Appendix A.

1. Джордж Вашингтон _____
2. Эмили Дикинсон _____
3. Чарли Чаплин _____
4. Марк Твейн _____
5. Коби Брайнт _____
6. Николас Кейдж _____

Translate the following names of American cities and states from Russian into English. Check your answers in Appendix A.

7. Детройт _____

8. Новый Орлеан _____

9. Синсинати _____

10. Бостон _____

11. Калифорния _____

12. Сан-Франциско _____

13. Сиэтл _____

14. Колорадо _____

15. Техас _____

16. Виксбург _____

17. Орегон _____

Based on the information from this chapter, transliterate your surname and your first name into Russian.

18. My name in Russian is _____

Chapter 3

Russian Pronunciation

Now that you are familiar with the Cyrillic alphabet, your next task is to master the sounds of the letters and explore how these sounds impact each other in words. This chapter explores the specific roles of Russian vowels and consonants, and silent signs are also covered. In this chapter, you will practice your reading skills with an introduction to Russian geography and learn several commonly used greetings and ways to say good-bye.

Pronunciation of Vowel Pairs

Scholars usually separate Russian vowels into two groups: those that contain a distinctive y-sound and those that do not.

Table 3-1

Vowel Pairs

Regular Vowels	Vowels with an Initial Y-Sound
А	Я
Э	Е
О	Ё
У	Ю

Vowels with an initial y-sound keep their original phonetic form if they occur at the beginning of a word or after another vowel. However, after a consonant the y-sound in these letters becomes less audible.

Table 3-2

TRACK 10

Pronunciation of Я, Е, Ё, Ю

Vowel	Initial Position	After Another Vowel	After a Consonant
Я	ярко (bright),	тихая (quiet),	Толя
Е	еда (food),	сырые (damp),	тема (theme)
Ё	ёлка (pine tree),	её (her),	Серёжа
Ю	Юля,	понимаю (I understand),	Нюра

Pronunciation of О, А, Е, Я

As you learned from the previous chapter, stress patterns influence the way you pronounce vowels. Typically, in a stressed position vowels are pronounced clearly, each sound retaining its individuality. In an unstressed position, vowels undergo what is often referred to as vowel reduction. This is a process that makes vowels less distinct as they lose some of their original phonetic qualities. It is important to remember that when "a" and "o" are stressed in Russian words, they are pronounced as "a" in "rather" and "o" in "autumn." However, if these vowels occur in the unstressed position, their pronunciation changes.

Table 3-3

O and A

Vowel	Stressed	Unstressed Before a Stressed Syllable	Other Unstressed Positions	
O	он (he)	as in autumn	Москва as in ox	молоко as in about and uh
A	старт (start) Марина as in father	хорошая as in mother	as in about and uh	

The vowels Е and Я also change their pronunciation depending on whether they are stressed or unstressed. Generally, when they are not stressed, they are reduced to a more neutral sound. Listen to Track 11 and try to hear differences in the way the vowels Е and Я are pronounced when they are in the stressed and unstressed positions.

Table 3-4

Examples of Vowel Reduction

TRACK 11

Vowel	Stressed	Unstressed
Е	тело (body)	перо (feather)
Е	дело (deed)	метро (metro)
Е	студент (student)	ребята (guys)
Е	сумасшедший (crazy)	вегетарианский (vegetarian)
Я	мясо (meat)	язык (language)
Я	яблоко (apple)	американская (American)
Я	яхта (yacht)	десятилетие (decade)
Я	ясли (nursery)	синяя (dark blue)

Silent Signs and Palatalization

You may have noticed two silent sounds in the Cyrillic alphabet in Table 2-1: the soft sign ь and the hard sign ъ. Their Russian names are respectively мягкий знак and твёрдый знак.

The Hard Sign

In modern Russian the hard sign is rarely used, but when it is its function is to separate a prefix from the root of the word and to insert an additional y sound. Listen to Track 12 to hear words with and without the hard sign.

TRACK 12

Table 3-5

The Hard Sign in Russian

With the Hard Sign	Translation	Without the Hard Sign	Translation
объявление	notice	обед	dinner
отъезд	departure	отец	father
подъезд	building entrance	падеж	grammatical case
съёмка	film shooting	сёмга	salmon
объезд	detour	обида	offense

The Soft Sign and Palatalization

The soft sign ь functions as an indicator that the preceding consonant is soft or palatalized, as in мать (mother) and спать (to sleep). In Russian, most consonants have two variants: hard and soft. Usually, English speaking students of Russian do not have many problems imitating the pronunciation of Russian hard consonants because they are in many ways similar to English consonants. However, this is not always true with Russian soft consonants.

To get an idea of what a soft or palatalized consonant is, pronounce the following English words: beautiful, pew, view, few, mew, and situation. As you pronounce them, consciously pay attention to how you articulate the following consonants: b, p, v, f, m, and t. You will notice that your pronunciation of these consonants is "softer" than when you say such words as boat, port, vote, fort, moat, and tote.

Palatalization is one of the biggest differences in the sound system between English and Russian. In English, it is rarely observed and has no semantic meaning. In Russian, it is a common feature that has a meaning-differentiating function as shown in Table 3-6.

F A C T

To pronounce a soft consonant in Russian, press the tip of your tongue against your hard palate. The hard palate is the flat surface on the top of your mouth. To locate your hard palate, move your tongue along the top of your mouth away from the ridge behind your teeth.

TRACK 13

Table 3-6

Words With and Without Palatalization

Palatalized	Translation	Non-Palatalized	Translation
быть	to be	быт	everyday life
ель	pine tree	ел	ate
Спорь!	Argue!	спор	debate
влить	pour in	влит	poured in
дань	tribute	дан	given
цель	goal	цел	safe and sound

The soft sign is only one of the three indicators of palatalization. The vowel sounds Я, Е, Ё, Ю, И also signal that the consonant preceding them is soft. Finally, there is a chain reaction that you must be aware of: palatalized consonants can make neighboring consonants soft, too.

TRACK 14

Table 3-7

Two Additional Methods of Palatalization

Я, Е, Ё, Ю, И	Translation	Palatalization Chain Reaction	Translation
мягко	soft	листья	leaves
нет	no	если	if
мёд	honey	видимость	visibility
Анюта	nickname for Anne	всласть	to one's heart's content
никогда	never	после	after

An understanding of the distinction between hard and soft consonants is essential even for the correct pronunciation of Russian first names. Your

Russian friends will be impressed if you were to try and pronounce their names the way they were meant to be: with soft and hard consonants. Without a doubt, you'll get preferential treatment if you can say "Ольга" instead of "Olga", "Юлия" instead of "Julia," and even your friend Boris will be happy to finally hear that soft 'r' in his name that he has been missing for years! Below is a table with some Russian names that require soft consonants.

Table 3-8

Palatalization and Russian First Names

Female Names	Male Names
Ольга	Владислав
Дарья	Пётр
Татьяна	Александр
Ксения	Виктор
Елизавета	Никита
Светлана	Борис

Voiced and Voiceless Consonants

Both in English and in Russian, some consonants are voiceless and some are voiced. When the vocal cords are together, the air flow makes them vibrate, resulting in the production of voiced consonants, for example, English consonants D and Z and Russian consonants Ж and Г. Other consonants do not rely on the vocal cords for pronunciation; think of the English consonants T and P and Russian consonants Ф and К. In Russian and in English, voiced and voiceless consonants can be classified into pairs as in the table below.

Table 3-9

Russian Voiced and Voiceless Consonants

Voiced	Voiceless
В	Ф
З	С
Ж	Ш
Б	П
Г	К
Д	Т

In contrast to English, Russian voiced and voiceless consonants are not always pronounced the way they are written. At the end of words, voiced consonants are pronounced like their voiceless counterparts.

Table 3-10

Devoicing Voiced Consonants

TRACK 15

Russian Word	Pronunciation of the Final Consonant	Translation
Рахманинов	[ф]	Rakhmaninov
город	[т]	city
клуб	[п]	club
друг	[к]	friend
враг	[к]	enemy
Петербург	[к]	Petersburg
сад	[т]	garden

Unlike English, Russian allows more consonant combinations within its words. This is why you will encounter words where you will see both voiced and voiceless consonants side by side, as in встреча (a meeting), субтитры (subtitles), and отдых (rest). Because it would be difficult to articulate both voiced and voiceless consonants side by side without a lot of effort, the language developed a conservation technique, also known as consonant assimilation.

Whenever there are adjacent voiced and voiceless consonants, the first consonant takes on the voicing quality of the second. In this manner, a voiced consonant can become voiceless, and a voiceless consonant can be transformed into a voiced consonant. This assimilation occurs not only within a word, but also within phrases. The assimilation rule does not apply to the words or phrases where the first consonant is voiceless and the second one is the voiced consonant B, as in "твой," a word that does not undergo assimilation.

Table 3-11

Consonant Assimilation

Russian Word/Phrase	Consonant Pronunciation	Translation
встр**е**ча	фст (voiced becomes voiceless)	meeting
суб**ти**тры	пт (voiced becomes voiceless)	subtitles
отдых	дд (voiceless becomes voiced)	rest
пр**о**сьба	зьб (voiceless becomes voiced)	request
в Калуге	ф Калуге (voiced becomes voiceless)	in Kaluga
твой	твой (no assimilation)	your
квас	квас (no assimilation)	kvas (a traditional Russian soft drink)

Pronunciation Patterns in Salutations

Now it's time to use your understanding of Russian pronunciation to learn several common greetings and ways to say good-bye in Russian.

As you learn Russian greetings, remember to apply the pronunciation rules that you have learned so far. Some Russian words might deviate from the rules. In such cases, this book will include a note on exceptions in the pronunciation of the words that you will be learning so that your Russian will sound authentic.

Russian Salutations: Cultural Notes

Russians have both informal and formal salutation and farewell expressions that correspond to the formal (вы) and informal (ты) forms of address. If you are meeting someone for the first time, or the person with whom you are speaking is older or much higher on the social ladder, it is always better to err on the side of caution and use the formal forms of saying hello and goodbye. Handshakes are an accepted form of salutation among men and are becoming more and more popular among women, especially in professional situations.

A very traditional way of saying goodbye is to exchange three kisses on the cheek followed by a hug. This ritual is only used with one's closest friends and immediate family or after the consumption of large quantities of liquor when the dividing lines have been irrevocably blurred. Whatever the situation might be, your best bet is to avoid excesses and stay more middle of the road.

If you greet a Russian friend with a casual "How are you?" or "What's up?" be prepared for a lengthy response. It's considered extremely rude to expect a two-word answer to these greetings. Your Russian friends will happily talk about their lives if you're genuinely interested, but they'll be offended if you ask such private questions without giving them the opportunity to engage in meaningful conversation.

Finally, remember that it is unnecessary to greet the same person several times during the day. Instead, you should say hello upon your first meeting of the day and then use eye contact or a head nod to acknowledge their presence throughout the day.

TRACK 17

Table 3-12

Greetings

Time	Formality	Greeting	Translation	Addressing
All day	Very Formal	Здравствуйте!	Hello	One or many
All day	Informal	Здравствуй!	Hello	One person
All day	Very Informal	Привет!	Hello	One or many
Morning	(In)formal	Доброе утро!	Good morning!	One or many
Afternoon	(In)formal	Добрый день!	Good afternoon!	One or many
Evening	(In)formal	Добрый вечер!	Good evening!	One or many

The Russian letter "В" in Здравствуйте is not pronounced.

Table 3-13

Saying Goodbye

TRACK 18

Time	Formality	Expression	Translation	Addressing
All day	(In)formal	До свидания!	Until we meet again!	One or many
All day	(In)formal	Всего хорошего!	All the best!	One or many
All day	Very Informal	Пока!	Bye!	One or many

Time	Formality	Expression	Translation	Addressing
All day	(In)formal	Счастливо!	All the best!	One or many
All day	Formal	До скорой встречи!	Until our next meeting!	One or many
All day	Formal	Прощайте!	Farewell!	One or many
All day	Informal	Прощай!	Farewell!	One
Night	Formal	Доброй ночи!	Have a good night!	One or many
Night	Informal	Спокойной ночи!	Have a quiet night! (before bed)	One or many

The Russian letter "Г" in Всего хорошего (in both words) is pronounced just like the Russian letter "В."

Reading Practice: Russian Geography

Now that you know how to pronounce Russian words, let's use Russian geographic names to introduce Russian spelling and pronunciation. You will know the Anglicized pronunciations of these Russian names, but the Russian pronunciation is somewhat different. For example, Russia is **Россия** in Russian, with the stress on the second syllable and a subsequent shift of the vowel pronunciation "О" into "А." The same rule applies to the pronunciation of the official name of the country: **Российская Федерация** (The Russian Federation).

Similar to some English geographic names, several Russian geographic names have meanings that can be directly translated into English. For example, **Новгород** (Novgorod), one of the oldest cities in Russia, can be literally translated in English as "New City." The Russian root **нов-** means "new," and **город** is "city."

The old Russian city **Владимир**, which also happens to be a male name, consists of the root **ВЛАД-**, meaning "to own" and the root **МИР**, which can mean either "peace" or "world" depending on the context in which it is used. Thus, **Владимир** could be interpreted as the "he who owns the world." It comes as no surprise that the name **Владимир** has been a very popular name for boys, with several of Russia's leaders associating it with a prophesy or a coincidence of sorts, depending on how you look at it. Just think about **Владимир Ленин** or the current president of **Российская Федерация**, **Владимир Путин**.

On a more serious note, several of the Russian cities that were founded during the imperial period in Russian history were given names to commemorate a specific tsar or tsarina or a city's patron saint. For example, Санкт-Петербург, founded by Peter the Great in 1703, was named after the biblical St. Peter, who was the tsar's patron saint. Several Russian cities, Санкт-Петербург among them, include -бург, a German borrowing that means "city," as their final component, or a Russian root -град or -город, which also means "city." Finally, there is the Russian city of Владивосток, which was founded to exert Russian imperial influence on Japan, China, and Korea. The city's name leaves no doubts about the political ambitions of the Russian empire: it is derived from two Russian roots (one of which you already know): влад- meaning "to own" and восток, which means "east."

Table 3-14

Russian Geographic Names

Russian	English
страна	country
Россия	Russia
Российская Федерация	Russian Federation
города	cities
Москва	Moscow
Санкт-Петербург	St. Petersburg
Новгород	Novgorod
Мурманск	Murmansk
Архангельск	Arkhangelsk
Волгоград	Volgograd
Астрахань	Astrakhan
Екатеринбург	Yekaterinburg
Новосибирск	Novosibirsk
Иркутск	Irkutsk
Владивосток	Vladivostok
Магадан	Magadan
горы	mountains
Урал	the Urals
реки	rivers
Москва-река	the Moskva River

Russian	English
Волга	the Volga
Дон	the Don
Обь	the Ob
Лена	the Lena
Амур	the Amur
моря и озёра	seas and lakes
озеро Байкал	Lake Baikal
Чёрное море	Black Sea
Берингово море	the Bering Sea

Chapter Review

Review the material covered in this chapter and complete the following exercises.

Chapter Quiz

Answer the following questions and check your answers in Appendix A.

1. How many Russian vowels include an initial y-sound? _____
2. What is the term that describes a change in the pronunciation of Russian vowels in the unstressed position?

   _____

3. Name two silent signs from the Russian Cyrillic alphabet.

   _____

   _____

4. List three indicators of palatalization in Russian consonants.

   _____

   _____

   _____

5. When should you pronounce Russian voiced consonants as their voiceless counterparts?

   _____

6. What happens to the pronunciation of words and phrases when there are adjacent voiced and voiceless consonants?

   _____

7. What is the official Russian name of Russia?

   _____

8. Name at least three Russian cities whose names have a clear meaning in Russian.

   _____

Pronunciation Practice

Identify soft consonants in these Russian names. Check your answers in Appendix A.

Female Names

1. Марья   _____
2. Наталья   _____
3. Людмила   _____
4. Юлия   _____
5. Анастасия   _____
6. Лидия   _____
7. Валентина   _____

Male Names

8. Владимир   _____
9. Николай   _____
10. Сергей   _____
11. Евгений   _____
12. Семён   _____
13. Кирилл   _____
14. Максим   _____

Practicing Russian Greetings

Which greeting(s) would you use in the following situations? Write down as many appropriate answers as possible.

1. You are meeting your new colleague from Russia. It's early in the morning.

   _____

2. You are saying goodbye to a close friend late at night.

   _____

3. You are meeting an acquaintance in the middle of the day.

   _____

4. You are saying "Good night!" to your child at bedtime.

   _____

5. Your friend is joining the circus, and you might never see him again.

   _____

Chapter 4

Surviving in Russia

Experienced travelers know that language skills increase the enjoyment of traveling and reduce the stress and anxiety of being in an unfamiliar environment. Knowing the correct words and phrases enhances cross-cultural understanding and prevents possible miscommunication. Familiarity with culturally acceptable ways of interacting with locals shows a degree of politeness which Russians will appreciate. This chapter introduces several key words and phrases frequently often heard at border crossings, airports, railway stations, and other means of public transportation.

Cognates

The emphasis in this chapter is on acquiring new words and phrases that might be helpful to you as you travel to Russia. As you learn these words, you will discover that some Russian words are similar to their English counterparts. Like many other languages spoken in the Western world, Russian and English have been greatly influenced by ancient Greek and Latin. As a result, a considerable section of the Russian and English lexicon consists of words that have the same Greco-Roman roots. Such words are known as cognates. Compare the following English and Russian words in Table 4-1.

Table 4-1

Latin and Greek Cognates in English and Russian

English	Russian
democracy	демокр**а**тия
demonstration	демонстр**а**ция
revolution	револю**ц**июя
bibliography	библиогр**а**фия
theater	те**а**тр
public	п**у**блика
conflict	конфл**и**кт
geography	геогр**а**фия
consensus	конс**е**нсус
agency	аг**е**нтство

French, Arabic, and Italian also have loaned numerous words both to English and Russian. Consider such terms as **метр**о – metro (from French), **а**лгебра – algebra (from Arabic), and макар**о**ны – macaroni (from Italian).

In addition to the cognates borrowed from other languages, there is a small group of basic terms that are shared by all Indo-European languages, including English and Russian. These terms are presumed to come from the so-called Proto-Indo-European language, an ancestral language that connects all Indo-European languages. Compare the following words in English and Russian: ночь (night), день (day), and три (three).

Although cognates have a shared ancestry that can be traced through linguistic analysis, their phonological form must accommodate the sound systems of different languages, resulting in differences in pronunciation. For example, Latin *schola* became school in English and **шкóла** in Russian; Russian **университéт** is connected through its Greco-Roman heritage to the English university.

QUESTION?

What is phonology?
Phonology is the system of classifying all allowable combinations of sounds in a particular language. Languages differ in their phonological systems as some languages make use of sounds that are simply not present in others.

Whereas many cognates have retained similar meanings, others have acquired independent meanings in two languages. These different semantic applications might lead to mistakes in translation when speakers assume that cognates have the same meaning in all languages. For example, "magazine" in English has acquired a meaning of "publication, journal," whereas the Russian **магазúн** is used in the sense of "shop, store."

As you learn more Russian words and phrases, remember that cognate recognition is an important skill that can be helpful in the development of your vocabulary in Russian; on the other hand, don't jump to conclusions when you see or hear words that look or sound similar. They just may happen to be your false friends. As Ronald Reagan once said in Russian (with a heavy American accent): **Доверяй, но проверяй!** (Be trustful, but always double check!)

Crossing the Border

To travel to Russia, you need to have a current **паспóрт** and a **вúза** (both words are cognates!). To obtain a visa, contact a Russian Consulate (**Консульство Российской Федерáции**) directly or work with a travel agency that specializes in trips to Russia. It usually takes a couple of weeks to process a visa application, so apply well in advance. Once all of the red tape is taken care of and your travel plans are finalized, you will be all set to begin your journey.

> It is always wise to make arrangements for transportation from the airport to your hotel in advance. Otherwise, be prepared to deal with an army of so-called gypsy cab drivers waiting to offer their services in the lobby of your terminal. Use your best judgment and don't be shy about bargaining!

If you are flying to Russia, your most likely point of entry will be Moscow or St. Petersburg. International airports in both cities do have bilingual signs, and many border officials are fluent in English. However, knowing several common words and phrases will provide some back-up to ensure a smooth border-crossing experience.

TRACK 19

Вот мой паспорт.
Here's my passport.

Я буду в России неделю / две недели / месяц.
I will be in Russia for a week / two weeks / a month.

Я – турист/туристка.
I am a tourist (male/female).

Я могу позвонить моему консулу?
Can I phone my consulate?

Мне нужно заполнить этот бланк?
Do I have to fill out this form?

У вас есть этот бланк на английском?
Do you have this form in English?

Note that the letter "Й" in the phrase "на английском" is silent.

Table 4-2

Crossing the Border: Helpful Vocabulary

Russian	English
граница	border
пограничники	border personnel
таможня	customs
таможенная инспекция	customs inspection
иммиграционная служба	immigration service
аэропорт	airport
рейс	flight
номер рейса	flight number
паспорт	passport
виза	visa
имя	(first) name
фамилия	last name
гражданство	nationality, citizenship
профессия	occupation
цель поездки	purpose of the trip
постоянное место жительства	permanent residence
возраст	age
дата рождения	date of birth
место рождения	place of birth
цвет глаз / волос	color of eyes / hair
подпись	signature

In Russian, Национальность refers to one's ethnicity. To indicate someone's nationality, Russians use the word Гражданство, which can be translated into English as either "nationality" or "citizenship."

Expressions of Politeness

Whether you are a fluent speaker or a have just begun learning Russian, don't underestimate the value of using polite language and gestures. A "thank you" said with a warm smile might just bridge that language barrier and perhaps make you new friends. This section introduces a list of basic polite expressions. Although they are not all-inclusive, these expressions will be appropriate in most situations.

ALERT!

The Russian language has more than its share of curses. You might hear them in traffic jams as drivers desperately lose their cool or see them in writing in urban graffiti. Hardcore obscenities are called мат. Although interesting from an anthropological standpoint, language learners are advised to avoid using them.

Russian has formal and informal forms of address, with the former usually reserved for interactions with strangers and figures of authority and the latter for conversations among peers and immediate family. It is better to tread lightly and use formal forms of address with all figures of authority(police, doctors, immigration officers, and customs officials) as well as with people with whom you are newly acquainted. In this chapter, all statements are made using the formal address. You will learn more about Russian formal and informal forms of address in Chapter 7.

Table 4-3

Expressions of Politeness

TRACK 20

Russian	English
Извините.	Excuse me.
Простите.	I am sorry.
Разрешите мне пройти.	May I pass through?
Спасибо.	Thank you.
Большое/огромное спасибо.	Thank you very much.
Благодарю вас.	Thank you.
Пожалуйста.	You are welcome.
Не за что.	Don't mention it.
Не стоит благодарности.	You are welcome (Literally: It's not worthy of gratitude).

Извините and простите are interchangeable, unlike "I'm sorry" and "Excuse me."

Taking Public Transportation: Asking for Directions

Although car rentals and private drivers are available in many big cities, taking public transportation will allow you to experience daily life as it is for many locals. It is also a great opportunity to practice your language skills. In Moscow, St. Petersburg, and other metropolitan areas, you will have a choice of subway, buses, trams, and trolleys.

Table 4-4

Public Transportation

Russian	English
метро	metro/Subway
автобус	bus
троллейбус	trolleybus
трамвай	tram
поезд	train
такси	taxi
остановка автобуса / троллейбуса / трамвая	bus / trolleybus / tram stop
станция метро	metro station
вокзал	train station
карта города	map of the city
центр (города)	(city) center, downtown
гостиница	hotel
отель	hotel
общежитие	dormitory
улица	street
площадь	square, plaza
ресторан	restaurant
кафе	café, coffee shop
музей	museum
театр	theater
кинотеатр	movie theater
аптека	pharmacy

Russian	English
университет	university
школа	school
магазин	store
библиотека	library
парк	park
стадион	stadium

At central locations where there are a lot of tourists, street names and maps both in Russian and English might be available. However, in other places, you might have to rely on directions from your fellow passengers and practice your speaking and listening skills. Here are some common phrases used for asking and expressing directions.

TRACK 21

Извините, пожалуйста, где гостиница / магазин / вокзал?
Excuse me, where is the hotel / store / train station?

Извините, вы не знаете где здесь остановка автобуса / трамвая / троллейбуса / метро?
Excuse me, do you know where a bus / tram / trolleybus / metro stop is around here?

Вы не знаете, где находится...?
Do you know where ... is?

Подскажите, пожалуйста, как пройти к...?
Can you please tell me how to get to...?

Я не знаю.
I don't know.

Это далеко/близко отсюда?
Is it far/close from here?

Идите прямо.
Go straight ahead.

Поверните налево / направо.
Turn to the left / right.

Это здесь / там.
It is around here / over there.

Перейд**и**те **у**лицу / дор**о**гу.
Cross the street / road.

Это в пят**и** / деся**т**и мин**у**тах ходьб**ы** отс**ю**да.
It's a five- / ten-minute walk from here.

Спас**и**бо за в**а**шу п**о**мощь.
Thank you for your help.

Understanding directions in a foreign language is not an easy task. Use gestures if you need to, and don't be shy to ask the person to speak slower: "Пож**а**луйста, говор**и**те пом**е**дленней," or to see if the person could repeat the directions in English: "Повтор**и**те, пож**а**луйста, по-английски."

Common Public Announcements and Signs

Whether you are traveling with a guide or independently, it is helpful to be able to understand common public announcements and signs. Being familiar with these expressions will give you more confidence to explore whatever destinations you choose to visit in Russia. While in the metro, stops will be announced as Сл**е**дующая ст**а**нция…. (The next stop is…) Bus stops are announced as Сл**е**дующая остан**о**вка.

FACT

Moscow's metro is known around the world as the most beautiful series of underground stations and connecting tunnels in the world. The Moscow metro opened its first station in 1935, and today it is the most efficient mode of transportation in this congested city of 14 million. The metro begins its daily service at 5:30 A.M. and stops running at 1 A.M.

It is also customary to warn passengers that the train is just about to leave the station by announcing that the doors of the train are closing:

Осторожно, двери закрываются. Onboard, you will see signs reminding passengers not to lean on the doors of the train: Не прислоняться (Don't lean). Look where you are sitting; a lot of seats are reserved for elderly people, pregnant women, passengers with young children, and the disabled. You can tell these seats by the stenciled: Места для пенсионеров, инвалидов и пассажиров с детьми (Seats for pensioners, the disabled and passengers with children).

Other signs that you are likely to see in many Russian cities and towns are roadside signs, including: Стоп (Stop), Осторожно (Caution), Объезд (Detour), and Дороги нет (Road Closed). In many public places, such as movie theaters, the theater, airports, and train stations, you will see two signs: "Вход" for Entrance and "Выход" for Exit. In Moscow, St. Petersburg, and other Russian cities, underground passageways are used to cross busy streets or to provide a connection to underground metro stations. These passages are announced by the sign Подземный переход.

If you are looking for a public bathroom, look for a sign that says Туалет. Women's bathrooms will be indicated by the sign with the letter "Ж" for женский туалет (women's bathroom). Men's bathrooms will bear the letter "М" for мужской туалет (men's bathroom).

Accidents and emergencies can happen to anyone. If you need to locate a police station, look for the sign that says Милиция. If you need to go to a hospital, you should ask for больница (hospital) or скорая помощь (ambulance). The following is a list of common expressions that may come in handy.

TRACK 22

Мне плохо.
I don't feel well.

У меня болит живот.
I have a stomachache.

На меня только что напали.
I was just attacked.

Меня только что обокрали.
I was just robbed.

Помогите мне!
Help me!

Пожар!
Fire!

Мне нужен врач.
I need a doctor.

У меня кровотечение.
I am bleeding.

Вызовите скорую помощь/милицию.
Call an ambulance / the police.

Мне необходимо переговорить с моим консулом.
I need to speak with my consul.

Пожалуйста, подождите здесь.
Please wait here.

Running Errands

Even in this age of ATMs and online banking, you may still need to find a bank during your stay in Russia. In Russian, a bank is called "банк." Many banks offer currency exchange services and cash machines. However, there are also many independent money exchange kiosks, easily recognizable by the sign обмен валюты (currency exchange).

If you need to mail some of your souvenirs back home or check your e-mail, ask for почта, a post office, which usually combines mailing, fax, the Internet, and utilities billing services.

Making, Accepting, and Declining Invitations

Your ability to speak Russian, combined with curiosity and a willingness to experience and appreciate a culture different from your own, will open up many opportunities for you to meet, interact, and hopefully build friendships with Russian people.

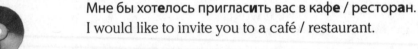

The basic way to indicate your agreement is "Да" for yes, and the easiest way of expressing your disagreement is by saying "Нет" for no.

Your Russian friends may invite you to their house, a local party, a restaurant, or a café. Or, you may want to invite your new friends for a cup of coffee or a beer. Here are some expressions that you can use when making or accepting invitations, or gracefully declining them.

TRACK 23

Мне бы хотелось пригласить вас в кафе / ресторан.
I would like to invite you to a café / restaurant.

Пожалуйста, приходите в гости.
Please come visit. (Literally: Please, come be our guests).

Мы будем очень рады.
We will be very glad.

Спасибо, с удовольствием.
Thank you. With pleasure.

Спасибо за приглашение.
Thank you for the invitation.

Спасибо, но я занят / занята*.
Thank you, but I am busy (male / female).

Спасибо, но сейчас у меня нет времени.
Thanks, but I don't have time now.

Может быть, в другой раз / завтра / на следующей неделе.
Perhaps next time time / tomorrow / next week.

*In Russian, adjectives have distinct forms when they refer to subjects of different genders. Stress patterns might vary in different forms of the same adjective.

Chapter Review

Review the material covered in this chapter and complete the following exercises.

Chapter Quiz

Answer the following questions and check your answers in Appendix A.

1. What are the words that have shared ancestry and are common in several languages? _____

2. What is the Russian word for swear words?

   _____

3. How would you say "thank you" in Russian?

   _____

4. How would you say "excuse me" in Russian?

   _____

5. How would you ask someone to speak slower?

   _____

6. How would you ask someone to explain whatever they are trying to say in English?

   _____

7. How would you thank someone for the help you received?

   _____

8. How would you ask in Russian where the bathroom is?

   _____

9. What do the letters "Ж" and "М" stand for on signs in public places in Russia?

   _____

10. How would you thank someone for inviting you?

    _____

11. Which signs are used to indicate an entrance and an exit in Russian?

_____

12. Which phrase is often used on the metro to announce the next stop?

_____

13. What are the basic ways of saying 'yes' and 'no' in Russian?

_____

14. What would a Russian "caution" sign look like?

_____

15. If you hear someone screaming "Пожар!", you will know that it's

_____

Vocabulary Building Exercise

Translate the following words into Russian using your knowledge of cognates:

1. Taxi   _____
2. Hotel   _____
3. Inspection   _____
4. Passport   _____
5. School   _____
6. University   _____
7. Visa   _____
8. Restaurant   _____
9. Center (of the city) _____
10. Stop   _____

Reading, Listening, and Pronunciation Practice

Read the following sentences as you listen to them on the CD. Use the blank lines to translate expressions of politeness and other conversation formulas from Russian into English. Check your answers in Appendix A.

TRACK 24

1. Извините, вы не знаете где здесь остановка автобуса?

_____

2. Это там. _____

3. Это далеко отсюда? _____

4. Нет, Это в пяти минутах ходьбы отсюда. Идите прямо. Потом поверните налево. _____

5. Спасибо за вашу помощь.

_____

6. Пожалуйста. _____

7. Мне бы хотелось пригласить вас в ресторан.

_____

8. Спасибо за приглашение.

_____

9. Мне бы хотелось пригласить вас в кафе.

_____

10. Спасибо, но сейчас у меня нет времени. Может быть, в другой раз

_____

Translation Practice

Translate the following sentences.

1. Excuse me, where is the men's bathroom?

_____

2. Sorry, I don't know.

_____

3. Call an ambulance.

_____

4. Please wait here.

_____

5. Please come visit.

_____

Chapter 5

Russian Cuisine: Introduction to Nouns and Adjectives

Tasting new foods and going to a market to buy ingredients for traditional recipes provide language learners with unique opportunities to experience Russian culture from within—especially if you use the Russian language to do them. Learning about traditional cuisine and acquiring necessary food-related vocabulary and grammar skills makes you a more proficient language learner and offers valuable insight into the workings of Russian culture. In this chapter, you'll learn the basics of Russian cooking, read about its staple dishes and beverages, and begin your exploration of Russian nouns and adjectives.

Russian Cuisine: Basic Vocabulary

Traditional Russian cooking or "**русская ку**хня" is famous for its variety. Spanning two continents, Russia has developed a cuisine that creatively blends elements from various cultures. Its most famous dishes include borsch (beet soup), blini (thin pancakes), caviar, and vodka. Jewish, French, Ukrainian, Georgian, and Middle Asian influences are evident in many dishes. The staple foods include potatoes, wheat, cabbage, and various meats. The following is a partial list of foods and beverages common in the Russian diet.

TRACK 25

Table 5-1

Foods and Drinks

Russian	English
еда	food
каша	kasha (porridge, cereals)
суп	soup
салат	salad
грибы	mushrooms
макароны	macaroni (plural)
мясо	meat
говядина	beef
свинина	pork
курица	chicken
рыба	fish
икра	caviar
колбаса	sausage
овощи	vegetables (plural)
капуста	cabbage
картофель	potatoes
морковь	carrot
помидор	tomato
огурец	cucumber or pickle
фрукты	fruits (plural)
яблоко	apple
груша	pear

Russian	English
апельси́н	orange
клубни́ка	strawberry
десе́рт	dessert
торт	cake
щокола́д	chocolate
конфе́та	candy
моро́женое	ice cream
молоко́	milk
хлеб	bread
ма́сло	butter
сыр	cheese
напи́тки	drinks (plural)
вода́	water
сок	juice
ко́фе	coffee
чай	tea
вино́	wine
во́дочка	vodka

You may already have many of these items in your kitchen. Practice saying the Russian words for these foods while shopping at your grocery store. To find authentic Russian food in your area, look up a Russian market in the phone book or online.

The Basics of Russian Nouns

Now that you have learned a number of Russian nouns, let's examine three of their basic grammatical characteristics: case, gender, and number.

Case

In Russian, nouns change their endings to indicate specific roles that they play in a sentence:

The student is reading. Студе́нт чита́ет.

"Student" is the subject of the sentence.

The teacher is asking the student. Преподава́тель спра́шивает студе́нта.

"Student" is the object of action performed by the teacher. Note that in English, the syntactic role of the noun "student" is shown through the word order: it appears at the beginning of the sentence when it is used as a subject, and it occurs after the verb as an object.

QUESTION?

What does "syntactic" mean?
Syntactic is an adjective formed from the noun "syntax," which denotes the structure of a language.

On the other hand, the Russian noun "студе́нт" has two different forms to correspond to its two different syntactic roles. Such forms are called cases, or declensions. There are six different cases in the Russian language:

- **Nominative:** This case is used to indicate that the noun is the subject of a sentence. Nouns given in a dictionary or in a vocabulary list are presented in the nominative case.
- **Accusative:** This case is used to indicate that the noun is the object of a sentence. It is also used to denote motion toward something when used after the prepositions в and на.
- **Genitive:** The genitive case is used to show possession, quantity, and negation.
- **Prepositional:** This case is used to describe location. As its name suggests, it uses prepositions; three of the most common are о, в, and на. These prepositions may be used with other cases, but their meaning is different.
- **Dative:** This case indicates the indirect object of a sentence. It is commonly used to indicate the giving of a gift and is also used to demonstrate motion toward another person ("to the teacher").

- **Instrumental:** This case is used to indicate the means used to accomplish an action. It is also used to indicate a noun's relationship to other nouns (with, above, below, in front, behind, among).

In addition to nouns, pronouns and adjectives also follow the case system. Adjectives also adopt the number and gender of the nouns they modify.

Grammatical Gender

One of the major grammatical differences between English and Russian is the use of gender. English nouns do not have a gender; they are neutral, or neuter. Russian nouns have one of three grammatical genders: masculine, feminine, or neuter. It is usually possible to tell the gender of a Russian noun by examining its last letter.

Table 5-2

Grammatical Gender of Russian Nouns

Masculine	Neuter	Feminine
consonant, Й, Ь	О, Е (Ё)	А, Я, Ь
суп	м**я**со	кап**у**ста
чай	мор**о**женое	вод**а**
карт**о**фель		морк**о**вь

Nouns ending in -ь have to be memorized! Some of them are masculine, and some are feminine.

There are several exceptions to the rules expressed in Table 5-3:

- Several nouns that refer to males end in -я or -а: **папа** (dad), **дядя** (uncle), and **дедушка** (grandfather).
- Several masculine first names have short names that end in -я or -а: **Коля** is short for **Николай** (Nicholas) and **Саша** is short for **Александр** (Alexander).
- Nouns ending in -мя are neuter: **имя** - first name, **племя** - tribe, **время** - time.
- Nouns borrowed from other languages might or might not follow the traditional pattern: **меню** - menu (neuter), **кофе** - coffee (masculine), **метро** - metro (neuter), **кафе** - café

Russian adjectives also have grammatical gender; however, their gender changes according to the noun they modify. This means that each Russian adjective usually has masculine, feminine, and neuter versions.

Number

Most Russian nouns have a singular and plural form. The number is indicated by the ending of the noun. In English, to express a plural form, the great majority of nouns take the -s ending, as in one dog – many dogs.

In Russian, there are several forms of the plural ending. In order to determine which ending you should use, remember that Russian nouns can be categorized based on their stem as either nouns with a hard stem or nouns with a soft stem. Hardness or softness of the stem is based on the phonetics quality of palatalization, which you learned about in Chapter 3. Some nouns take what is called a "zero ending."

Table 5-3

Singular and Plural Forms of Nouns in the Nominative Case

Hard Stemmed Nouns		
Masculine: Singular/Plural	Feminine: Singular/Plural	Neuter: Singular/Plural
Zero ending / -Ы or -И	-А / -Ы or -И	-О / -А
суп – супы	конфета – конфеты	вино – вина
универмаг - универмаги	груша – груши	
Soft Stemmed Nouns		
Masculine: Singular/Plural	Feminine: Singular/Plural	Neuter: Sing./Plural
-Й or –Ь / -И	-Я or –Ь /-И	-Е / -Я
музей – музеи	таможня - таможни	варенье – варенья

In some nouns, the stress pattern might change in the plural form.
Masculine nouns in the nominative case that have a zero ending end in a consonant.

How do you choose between the ending of -Ы or -И? Make your selection based on the spelling rule: choose "И" after the consonants К, Г, Х, Ж, Ч, Ш, and Щ. This spelling rule is known as Spelling Rule 1. It is used in many other situations when you have to choose between the vowels И and Ы.

Several Russian nouns have irregular plural forms that must be memorized:

- Some nouns have a fleeting vowel, as in огурец – огурцы (cucumber - cucumbers). Also, отец – отцы (father - fathers), церковь – церкви (church - churches), напиток – напитки (drink - drinks), and американец - американцы (American male - Americans).
- Some nouns do not have a plural form and are only used in singular, as in мясо, мороженое, молоко, and масло. Some of these words also do not have a plural form in English, for example, milk and butter. However, be careful: some nouns that are uncountable in English are countable in Russian and vice versa.

Knowing the gender, number, and case of a noun is essential in determining what form a modifying adjective needs to take.

Russian Meals

The most important meal of the day is served in the afternoon, sometime between 1 P.M. and 3 P.M. It is called "обед," and it includes soup, an entrée, and possibly tea with dessert. Breakfast, or in Russian "завтрак," consists of tea or coffee with a slice of bread served with cheese or salami, or a bowl of hot kasha with milk. Блины (pancakes) are often reserved for Sunday brunch or a holiday breakfast. Thin and light, блины are different from American pancakes and, depending on one's preference, can be eaten with different types of варенье (jam) or икра (caviar).

Between завтрак and обед, many people like to have a small snack, often referred to as "полдник." The British tradition of tea is not known as British in Russia, but it is popular with many Russians. In fact, tea drinking, or in Russian "чаепитие," is considered a national pastime.

FACT

"Чай," or tea, was not well known in Russia until the nineteenth century when the construction of railroads allowed for an uninterrupted supply from China and India. As prices for tea decreased, its popularity soared, and black tea became a staple of the Russian diet. Russians brew strong tea, called заварка, in a small teapot. The tea is diluted with hot water in individual cups. Sugar and milk are added to taste.

Between 7 P.M. and 8 P.M. families gather for a hearty dinner, which might be similar to об**е**д in the dishes served. The following language formulas are frequently used to encourage guests and family members to enjoy their meal and to thank hosts:

TRACK 26

При**я**тного аппет**и**та!
Bon appetit!

К**у**шайте на здор**о**вье!
Enjoy your meal! (Literally: Eat to your health!)

Очень вк**у**сно!
Delicious!

Спас**и**бо за вк**у**сный з**а**втрак / об**е**д / **у**жин!
Thank you for a delicious breakfast / lunch / dinner!

You can practice these phrases at your own dinner table with friends or family. Try cooking a traditional Russian meal for all to enjoy.

Traditional Russian Dishes and Beverages

The philosophy behind Russian cuisine is that a meal should provide an opportunity not only to satisfy one's hunger, but also to engage in pleasant conversation with others. Evening meals with family or friends are considered an important social activity. Except for breakfast, Russian meals incorporate starters or "зак**у**ски"—small dishes served all at once as an accompaniment to a pre-meal shot of vodka or a glass of wine.

Пир**о**ги (small, oval-shaped pies stuffed with meat, mushrooms, jam, potatoes, or a rice and egg mixture) are equally as popular as зак**у**ски at the beginning of the meal or as an afternoon snack with tea.

Закуски provide a way to simultaneously tempt one's palate before the real meal arrives and to get a conversation going. Pickled vegetables and mushrooms together with a selection of cheeses and cold meats are often served as закуски.

The next dish is usually суп (soup); щи, a cabbage beef soup, or борщ, a soup made out of beets and other vegetables, are common. Soups are served hot with a small serving of сметана (sour cream) and chopped parsley. After the soup comes the main dish. One of the most popular main dishes is пельмени, Russian dumplings, which are usually stuffed with a mixture of beef and pork and seasoned with соль (salt, (feminine)) and перец (pepper).

Although today Russian stores carry a wide selection of pre-made frozen пельмени, many families prefer to make their own in keeping with old family traditions. A mundane activity on the surface, for many Russians it has become a family ritual symbolizing unity and cooperation. Another popular dish is грибы с картошкой, fried mushrooms with potatoes.

ALERT!

In Russian, there are two words for potatoes: картофель (masculine) and картошка (feminine). The two forms are interchangeable, and the second one is less formal. Both words are usually used in the singular.

Russians are known for their love of хлеб (bread). It is offered with every meal, and there are usually at least two types to choose from: white wheat and dark rye. Many Russians believe that a meal without bread is not a nourishing meal.

The significance of bread in Russian culture is such that sharing bread and salt has become a common metaphor for friendship and trust. Bread symbolizes all the good of the world, and salt stands for the tears shed due to earthly turmoil. This is why in traditional Russian culture, hosts offer bread and salt to distinguished guests upon their arrival. Related to bread is квас, a mildly alcoholic beverage made by the natural fermentation of rye or wheat bread. It is sometimes flavored with fruits and berries, and because its alcoholic content is extremely low (no more than 1.5 percent), is enjoyed by people of all ages.

Eating Out

You will find a wide selection of restaurants in big Russian cities, from very affordable mom-and-pop stands to trendy sushi bars and French bistros. American-style fast food is everywhere, but gets a lot of competition from local chains such as Ёлки-Палки which sells блины, пироги, and other traditional Russian dishes. For lunch, office workers and students often go to a кафетерий or столовая (cafeteria). In the afternoon, stop for a coffee at a trendy кафе (café) and remember to order Turkish coffee and Russian ice cream, an unbeatable combination for any lover of caffeine and sweets.

As dark descends upon the town, it's time to check out a more upscale venue: a traditional Russian ресторан (restaurant) where you will be treated to a dinner with live music played in the background. Don't be surprised to see couples dancing between different courses! Relax and savor the atmosphere, but remember that the night is young, and you still have time to visit one of the big city's салса-бар (salsa bars) or ирландский паб (an Irish pub) or have a couple of beers in a пивная (a Russian bar). If you are happy with the service, remember to leave чаевые (a tip, literally "tea money"). The following is a list of words and phrases that might be helpful as you navigate your way through a menu in Russian.

QUESTION?

Are American soft drinks popular in Russia?
Yes, Coca-Cola, Pepsi, and other soft drinks are readily available. Diet drinks are less popular and sometimes harder to find. If you crave a Diet Coke, don't despair. Ask for "Кока-кола лайт" (Coke Light).

Table 5-4

Ordering Food in a Restaurant

Russian	English
ресторан	restaurant
бар	bar
кафетерий	cafeteria
столовая	cafeteria

Russian	English
меню	menu
список вин	wine list
официант	waiter
официантка	waitress
заказать обед	to order dinner
коктейль	cocktail (masculine)
закуски	starters
горячие блюда	main dishes
первые блюда	first dishes
вегетарианские блюда	vegetarian dishes
специи	spices
десерт	dessert
счёт	bill
заплатить по счету	to pay the bill
чаевые	tip (noun)

It's possible to sample many different dishes in Russia, and you don't have to limit yourself to Russian specialties. Caucasian, Central Asian, East Asia, and South Asian restaurants are common, especially in urban areas. It's also not hard to find European restaurants.

Introduction to Russian Adjectives

In Russian, adjectives serve the same syntactic role as in the English language: to describe qualities of objects. The following adjectives are often used to describe different food tastes:

Table 5-5

Food-Related Adjectives

TRACK 27

Russian	English	Russian	English
вкусный	tasty	невкусный	not tasty
хороший	good	плохой	bad
новый	new	старый	old

Russian	English	Russian	English
го́рький	bitter	сла́дкий	sweet
солёный	salty	пре́сный	fresh
све́жий	fresh	несве́жий	not fresh
горя́чий	hot	холо́дный	cold
мя́гкий	soft	твёрдый	hard

It is important to remember that Russian adjectives agree with the nouns that they denote in gender, number, and case, for example, све́жий хлеб (masculine) – све́жая клубни́ка (feminine) – све́жее молоко́ (neuter). Russian adjectives are grouped according to the palatalization of their stem into hard-stemmed adjectives and soft-stemmed adjectives.

Table 5-6

Adjectives in the Nominative Case

Hard Stem			
Masculine	Feminine	Neuter	Plural
-ЫЙ / -ИЙ (stress on the stem) –ОЙ (stress on the ending)	-АЯ	-ОЕ	-ЫЕ (stress on the stem)/ -ИЕ (stress on the ending)
Soft Stem			
Masculine	Feminine	Neuter	Plural
-ИЙ	-ЯЯ	-ЕЕ	-ИЕ
горя́чий суп	горя́чая ка́ша	горя́чее блю́до	горя́чие макаро́ны

Use Spelling Rule 1 to choose between И and Ы.

Chapter Review

Review the material in this chapter and complete the following exercises.

Chapter Quiz

Answer the following questions and check your answers in Appendix A.

1. List at least three products that are considered typical of the Russian diet. _____

2. How can you tell the syntactic roles of Russian nouns?

   _____

3. How many cases does Russian have? _____

4. What is the function of the nominative case?

   _____

5. What genders are assigned to Russian inanimate nouns?

   _____

6. What are the typical endings of Russian feminine nouns?

   _____

7. Name all typical daily Russian meals in Russian.

   _____

8. Explain what "закуски" are.

   _____

9. Name several typical Russian dishes.

   _____

10. Wish someone *Bon appetit!* in Russian.

    _____

11. Compliment a dish by saying that it is very delicious.

    _____

12. What does sharing bread and salt symbolize in Russian culture?

    _____

13. In which grammatical categories do Russian adjectives agree with Russian nouns?

    _____

14. Why is it important to know whether a particular adjective has a hard or a soft stem?

    _____

Grammar Drill

Denote the grammatical gender of the nouns listed below. Check your memory to make sure that you remember the meaning of these words by writing down their meanings in English.

1. обед _____
2. варенье _____
3. икра _____
4. сок _____
5. хлеб _____
6. клубника _____
7. картофель _____
8. колбаса _____
9. мясо _____
10. вино _____
11. ресторан _____
12. меню _____
13. счёт _____
14. десерт _____

Translation Drill

Translate the following phrases into Russian, taking into consideration what you have learned in this chapter about the grammatical agreement between Russian nouns and adjectives.

1. good wine _____
2. new menu _____
3. salty sausage _____
4. bitter chocolate _____
5. tasty dinner _____
6. soft bread _____
7. salty cucumbers _____
8. fresh tomatoes _____
9. good soup _____
10. bad Russian dumplings _____

Reading, Listening, and Pronunciation Practice

Read the following menu of a typical Russian restaurant as you listen to the CD. Translate each item from Russian into English. To improve your pronunciation, try to imitate the accent and stress patterns that the actor uses on the CD. Check your answers in Appendix A.

TRACK 28

Russian Menu – Ру́сское меню́

1. Заку́ски: солёные огурцы́ и помидо́ры, икра́, сыр и колбаса́.

   _____

2. Пе́рвые блю́да: суп (щи и борщ).

   _____

3. Горя́чие блю́да: грибы́ и карто́фель, говя́дина и макаро́ны, пельме́ни, свини́на и о́вощи.

   _____

4. Десе́рт: торт, моро́женое.

   _____

5. Напи́тки: чай, ко́фе, вода́, квас, Ко́ка-ко́ла лайт.

   _____

6. What would you choose for dinner? Write down your selection in Russian.

   _____

Chapter 6

Russian Names and Family

Reading Dostoyevsky or Tolstoy is a wonderful way to explore Russian heritage, but readers who are unfamiliar with the Russian language often find it difficult to decode important cultural information embedded in the names of the characters. Examining the structure of Russian names will allow you to pick up on cultural nuances and will introduce you to the dynamics of Russian family life. In this chapter, you will learn new vocabulary dealing with family relations, discover the basics of Russian verbs, and learn about Russian personal pronouns.

Russian Family Life

The Russian family has undergone major social changes over the last hundred years. Historically, Russia is a society that values extended family, but it has become a country where a rate of divorce approximates or exceeds that of the United States.

Despite these dramatic changes, the traditional value of respect toward the elderly is still alive. Grandparents, or in Russian **бабушки и дедушки** (grandmothers and grandfathers), occupy a revered place in the Russian family.

Following is a vocabulary list with words to describe family relations. Note the conceptual difference between English and Russian ways of referring to in-laws. English uses generic terms that apply to both sides of the family, e.g. mother-in-law, while Russian has specific terms that help to identify who is who on what side of the family, e.g. **тёща** – the mother-in-law on wife's side, and **свекровь** – the mother-in-law on the husband's side. The concept of "son- or daughter-in-law" is expressed in Russian through terms that bear no similarities to that of "son or daughter." Compare the following pairs: **сын** – son, **зять** – son-in-law; **дочь** – daughter, **невестка** – daughter-in-law.

Table 6-1

Family Relations

TRACK 29

Russian	English
семья	family
мать / мама (informal)	mother
отец / папа (informal)	father
сын	son
дочь / дочка (informal)	daughter
сестра	sister
брат	brother
двоюродная сестра	cousin (female)
двоюродный брат	cousin (male)
бабушка	grandmother
дедушка	grandfather
внук	grandson
внучка	granddaughter

тётя	aunt
дядя	uncle
племянник	nephew
племянница	niece
отчим	stepfather
падчерица	stepdaughter
пасынок	stepson
сирота	orphan (male/female)
муж	husband
жена	wife
свекровь	mother-in-law (husband's mother)
свёкр	father-in-law (husband's father)
невестка	daughter-in-law
тёща	mother-in-law (wife's mother)
тесть	father-in-law (wife's father)
зять	son-in-law
невеста	bride
жених	groom
вдова	widow
вдовец	widower

The form "мать" is used only in formal paperwork. In nearly all other situations, the form "мама" is more appropriate.
Be careful with similarly sounding words "невеста" (bride) and "невестка" (daughter-in-law).

Russian Names

Russians have three names: a first or given name (**имя**), patronymic (**отчество**), and the surname (**фамилия**). For instance:

Михаил (first name) **Сергеевич** (patronymic) **Горбачёв** (last name)

Анна (first name) **Андреевна** (patronymic) **Ахматова** (last name)

These three names constitute an individual's legal name, the one that appears on all official papers, including passport, birth certificate, and court proceedings.

First Names

Имя, in English a first name, is the given name selected for the baby by the parents. As in English, many Russian names have full and short or diminutive forms. Compare the following names: **Александра** (feminine) – **Александр** (masculine), **Мария** (feminine)– **Григорий** (masculine), **Нина** (feminine)- **Игорь** (masculine). The general rule is that first names referring to males usually end in a consonant, a soft sign, or -Й. First names referring to females usually end in -А or -Я. There are very few exceptions to this rule: **Данила** and **Никита** end in -а, but they are male names. All Russian short names, regardless of whether they are masculine or feminine, end in -Я or -А.

Following are two tables with popular Russian first names for men and women. Both full and short names are included. Note that some Russian names have a literal meaning: **Вера** (Faith), **Слава** (Glory).

TRACK 30

Table 6-2

Masculine First Names

Russian Name	Short Name(s)	English Equivalent
Александр	Саша, Шура	Alexander
Алексей	Алёша, Лёша	Alexei
Андрей	Андрюша	Andrew
Валентин	Валя	Valentin
Василий	Вася	Basil
Виталий		Vitaly
Владимир	Володя	Vladimir
Георгий	Гоша, Жора	George
Григорий	Гриша	Gregory
Данила	Даня	Daniel
Дмитрий	Дима, Митя	Dmitry
Иван	Ваня	Ivan
Евгений	Женя	Eugene
Никита	Ника	Nikita
Николай	Коля	Nicholas
Матвей	Матюша	Matthew
Михаил	Миша	Mikhail/Michael

Олег	Олежка	Oleg
Павел	Павлик, Паша	Paul
Пётр	Петя, Петруша	Peter
Фёдор	Федя	Fyodor/Theodor
Сергей	Серёжа	Sergei
Станислав	Стас	Stanislav

Remember that although the names Данила and Никита end in –a, they are male names.

TRACK 31

Table 6-3

Feminine First Names

Russian Name	Short Name(s)	English Equivalent
Александра	Саша, Шура	Alexandra
Анна	Аня, Анюта, Нюра	Anna
Алла	Аля	Alla
Анастасия	Настя	Anastasia
Валентина	Валя	Valentina
Вера		Vera (Faith)
Дарья	Даша	Daria
Евгения	Женя	Eugenia
Екатерина	Катя	Catherine
Елизавета	Лиза	Elizabeth
Ирина	Ира	Irina
Ксения	Ксюша	Xenia
Любовь	Люба	Lyubov (Love)
Людмила	Люда	Ludmila
Марина		Marina
Мария	Маша, Маруся	Maria
Надежда	Надя	Nadia (Hope)
Наталья	Наташа	Natalia
Нина		Nina
Ольга	Оля	Olga
Светлана	Света	Svetlana
Татьяна	Таня	Tatiana
Юлия	Юля	Julia

Patronymics

Отчество, or a patronymic, is derived from the father's first name. The literal translation of the patronymic is "the son of" or "the daughter of." It is always put after the individual's full first name. To form a patronymic, add a gender-specific suffix to the first name. For example, **Юлия Петровна** is a woman whose first name is **Юлия** and whose patronymic name is **Петровна**, which means her father's name is **Пётр**.

Table 6-4

Forming a Patronymic

Father's Name	Son's Patronymic	Daughter's Patronymic
Father's Name	+ -ович / -евич	+ -овна / -евна
Борис	Борисович	Борисовна
Александр	Александрович	Александровна
Николай	Николаевич	Николаевна
Григорий	Григорьевич	Григорьевна
Валентин	Валентинович	Валентиновна

Patronymics are never used with short names or nicknames. They are used to address or refer to adults in formal and professional situations. They show respect and sometimes a certain degree of social distance. For example, students will address their teacher with a combination of her full first name and patronymic, or in Russian **имя-отчество**. All official documents used internally in Russia also require a patronymic.

Last Names

Фамилия, or "last name" in English, usually has both masculine and feminine variants, as in **Сидоров – Сидорова** and **Волчонков – Волчонкова**. The basic rule to remember is that if the male form of the last name ends in a consonant, the female form ends in -a, or if the male form of the last name ends in -**ий**, the female form ends in -**ая**. Foreign surnames do not follow this pattern and retain the same form for both genders: **Шевченко** (Ukrainian), **Рено** (French), and **Смит** (English).

Table 6-5

Common Russian Last Names

Male Form	Female Form
Ending in a consonant or -Й	Ending in -А or -Я
Ивано**в**	Ивано**ва**
Кузнец**ов**	Кузнец**ова**
Вр**о**нский	Вр**о**нская
Кипр**е**нский	Кипр**е**нская

Personal Pronouns: Subject and Direct Object Forms

Now that you have learned about Russian names, let's figure out how to ask people what their names are. First we must go over some of the basics of Russian personal pronouns.

Personal pronouns are pronouns that can be used in place of a noun, for example, "boy" (noun) or "he" (personal pronoun). In both English and Russian, personal pronouns change their form to indicate their role in the sentence, such as that of a subject or a direct object.

She calls for / is calling him. **Он**а зовёт е**го**.

He calls for / is calling her. **Он** зовёт е**ё**.

You can see that the forms of the personal pronouns "he" and "she" are different in these sentences in both languages. This is because in the first sentence, the pronoun "she" is used as a subject, whereas in the second it is a direct object, and vice versa for the pronoun "he." In the previous chapter, you learned that Russian nouns have a case system, also known as declensions. This case system also applies to pronouns. The following tables show the subject and direct object forms of Russian personal pronouns. These tables introduce you to the nominative and accusative cases of Russian personal pronouns.

Table 6-6

Subject Personal Pronouns: Nominative Case

	Singular	English	Plural	English
1st person	я	I	мы	we
2nd person	ты/вы (familiar/formal)	you	вы	you
3rd person	он/она/оно	he/she/it	они	they

In Russian, the first person singular is never capitalized unless it is the first word in the sentence.

Table 6-7

Direct Object Personal Pronouns: Accusative Case

	Singular	English	Plural	English
1st person	меня	me	нас	us
2nd person	тебя/вас	you	вас	you
3rd person	его/её/его	him/her/it	их	them

The form "его" is pronounced [yivo]. The form её is pronounced [yeyo].

ALERT!

The personal pronoun вы can refer either to formal *you* (second person singular) or to *"you all"* (second person plural). You can deduce the meaning through context.

Russian has two forms of the second person singular: familiar you, "ты," and formal you, "вы." Use the familiar "ты" when addressing someone you know very well, such as a relative, a child, or a pet. Remember that this form can only be used when addressing one person or animal. Use the formal you, "вы," to address a person whom you do not know well, an elderly person, or a person of authority. The rule of thumb is to use "вы" whenever you are in a formal situation or you would like to show respect.

Introduction to Russian Verbs: What Is Your Name?

The structure used in Russian to ask someone about his or her name is different than in English. There are two important elements in this structure: the use of the direct object personal pronoun, and the use of the verb "звать," or in English "call," which you'll learn here.

The form of the verb you will find in the dictionary is called the infinitive. "Звать" is an example of the infinitive in Russian. Examples in English are write, read, and play. In English, the infinitive is often used with a particle "to," as in "to call." In Russian, most infinitive forms end in –ть.

The literal translation of the Russian structure corresponding to the English "What is your name?" is "How do they call you?", or in Russian "Как тебя зовут?" A standard response is "Меня зовут + Name." When you are reporting on the name of another person or persons, you can also use the construction "This is / These are . . . ," which is translated into Russian with only one word, "Это . . . " If you are not sure who the person in front of you is, you can also ask the question "Кто это?", meaning "Who is this/that?"

Note that in the present tense of the Russian verb, "to be" is often omitted, as in "Кто это?" / "Это Маша." or "Who is this?" / "This is Masha." In sentences where both the subject and the predicate are nouns, a dash is used to indicate the omission of the verb "to be" as in "Мария – жена и мама," or "Maria is a wife and a mother."

The following are some examples of questions and answers you might hear as people discuss their names.

TRACK 32

Как тебя зовут?
What is your name? (familiar)

Меня зовут Слава.
My name is Slava.

Как вас зовут?
What is your name? (formal)

Меня зовут Андрей Михайлович Суриков.
My name is Andrei Mikhailovich Surikov.

Как его зовут?
What is his name?

Его зовут / Это Фёдор.
His name is / This is Fyodor.

Как её зовут?
What is her name?

Её зовут / Это Светлана Николаевна Тихомирова.
Her name is / This is Svetlana Nikolayevna Tikhomirova.

Как вас зовут?
What are your names?

Нас зовут Мария и Виталий.
Our names are Maria and Vitaly.

Как их зовут?
What are their names?

Их зовут / Это Наташа и Аня.
Their names are / They are Natasha and Anya.

Verbs in Russian change their form depending on the person who accomplishes the action the verbs denote. Compare in English: I call / she calls / they call, and in Russian: я зову / она зовёт / они зовут. Russian verbs have six distinctive forms, or conjugations, to go with six grammatical persons:

- 1st person singular   (I / я)
- 2nd person singular   (you / ты/вы)
- 3rd person singular   (he/she/it / он/она/оно)
- 1st person plural   (we / мы)
- 2nd person plural   (you all / вы)
- 3rd person plural   (they / они)

The conjugation for the formal you is the same as that for the second person plural. In the Russian structure "Как тебя/вас/его/её/их зовут?", we are using the third person plural form of the Russian verb "звать." You will learn more about Russian verbs and their conjugations in the next chapters. Meanwhile, to practice the use of the structures that you have learned in this chapter, read aloud the following dialogue between a teacher and her students on the first day of school.

ALERT!

The Russian conjunction "a" is used to connect sentences that contain slightly contrasting ideas and is translated either as "and" or "but," depending on the context. The conjunction "и" can only be translated as "and." It connects ideas of equal status that do not contrast with one another.

Teacher: **Добрый день, дети! Меня зовут Валентина Петровна. А как вас зовут?**
Good afternoon, children! My name is Valentina Petrovna. And what are your names?

Student 1:   **Меня зовут Люда.**
My name is Lyuda.

Student 2:   **Меня зовут Даша.**
My name is Dasha.

Teacher: **А как тебя зовут?**
And what is your name?

Student 3: **Меня зовут Вася.**
My name is Vasya.

Teacher (pointing at a boy who has been silent so far): **А как его зовут?**
And what is his name?

Student 2: **Это Коля Серов.**
That's Kolya Serov.

This example highlights the traditional ways of introducing yourself and others. Notice that the teacher introduced herself with her given name and her patronymic, the three students introduced themselves with their short names, and the fourth student was introduced by another student who used his short name and surname.

Chapter Review

Review the material covered in this chapter and complete the following exercises.

Chapter Quiz

Answer the following questions and check your answers in Appendix A.

1. Who are considered the guardians of traditional values in Russian families? _____

2. If you were to rely on English to pronounce the Russian word for grandmother, what mistake are you likely to make?

_____

3. Name one of the differences in the conceptualization of family relations in English and Russian as evidenced in family-related vocabulary.

_____

4. List all of the forms used in Russian to refer to mother and father.

_____

5. How many names does a Russian person have? _____

6. Are there any Russian full first names that can be used both for men and women? _____

7. Give at least one example of a Russian full first name that is masculine, but ends in a typically feminine ending.

   _____

8. What is the literal translation of a patronymic?

   _____

9. What suffixes are used to form a patronymic?

   _____

10. As a foreign visitor to Russia, are you expected to introduce yourself with a patronymic name? _____

11. What is one major difference between English and Russian last names?

    _____

12. What is the culturally acceptable way to address a Russian doctor or teacher? _____

13. What form of the second person singular would you use when talking with your best Russian friend? With the grandfather of your best Russian friend? With your professor at the University?

    _____

14. In most cases, how can you tell the infinitive form of a Russian verb?

    _____

15. Give at least one example of a sentence in Russian where the verb "to be" is omitted.

    _____

Name Recognition and Vocabulary Drill

The following list of names reflects three generations of two different families. Remember that many Russian women take their husband's last name. Figure out who is related to whom and in what capacity. Write down your answers in English and then translate terms indicating family relations in Russian.

1. Мария Петровна Сергеева _____
2. Пётр Николаевич Сергеев _____
3. Владимир Сергеевич Никаноров _____
4. Ксения Борисовна Сергеева _____
5. Николай Дмитриевич Сергеев _____
6. Станислав Сергеевич Никаноров _____
7. Борис Алексеевич Никаноров _____
8. Александр Петрович Сергеев _____
9. Сергей Матвеевич Никаноров _____
10. Наталья Петровна Сергеева _____

Grammar Drill

Translate the following phrases into Russian, applying what you have learned in this chapter about Russian personal pronouns and Russian verbs.

1. My name is Ivan. _____
2. What is his name? _____
3. His name is Vladimir. _____
4. Who is this? _____
5. This is Marina. She is a mother and a wife.

_____

6. What are their names? _____
7. Their names are Alexander and Maria. _____

Listening Comprehension

TRACK 33

Listen to the corresponding CD track and fill out the missing patronymics.

1. Наталья _____ Иванова
2. Николай _____ Сидоров
3. Екатерина _____ Миронова
4. Сергей _____ Михалков
5. Марина _____ Левина

Chapter 7

Descriptions and Possessions

The goal of this chapter is to introduce the expressions and grammar you need to express possession and describe objects and people. We will focus on possessive pronouns, adjectives, and nouns referring to professions and common household objects. You will learn how to describe your family, talk about their professions, and make and accept compliments. You will also find out how to use culturally appropriate terms to address people of different ages and genders, even if you don't know their names. You will explore differences and similarities in making statements, posing questions, and constructing negative sentences.

Possessive Pronouns

Possessive pronouns express who or what possesses the nouns they modify. Compare the following expressions in English and in Russian: **мой папа** (my father), **моя мама** (my mother), **моё вино** (my wine), **мои родственники** (my relatives). As you can see from these examples, the possessive pronoun "**мой**" agrees in gender and number with the noun that it modifies.

ALERT!

Keep in mind that grammatical agreement in Russian includes gender, number, and case. Adjectives change form depending on the gender of the noun they modify. They also change depending on whether the noun is singular or plural. You will learn more about cases of nouns, adjectives, and pronouns in the following chapters.

Following is a table with Russian possessive pronouns and their forms in the nominative case. Although there are many forms to remember, note that third person possessives **его**, **её**, and **их** have only one form. However, don't confuse these possessive pronouns with the accusative case of the personal pronouns *he*, *she*, *it*, and *they* that were covered in Chapter 6.

Table 7-1

Possessive Pronouns: Nominative Case

English Personal Pronoun	Russian Personal Pronoun	Masc.	Fem.	Neuter	Plural
I	я	мой	моя	моё	мои
you	ты	твой	твоя	твоё	твои
he	он	его	его	его	его
she	она	её	её	её	её
it	оно	его	его	его	его
we	мы	наш	наша	наше	наши
you	вы	ваш	ваша	ваше	ваши
they	они	их	их	их	их

The possessive ваш can refer either to formal you (second person singular polite) or to you all (second person plural).

Describing Your Family

Following is a list of adjectives that people often use to describe family members. Russian adjectives have several forms because they agree in gender, number, and case with the nouns they modify. The form you will encounter in the dictionary is masculine, singular, and in the nominative case.

Table 7-2

Pronouns, Adjectives, and Nouns: Describing Family Members

TRACK 34

Russian Adj.	Example	English Translation
молод**ой**	молод**ая** мама	young mother
ст**а**рый	ст**а**рый дедушка	old grandfather
крас**и**вый	крас**и**вая жена	beautiful wife
хор**о**ший	хор**о**ший муж	good husband
симпат**и**чный	симпат**и**чный брат	good-looking brother
умный	**у**мная сестр**а**	smart sister
тал**а**нтливый	тал**а**нтливый сын	talented son
ст**а**рший	ст**а**рш**ие** д**е**ти	elder children
мл**а**дший	мл**а**дший брат	younger brother
люб**и**мый	люб**и**мая тётя	favorite aunt

Nouns: Professions

When describing your relatives, you might also want to mention their professions. Following is a list of Russian terms for various professions and occupations. Note that some names of professions have distinctive masculine and feminine forms; others, on the other hand, remain invariable, and it doesn't matter whether they are applied to men or women.

Table 7-3

Professions

TRACK 35

Masculine	Feminine	English Translation
уч**и**тель	уч**и**тельница	teacher
преподав**а**тель	преподав**а**тельница*	instructor (university/ college)

писатель	писательница*	writer
художник	художница*	painter
поэт	поэтесса*	poet
повар	повариха*	cook
студент	студентка	student
спортсмен	спортсменка	athlete
певец	певица	singer
актёр	актриса	actor/actress
артист	артистка	performer
официант	официантка	waiter/waitress
продавец	продавщица	salesman/saleswoman
стюард	стюардесса	flight attendant
военный	военная	military serviceman
рабочий	рабочая	manual worker
врач, доктор		doctor
инженер		engineer
строитель		builder
водитель		driver
фармацевт, аптекарь		pharmacist
ветеринар		veterinarian
профессор		professor
бухгалтер		accountant
менеджер		manager
директор		director
учёный		scientist
президент		president
офицер		officer
солдат		soldier
пилот		pilot

An asterisk indicates professions for which some women prefer to use the masculine form when referring to their own occupation as a way to express their equal status.

Making Compliments

When people describe their family to their friends, it is customary to compliment newly introduced family members by commenting on their youthful appearance, beauty, or other positive qualities. Here is how you can do this in Russian:

Какая у вас/ у тебя умная / красивая сестра!
What a smart / beautiful sister you've got! (informal)

У вас такой симпатичный / талантливый брат!
What a cute / talented brother you've got! (formal)

Ваш муж такой умный!
Your husband is so smart!

If you are introducing your family members to someone else, you can do so with the construction **Это** . . . , which was first introduced in Chapter 6. To compliment someone's relatives, use the construction **У вас такой** . . . , which literally means "By you, there is . . . "

Read the following dialogue to learn more about how to introduce family members and make compliments. The dialogue is between two friends, **Игорь** and **Евгений**, who are students at Moscow State University. **Игорь** is showing a picture of his family to **Евгений**.

Игорь: Евгений, это моя мама. (Igor, this is my mother.)

Евгений: У тебя такая молодая мама! Как её зовут?
(Your mother is so young! What is her name?)

Игорь: Её зовут Нина Александровна. Она – врач.
(Her name is Nina Alexandrovna.)

Евгений: А это кто?
(And who is this?)

Игорь: Это моя невеста, Настя. Она - студентка.
(This is my fiancée, Nastya. She is also a student.)

Евгений: У тебя такая красивая невеста! А это кто?
(You have such a pretty fiancée! And who is this?)

Игорь: Это мой папа. Он – профессор.
(This is my father. He is a professor.)

If you would like to compliment someone directly, learn the following words and expressions:

TRACK 36

Table 7-4

Making Face-to-Face Compliments

Russian	English
женщина	woman
девушка	young girl
мужчина	man
молодой человек	young man
человек	person
мальчик	boy
девочка	girl
дети	children
Вы / Ты – такой умный!	You are so smart!
Вы / Ты – такая талантливая женщина!	You are such a talented woman!

Treat такой as an adjective. It can be translated as "such" or "so." Remember to make sure it agrees with the noun it defines.

The general structure for making compliments is as follows: pronoun, adjective, noun. If you are going to use **такой** for emphasis, it should be placed before the main adjective(s).

Note that if you don't know the person's name, it is acceptable to address him or her with nouns and adjectives indicating their gender and age, such as **молодой человек** (only for men), **мужчина**, **девочка**. However, be careful with the use of **женщина**—many Russian women prefer to be called **девушка** well into their golden years! It is advisable to rely exclusively on the formal pronoun **вы** as a way to address all people you don't know. Children are the exception; use the familiar **ты** to address children you do not know.

During Soviet times, it was common to use the terms **товарищ** / **товарищи** (comrade/s) or **гражданин** / **гражданка** / **граждане** (citizen: masculine, feminine, plural) to address others. Today, these terms are outdated. The terms **господин** / **госпожа** / **господа** (mister, missus, generic plural) are slowly being resurrected, but they are more commonly used in formal settings than in everyday interactions.

The Russian "**девушка**" and "**молодой человек**" are also equivalents to the English "girlfriend" and "boyfriend." A boyfriend can be also referred to as "**друг**" (friend). Today some young Russians use the English terms "boyfriend" and "girlfriend" in place of their Russian equivalents.

Statements, Questions, and Negative Sentences

As opposed to English, in order to form a question in Russian, you don't have to change the order of words. Listen to the CD and compare the following examples:

TRACK 37

Это твой сын.	This is your son.
Это твой сын?	Is this your son?
Это его внучка.	This is his granddaughter.
Это его внучка?	Is this his granddaughter?
Это её муж.	This is her husband.
Это её муж?	Is this her husband?

Remember the word for "yes" in Russian is да, and the word for "no" is нет. To form a negative statement or question, add the particle не in front of the word that you are negating, as in **Э**то не моя жена. (This/That is not my wife.)

Use different intonation to indicate the difference between a statement and a question. Generally, statements are pronounced with a falling pitch, while questions have a rising pitch with a stress on the word that is the focus of the question. Add an appropriate question word at the beginning of the sentence to form questions that require more than a yes-no answer:

Table 7-5

Question Words

Russian	English
Кто	Who
Кто там?	Who is there?
Что	What
Что там?	What is there?
Какой	Which / What kind
Какой это город, Москва или Санкт-Петербург?	Which city is this, Moscow or St. Petersburg?
Как	How
Как дела?	How are things going? / How are you?

The "I Have" Construction

Earlier in this chapter, you learned to compliment other people's relatives by using the У вас такой . . . construction. In this section, we will examine a similar construction that allows us to express possessions:

У меня есть мама и папа.
I have a mother and a father.

У тебя есть брат и сестра.
You have a brother and a sister.

The literal translation of this construction is "By me/you, there is . . . " The construction includes the verb есть ("to be"), which can be translated as "to have" in this context. The first part of the construction is a preposition "у" (by) plus the appropriate personal pronoun in the genitive case followed by есть and a noun in the nominative case.

Table 7-6

Personal Pronouns: Genitive Case

Singular	English	Plural	English
First person			
меня	me	нас	us
Second person			
тебя/вас	you((in)formal)	вас	you
Third person			
его/её/ его	him/her/it	их	them

The form "его" is pronounced [yivo]. The form её is pronounced [yeyo]

Note that the third person singular and plural forms of pronouns acquire an additional initial letter "н" when preceded by the preposition "у": у него, у неё, у нас, у них. Also, remember that you already know another way to express possession through the use of possessive pronouns, which you learned in Chapter 6. Following is a list of sentences with examples of how to express possessions using either the есть formula or possessive pronouns.

TRACK 38

У меня есть кот и собака.	I have a cat and a dog.
Это мои кот и собака.	These are my cat and dog.
У меня есть машина.	I have a car.
Это моя машина.	This is my car.
У тебя есть хлеб, молоко и сыр.	You have bread, milk, and cheese.
Это мой хлеб, молоко и сыр.	This is my bread, milk, and cheese.

Common Possessions

To increase your vocabulary, study the following words and expressions that will help you describe what you and others have:

Table 7-7

Everyday Objects and Possessions

Russian	English
машина	car
мотоцикл	motorcycle
велосипед	bicycle
дом	house
квартира	apartment
дача	country house (dacha)
телевизор	TV set
компьютер	computer
телефон	telephone
мобильный телефон	cell phone
собака	dog
кот	cat (male)
попугай	parrot

Other Uses for есть

You can also use the **есть** construction to talk about "**деньги**" (money) and "**время**" (time) as illustrated in the following dialogue:

Пётр: У тебя есть время?
Do you have time?

Виктор: Да. Чем я могу тебе помочь?
Yes. How can I help you?

Пётр: У тебя есть деньги? Я могу у тебя взять в долг десять рублей?
Do you have money? Can I borrow ten rubles from you?

Виктор: Да, конечно.
Yes, certainly.

Пётр: Огромное спасибо.
Thank you so much.

Expressing the Lack of Possession

If you would like to provide a short negative answer to a question about a possession, simply reply "нет" (no) to the question, as in

У теб**я** есть чай? – Нет.
Do you have tea? – No.

Giving a full-sentence negative answer requires knowledge of the genitive case of nouns, which will be covered later.

Describing Possessions

Memorize the following adjectives to describe your possessions and to praise or criticize things that belong to others. Note that in Russian you can almost always form an adjective with the opposite meaning by simply adding the particle "не" to the adjective.

TRACK 39

Table 7-8

Russian	English	Russian	English
уд**о**бный	comfortable	неуд**о**бный	uncomfortable
крас**и**вый	beautiful	некрас**и**вый	not beautiful
стр**а**шный	scary	нестр**а**шный	not scary
больш**о**й	big	небольш**о**й	not big
м**а**ленький	small	нем**а**ленький	not small
дорог**о**й	expensive	недорог**о**й	inexpensive
Russian	**English**	**Russian**	**English**
дешёвый	cheap	недешёвый	not cheap
хор**о**ший	good	нехор**о**ший	not good
плох**о**й	bad	неплох**о**й	not bad
интер**е**сный	interesting	неинтер**е**сный	not interesting

The adjective "неплох**о**й" is usually used in the sense of "satisfactory" or "average." It is a modest way of praising something or somebody. Use the word "**о**чень" (very) to intensify your statements.

Use the words "там"(over there) and "здесь"(here) to generally indicate the location of the object that you are referring to. For example: Где твой дом? - Мой дом — там. (Where is your house? - My house is over there.)

Coordinating Conjunctions

In Chapter 6, you learned about two Russian conjunctions, "**a**" (and/but) and "**и**" (and). These conjunctions are called coordinating conjunctions because they connect words and/or sentences of equal importance: "**и**" connects a series of parallel ideas that cannot be contrasted, whereas "**a**" links ideas of slight contrast. Another very common coordinating conjunction is "**но**" (but), which is used to connect contrasting ideas. See the following sentences for examples of how to use these three conjunctions appropriately.

Саша – **о**чень хор**о**ший муж и от**е**ц.
Sasha is a very good husband and father.

Борис Петр**о**вич – не преподав**а**тель, а инжен**е**р.
Boris Petrovich is not a teacher but an engineer.

Это Л**е**на, мо**я** мл**а**дшая сестр**а**. А **э**то Н**и**на, мо**я** ст**а**ршая сестр**а**.
This Lena, my younger sister. And this is Nina, my elder sister.

Это мо**я** маш**и**на. Он**а** – м**а**ленькая, но **о**чень хор**о**шая.
This is my car. It is small but very good.

Chapter Review

Review the material covered in this chapter and complete the following exercises.

Chapter Quiz

Answer the following questions and check your answers in Appendix A.

1. Explain the notion of grammatical agreement as it applies to Russian nouns, pronouns, and adjectives.

   _____

2. List all Russian possessive pronouns that do not follow the general rules of grammatical agreement and keep their form invariable.

   _____

3. Identify one Russian personal and possessive pronoun that can refer to one person or several people. _____

4. In which form will you find Russian adjectives in the dictionary?

   _____

5. How would you compliment a smart and pretty sister of your good friend, Ivan?

   _____

6. What is the most foolproof way to address strangers in Russian?

   _____

7. What are current substitutes for the Soviet **товарищ / гражданин / гражданка / граждане**? _____

8. Which verb do we use to express possession in Russian?

   _____

9. How can you tell a statement from a question in Russian?

   _____

10. How can you make a positive sentence into a negative one?

    _____

11. How would you give a negative answer about having something? How would you give a positive answer? _____

12. Do all terms for professions have distinct masculine and feminine forms? _____

13. List three common coordinating conjunctions in Russian.

_____

14. Explain the meaning of the Russian adjective "неплохой."

_____

_____

Grammar and Vocabulary Drill

Translate the following expressions to practice describing family members. Pay specific attention to possessive pronouns and grammatical agreement between nouns, adjectives, and pronouns.

1. Your pretty sister _____

2. His good-looking son _____

3. My talented daughter _____

4. His mother-in-law and father-in-law _____

5. Her old grandfather _____

6. Your (formal) smart husband _____

7. You are so cute! (addressing a woman) _____

8. You are so handsome! (addressing a man)

_____

9. What a nice husband you've got! (formal)

_____

10. What a talented and beautiful daughter you've got!

_____

11. This is my younger sister. Her name is Lena. She is a student.

_____

12. Who is this? – This is my wife, Vera. She is a talented scientist and a good teacher.

_____

Reading Practice

Read the following sentences in which people talk about their possessions. Translate new vocabulary and conversation formulas from Russian into English. Check your answers in Appendix A.

1. **Э**то тво**я** маш**и**на?

_____

2. Нет, **это его** маш**и**на. А **это** твой мотоц**и**кл?

_____

3. Да. Он ст**а**рый, но **о**чень хор**о**ший. А **это** твой дом?

_____

4. Да. Он – м**а**ленький, но уд**о**бный.

_____

5. **Э**то мо**я** кварт**и**ра. У мен**я** есть телеф**о**н, хор**о**ший телев**и**зор и ст**а**рый комп**ь**ютер. А у теб**я** есть кварт**и**ра?

_____

6. Нет, у мен**я** есть небольш**о**й дом. Там у мен**я** есть м**а**ленький телев**и**зор и телеф**о**н.

_____

7. Кто **это**?

_____

8. **Э**то мой муж, Никол**а**й Фёдорович. Он – **о**чень хор**о**ший инжен**е**р. А **это** мо**я** дочь, М**а**ша. Он**а** – студ**е**нтка. А **это** её жен**и**х, В**а**ся.

_____

9. В**а**ся – **о**чень симпат**и**чный. Он студ**е**нт?

_____

Listening Comprehension

TRACK 40

Listen to the questions on the corresponding CD track and write down positive full-sentence answers in the spaces below.

1. Question: **Это Москва**? Answer: _____

2. Question: **У вас есть время**? Answer: _____

3. Question: **Это ваша собака**? Answer: _____

4. Question: **У вас есть деньги**? Answer: _____

Chapter 8

Introduction to Russian Verbs and Numerals

This chapter introduces the very basics of Russian verbs. It establishes their major conjugation groups in the present tense and offers examples of both regular and irregular verbs. Once you understand the basics, apply your new knowledge of Russian verbs to learn how to discuss your hobbies and ask others about their favorite seasonal pastimes. Finally, do your math in Russian and find out Russian names for the days of the week and months.

Verb Groups I and II

Russian verbs are listed in the dictionary in their infinitive forms. Verbs in their infinitive forms have two parts, a stem and a suffix. Infinitive verbs usually end in –ть.

In Russian, each verb has two stems: the infinitive stem derived by chopping of the –ть ending from the infinitive form of the verb and the present tense stem found by cutting off the conjugation ending from any of the conjugation forms of the verb in the present tense.

Infinitive verbs are not meant to show the tense, person, or number of the verb. All of that must be accomplished through conjugation. In this chapter, we will focus on conjugating verbs in the present tense.

Russian verbs are usually classified into two large groups, each following a distinctive pattern in their conjugations. The groups are known as Group I, or the Е Group, and Group II, or the И Group. The letters е and и are the so-called thematic vowels. Group I verb stems take on the letter Е in their conjugations, and Group II verb stems end with the letter И.

The secret to forming correct conjugations of Russian verbs in the present tense is to remember that conjugation endings are added to the present tense stem of the verb, not to its infinitive stem. Whenever these stems are different (which happens often), you must memorize the forms of both stems.

The following charts provide conjugations for the verb читать (to read), which falls within Group I, and the verb говорить, which belongs to Group II. If you memorize the endings of these two verbs, you will be able to conjugate most Russian verbs. Remember that verbs taking -ю and -ют endings are known as Group I or Group II Model 1 verbs. Verbs that have the endings -у and -ут or -ат are known as Group I or Group II Model 2 verbs.

TRACK 41

Table 8-1

Group I: Читать– The Present Tense Stem Чита-

Person	Singular	Plural
I	чита**ю** - ю/у	чита**ем** - ем
II	чита**ешь** - ешь	чита**ете** - ете
III	чита**ет** - ет	чита**ют** - ют/ут

Note that the endings "-у" and "-ут" are less common.

Verbs that follow Group I pattern include verbs with the present tense stem ending in vowels. The following are examples of Group I Model 1 verbs. Note that infinitive stems and present tense stems for these verbs are identical.

понима**ть**	to understand
раб**о**тать	to work
игр**ать**	to play
отдых**ать**	to rest, to be on vacation
пл**а**вать	to swim
д**е**лать	to do
д**у**мать	to think
гул**ять**	to walk, to take a stroll
ум**е**ть	to know how to do something
счит**ать**	to count

Now let's examine the conjugation pattern for Group II verbs.

Table 8-2

Group II: Говорить – The Present Tense Stem Говор-

TRACK 42

	Singular	Plural
I	говор**ю** - ю/у	говор**им** - им
II	говор**ишь** - ишь	говор**ите** - ите
III	говор**ит** - ит	говор**ят** - ят/ат

Note that the endings "-у" and "-ат" are less common.

Verbs that follow Group II pattern include verbs with the present tense stem ending in a consonant with the -**ить** and sometimes -**ать** endings in the infinitive form, for example:

смотр**еть**   to watch
плат**ить**   to pay

Beware that in some verbs stress patterns change in different conjugations. For example, take the verb смотр**еть**: я смотр**ю**, ты см**о**тришь, он см**о**трит, мы см**о**трим, вы см**о**трите, они см**о**трят. In these cases, you must memorize the stress patterns in addition to the conjugation endings.

Keep in mind that the differences between the pronouns ты and вы: the form ты чит**а**ешь is used to address family members, relatives, friends, children, and pets, whereas the вы чит**а**ете form is reserved for formal address or to refer to several people.

Stem Variations in the Present Tense

Remember that some variation is possible within Group I and II regular verbs. For example, although the verb пис**ать** (to write) belongs to Group I Model 2, its present tense stem is different from its infinitive stem, resulting in the consonant variation in the present tense in all persons:

Table 8-3

Писать (Group I, Model 2) – The Present Tense Stem Пиш-

Person	Singular	Plural
I	пиш**у**	п**и**шем
II	п**и**шешь	п**и**шете
III	п**и**шет	п**и**шут

Note the stress shift in the present tense.

Finally, in the verb любить (to like, love) that belongs to Group II, an additional consonant –л is added to form its present tense stem, resulting in the following conjugation in the present tense:

TRACK 44

Table 8-4

Любить (Group II, Model 1) – The Present Tense Stem Любл-

Person	Singular	Plural
I	люблю	любим
II	любишь	любите
III	любит	любят

Note the shift in the stress pattern of this verb. Use this verb to form infinitive constructions, as in "я люблю работать."

Based on variations in their present tense stems, Russian verbs are classified in additional subclasses. You will learn more about this in the following chapters.

Russian Present Tense: The Specifics

Now that you know the basics of the conjugations of Russian verbs in the present tense, let's examine the differences and similarities between how this tense is used in Russian and English.

QUESTION?

What does the word "tense" mean?
Tense is a grammatical concept that expresses the time when an action takes place. There are three basic tenses: present, past, and future. In English, there are many additional tenses formed using auxiliary verbs and participles. Russian has only three grammatical tenses but uses other ways to indicate an attitude toward action in time.

In English, there are several grammatical tenses that describe present actions, including the simple present (I write), the present continuous (I am writing), and the present perfect (I have been writing). In Russian, there is only one present tense, and all of the above sentences are translated as "я пишу." The Russian present tense denotes actions that are happening at this moment, continuous actions, actions that have begun in the past and are continuing now, and habitual or repetitive actions.

Reflexive Verbs

Russian has reflexive verbs, just like English. Reflexive verbs express actions that reflect back on the performer. For example, "I washed myself" (reflexive) as opposed to "I washed my dog" (non-reflexive). In Russian, reflexivity is expressed through the addition of the particle -ся as in смотреть (to look, watch) – смотреться (to look at oneself / to appear to others (colloquial)). The reflective particle is added at the very end of the verb. Note that some verbs that are reflexive in English are not reflexive in Russian, and vice versa. Russian reflexive verbs follow the same conjugation rules as their non-reflexive counterparts. Below is a conjugation table for the verb кататься (to ride or roll / skate oneself), a verb that is used in several idiomatic expressions that you will learn in the following section of this chapter

Table 8-5

Кататься (Group I, Model 1) – The Present Tense Stem Ката-(ся)

Person	Singular	Plural
I	катаюсь -юсь/усь	катаемся -емся
II	катаешься -ешься	катаетесь -етесь
III	катается -ется	катаются -ются/-утся

Note that the particle –ся changes to –сь in the first person singular and second person plural.

Another reflexive verb to remember is заниматься (to occupy oneself) (Group I, Model 1) – the present tense stem занима-(ся).

Recreational Activities and Seasons

Sports, arts, and reading are popular recreational activities in Russia. Russians are proud of their accomplishments in international competitions in chess, tennis, and gymnastics, and many people choose these sports as hobbies. Hockey and soccer remain the most popular team sports and pastimes for boys all over the country. One famous Soviet song goes, "В хоккей играют настоящие мужчины . . . " (Real men play hockey), and that attitude still portrays a typical, somewhat macho, attitude toward this sport. Volleyball and basketball are equally popular among men and women and are often played with teams consisting of members of both genders.

Figure skating and skiing continue to be popular winter activities for many Russians, some of whom choose to pursue these sports on the professional level, reaching the very top in international competitions. The following is a list of expressions with the verbs **играть**, **читать**, and **слушать** that describe some popular hobbies and recreational activities.

TRACK 45

Играть в ш**а**хматы / футб**о**л / баскетб**о**л / волейб**о**л / хокк**е**й / **т**еннис / бейсб**о**л / америк**а**нский футб**о**л
to play chess / soccer / basketball / volleyball / hockey / tennis / baseball / football

Игр**а**ть на пиан**и**но / скр**и**пке / саксоф**о**не / гит**а**ре
to play piano / violin / saxophone / guitar.

Чит**а**ть кн**и**ги / журн**а**лы / газ**е**ты
to read books / magazines / newspapers

Рис**о**в**а**ть акв**а**р**е**лью
to paint watercolors

Сл**у**шать м**у**зыку
to listen to music

Кат**а**ться на конькáх / л**ы**жах / велосип**е**де / мотоц**и**кле
to skate / to ski / to bike / to ride a motorcycle.

Пл**а**вать в басс**е**йне
to swim in a swimming pool

Заниматься спортом
to do sports

Танцевать дискотеке в клубе
to dance at a disco club

Read the following dialogue between two friends, **Коля** and **Борис**, who are discussing their favorite things to do.

Коля: Что ты любишь делать в свободное время?
What do you like to do in your free time?

Борис: Я люблю кататься на лыжах и играть в футбол. А ты?
I like to ski and play soccer. And you?

Коля: А я люблю играть в хоккей и читать книги.
And I like to play hockey and read books.

Борис: А чем любит заниматься твоя сестра Аня в свободное время?
And what does your sister Anya like to do in her free time?

Коля: Аня любит танцевать и рисовать. А ещё, она играет в баскетбол и любит кататься на коньках.
She likes to dance and draw. And also, she plays basketball and likes to skate.

Борис: Я тоже люблю танцевать и играть в баскетбол.
I also like to dance and play basketball.

Hobbies and Seasons

Many hobbies are seasonal. We like to go skating in the winter and swimming in the summer. The following is a vocabulary list with words that will help you describe the hobbies you like to pursue in different seasons of the year. Note that the instrumental case is required to express the season when you enjoy a particular activity.

Table 8-6

Seasons: Времена года

Russian	English	Russian	English
(Nominative Case)		(Instrumental)	
время года	season		
зима	winter	зимой	in the winter
весна	spring	весной	in the spring
лето	summer	летом	in the summer
осень (feminine)	fall	осенью	in the fall

Here is a dialogue between Саша and Наташа about their hobbies during different times of the year.

Саша: Наташа, что ты любишь делать летом?
Natasha, what do you like to do in the summer?

Наташа: Летом я люблю играть в баскетбол.
In the summer, I like to play basketball.

Саша: А зимой?
And in the winter?

Наташа: А зимой, мой муж и я любим кататься на лыжах в парке. Саша, а ты любишь кататься на лыжах?
And in the winter, my husband and I like to ski in the park.
Sasha, do you like to ski?

Саша: Нет, но я люблю кататься на коньках.
No, but I like to ice skate.

Additional Idiomatic Phrases

Just like English, Russian is full of metaphoric and idiomatic expressions: these are phrases that use images to produce colorful associations between the things being described and our experiences. The following are several examples of such expressions with the verbs that you have learned in this chapter:

играть на нервах

to irritate someone, literally "to play on someone's nerves"

заниматься ерундой

to waste time by doing something inconsequential, literally "to engage in nonsense"

читать лекцию

to lecture someone, literally "to read a lecture"

Любишь кататься – люби и саночки возить.

If you are enjoying something, be ready to deal with the consequences; literally "If you like to ride in the sled, then you should like dragging it along, too."

Cardinal and Ordinal Numerals

Do you like to count, or in Russian, Вы любите считать? If you are mathematically inclined, study this section to learn cardinal and ordinal numbers in Russian from one to 100. Note that some numerals are similar to the ones in English. Compare два (two), три (three), and шесть (six). These similarities can be explained through the common Indo-European ancestry of the English and Russian languages.

Table 8-7

Cardinal and Ordinal Numbers

TRACK 46

Numeral	Cardinal	Ordinal
0	ноль	
1	один	первый
2	два	второй
3	три	третий
4	четыре	четвёртый
5	пять	пятый
6	шесть	шестой
7	семь	седьмой
8	восемь	восьмой
9	девять	девятый
10	десять	десятый
11	одиннадцать	одиннадцатый

Numeral	Cardinal	Ordinal
12	двен**а**дцать	двен**а**дцатый
13	трин**а**дцать	трин**а**дцатый
14	чет**ы**рнадцать	чет**ы**рнадцатый
15	пятн**а**дцать	пятн**а**дцатый
16	шестн**а**дцать	шестн**а**дцатый
17	семн**а**дцать	семн**а**дцатый
18	восемн**а**дцать	восемн**а**дцатый
19	девятн**а**дцать	девятн**а**дцатый
20	дв**а**дцать	дв**а**дцатый
21	дв**а**дцать од**и**н	дв**а**дцать п**е**рвый
22	дв**а**дцать два	дв**а**дцать втор**о**й
30	тр**и**дцать	тр**и**дцатый
31	тр**и**дцать од**и**н	тр**и**дцать п**е**рвый
40	с**о**рок	сороков**о**й
50	пятьдес**я**т	пятидес**я**тый
60	шестьдес**я**т	шестидес**я**тый
70	с**е**мьдесят	семидес**я**тый
80	в**о**семьдесят	восьмидес**я**тый
90	девян**о**сто	девян**о**стый
100	сто	с**о**тый

The pattern of forming complex ordinal numerals from twenty-one on consists of putting an appropriate cardinal number together with an ordinal number (one through nine).

The dialogue below illustrates how to ask someone for their telephone number. Remember that in Russian, telephone numbers can be given using simple numbers (zero through ten). Make logical pauses to indicate the sequences of numbers when reading out a telephone number. If you have to call Russia, the country code is **семь** (seven) and the city code for Moscow is **чет**ы**ре д**е**вять пять** (495).

Ольга: У вас как**о**й н**о**мер телеф**о**на?
What is your telephone number?

Дарья: Два три пять – чет**ы**ре од**и**н – в**о**семь три.
Two three five – four one – eight three.

Writing a Date in Russian

In Russian, the day is written before the month, just like in other European countries, which means 3/12 is the 3rd of December, not March 12.

The following is a vocabulary list with the seven days of the week in Russian. The Russian week begins with Monday, not Sunday. Typically, people have Saturday and Sunday as their days off, or выходные дни.

Table 8-8

Russian Days of the Week: Дни Недели

TRACK 47

Russian	English
неделя	week
день (masculine)	day
сегодня	today
завтра	tomorrow
вчера	yesterday
понедельник	Monday
вторник	Tuesday
среда	Wednesday
четверг	Thursday
пятница	Friday
суббота	Saturday
воскресенье	Sunday

Note the pronunciation of the word сегодня – the letter "г" is pronounced as the consonant "в."

TRACK 48

Read the models below to learn how to ask about the day of the month and the day of the week for today, tomorrow, and yesterday.

Сегодня какой день недели? – Четверг.
What day of the week is it today? – Thursday.

Завтра какой будет день недели? – Пятница.
What day of the week will it be tomorrow? – Friday.

Вчера какой был день недели? – Среда.
What day of the week was yesterday? – Wednesday.

Какое сегодня число? – Сегодня пятое мая.
What date is it today? – Today is May 5.

Как**о**е числ**о** б**у**дет з**а**втра? – З**а**втра б**у**дет шест**о**е м**а**я.
What will the date be tomorrow?   Tomorrow will be May 6.

Как**о**е числ**о** б**ы**ло вчер**а**? – Вчер**а** б**ы**ло четвёртое м**а**я.
What date was yesterday? – Yesterday was May 4.

Note that in Russian word order is much more flexible than in English. Russian uses endings to indicate the syntactic roles that words play in the sentence, while English relies more on word order.

Russian Months

Study the following list to learn the Russian names for months. You will notice that many of them are very similar to the ones used in English. Be aware that you will have to know the genitive case forms to express the date in Russian. Compare: May – май (nominative case), the 1st of May – п**е**рвое м**а**я (genitive case). The genitive case is used to express the same notion that is conveyed in English through the preposition "of," and it is discussed in detail in Chapter 15. Observe the stress shift in several genitive forms.

Table 8-9

Months of the Year: М**е**сяцы г**о**да

Nominative Case Form	Genitive Case Form	English
янв**а**рь	январ**я**	January
февр**а**ль	феврал**я**	February
март	м**а**рта	March
апр**е**ль	апр**е**ля	April
май	м**а**я	May
и**ю**нь	и**ю**ня	June
и**ю**ль	и**ю**ля	July
август	**а**вгуста	August
сент**я**брь	сентябр**я**	September
окт**я**брь	октябр**я**	October
но**я**брь	ноябр**я**	November
дек**а**брь	декабр**я**	December

None of the months are capitalized. They are all masculine.

To indicate the date, or "**число**," numerals must be used as neuter forms of adjectives. Consider the following examples.

Восьм**ое** м**а**рта	the 8th of March
Дев**я**тое ма**я**	the 9th of May
Тр**и**дцать п**е**рвое декабр**я**	the 31st of December

Chapter Review

Review the material covered in this chapter and complete the following exercises.

Chapter Quiz

Answer the following questions and check your answers in Appendix A.

1. How many conjugation groups are in the Russian language?
   _____

2. In addition to remembering the endings for the two conjugation groups of Russian verbs, what else do you need to remember to form the correct present tense? _____

3. How can you tell a Russian reflexive verb from a non-reflexive verb?
   _____

4. How many grammatical tenses does the Russian language have?
   _____

5. Is it appropriate to address an adult that you have never met before using the **ты говор́ишь** form? _____

6. Which form of the pronoun/verb would you use to address a group of young children? _____

7. How can you tell who the implied subject in the sentence is even when the grammatical subject is omitted? _____

   Conjugate the following verbs:

8. **д́у**мать _____

9. занима**ть**ся _____

10. смотр**е**ть _____

11. люб**и**ть_____

Answer the following questions in Russian using the expressions in parentheses:

12. Что ты л**ю**бишь д**е**лать в своб**о**дное вр**е**мя л**е**том? (to swim in the pool)
_____

13. Что ты л**ю**бишь д**е**лать в своб**о**дное вр**е**мя зим**о**й? (to skate and ski)
_____

14. Что ты л**ю**бишь д**е**лать в своб**о**дное вр**е**мя зим**о**й? (to read books, play piano, and do sports) _____

Writing Dates

Write the following dates in Russian:

1. Monday, November 1st

_____

2. Sunday, May 17th

_____

3. Thursday, September 4th

_____

4. Saturday, February 7th

_____

5. Tuesday, March 9th

_____

6. Wednesday, October 11th

_____

7. Friday, January 22nd

_____

8. My birthday is

_____

Chapter 9

Making Connections:
Nouns, Verbs,
and Pronouns

This chapter introduces the basic uses of all six cases in Russian. It then focuses on the specifics of the prepositional case, discussing ways to express location and objects of thought or speech. Special attention is given to prepositions, idiomatic expressions, and demonstrative pronouns. Verb conjugations and vocabulary to describe people's language abilities are also provided. The cultural focus in this chapter is on typical Russian housing in urban settings.

Declensions and the Case System

Russian nouns change their endings to reflect their role in the sentence. As you learned in Chapter 5, Russian nouns have six cases to express all of the roles they can possibly assume in any grammatically correct sentence. These noun endings are called declensions. There are three major declension patterns for Russian nouns, also known as the first, second, and third declensions.

Russian pronouns and adjectives also follow the case system. They have their own declension patterns. Russian adjectives must agree with the nouns they modify not only in case but also in number and gender.

It is possible to predict which declension pattern any noun would follow by considering the final letter in the nominative case and its grammatical gender.

- **First declension:** Masculine nouns ending in a consonant, a soft sign, or "й" (e.g. хлеб - bread, тесть - father-in-law on the wife's side, музей - museum) and neuter nouns ending in -о/-е (e.g. молоко - milk, здание - building) follow the first declension pattern.
- **Second declension:** Feminine and masculine nouns ending in –а/-я (e.g. вода - water, неделя - week, папа - dad, дядя - uncle) belong to the second declension.
- **Third declension:** Feminine nouns ending in a soft sign (морковь - carrot) follow the third declension pattern.

Although masculine nouns ending in -а/-я are not common, many masculine short names end in -а/-я: Валя (Валентин) Дима (Дмитрий), Витя (Виктор). Several nouns denoting male relatives also end in -а/-я. See Chapter 5 for review.

Review the complete model of Russian declensions in the following table for the singular and plural forms of the nouns **стол** (masculine, table), **вода** (feminine, water), and **тетрадь** (feminine, notebook).

Table 9-1

Simplified Table of Declension Patterns

Case	First	Second	Third	Plural
Nominative	стол	вода	тетрадь	столы/воды/тетради
Accusative	стол	воду	тетрадь	столы/воды/тетради
Genitive	стола	воды	тетради	столов/вод/тетрадей
Prepositional	столе	воде	тетради	столах/водах/тетрадях
Dative	столу	воде	тетради	столам/водам/тетрадям
Instrumental	столом	водой	тетрадью	столами/водами/тетрадями

Now that you have an idea of how each case is formed, let's briefly review their main functions:

- **Nominative Case:** This is the case used for the subject of a sentence or clause.
- **Accusative Case:** This is the case used for direct objects. Several prepositions also require that nouns take the accusative case.
- **Genitive Case:** This is the case used to show possession. Several prepositions also require that nouns take the genitive case.
- **Prepositional Case:** This is the case used to express location. It is always accompanied by a preposition.
- **Dative Case:** This is the case used with indirect objects. Several prepositions also require that nouns take the dative case.
- **Instrumental Case:** This is the case that shows the means, manner, or agent of the action. Several prepositions also require that nouns take the instrumental case.

You already learned about the nominative case in Chapter 5. This chapter focuses on the prepositional case, and you will master the other cases in the following chapters.

Prepositional Case

The main function of the prepositional case is to express location of an object or a person. Compare the following examples:

TRACK 49

Учительница рабОтает в шкОле.   The teacher works at a school.

В шкОле рабОтает мой муж.   My husband works at a school.

Тетрадь лежит на столе.   The notebook is on the table.

На столе лежит тетрадь.   There is a notebook on the table.

These examples illustrate the basic use of the prepositional case and show that Russian sentences are structured so that the new information is usually put at the end of the sentence. When answering who, what, or where questions, Russian allows shortened answers just like English.

Что лежит на столе? – Тетрадь.
What is on the table? – A notebook.

Где лежит тетрадь? – На столе.
Where is the notebook? – On the table.

Где рабОтает твой брат? – На завОде.
Where does your brother work? – At the factory.

Кто рабОтает на завОде? – Мой брат.
Who works at the factory? – My brother.

The prepositional case is expressed through specific endings:

- Most nouns that follow the first and second declension patterns take the ending -е, as in класс – в клАссе (classroom – in the classroom), окнО – в окнЕ (window – in the window), шкОла – в шкОле (school – in the school).

- Masculine nouns from the first declension pattern that end in -ий, -ия, and -ие and feminine nouns that follow the third declension pattern take the ending -и, as in **санаторий – в санатории** (sanatorium – in a sanatorium),
- Several nouns that belong to the first declension pattern take the ending -у, which is always stressed, as in **сад – в саду** (garden – in the garden), **лес – в лесу** (forest – in the forest), **пол – на полу** (floor – on the floor).

The endings of the prepositional case are added to the stem of the noun, as in **тетрадь – в тетради** (notebook – in the notebook), **школа – в школе** (school – in the school).

In addition to the endings, the prepositional case is always formed using prepositions. Use the prepositions **в** (in, at) or **на** (on, at, in) to express location. There is one basic difference in meaning between these two prepositions: **в** usually expresses the location of the object inside of something, and **на** shows that the location of the object is on the surface of something. Compare:

стол – в столе	table – in the table (drawers)
стол – на столе	table – on the table (top)

Generally, when referring to the location in a city, town, or county, the preposition **в** is used, as in **Москва – в Москве** (Moscow – in Moscow), **Нью-Йорк - в Нью-Йорке** (New York – in New York), **Россия – в России**. In many other cases, the choice between the two prepositions must be memorized:

TRACK 50

Table 9-2

Proper Use of Prepositions with Nouns in the Prepositional Case

Preposition В	English	Preposition На	English
институт - в институте	at the institute	остров - на острове	on an island
университет - в университете	at the university	площадь - на площади	in the square
школа - в школе	at school	стадион - на стадионе	at a stadium
кино -в кино	at the cinema	завод - на заводе	at a plant
театр - в театре	at the theater	станция - на станции	at a station
гостиница - в гостинице	at a hotel	концерт - на концерте	at a concert
ресторан - в ресторане	at a restaurant	урок - на уроке	in class
дом - в доме	at the house	улица - на улице	on a street
санаторий - в санатории	at the sanatorium	вечер – на вечере	at a party

The prepositional case forms for personal pronouns are мне, тебе, нём (masculine)/ней (feminine)/нём (neuter), нас, вас, них. When substituting a pronoun for a noun, keep in mind that all Russian nouns have grammatical gender, irrespective of whether they are animate or inanimate. Choose an appropriate pronoun so that it agrees with the gender and number of the noun it stands for.

TRACK 51

In addition to expressing location, the prepositional case is used to express the object of thought or speech, as in:

Я говорю о Маше.
I am talking about Masha.

Он думает о его невесте.
He is thinking about his bride.

Мы думаем об экскурсии.
We are thinking of the excursion.

Николай Петрович говорит о заводе, где он работает.
Nikolai Petrovich is talking about the factory where he works.

Света думает о доме.
Sveta is thinking about home.

Note that the prepositional case expressing the object of thought or speech requires the use of the prepositions о / об (about): об is reserved for the nouns beginning with the vowels а, и, о, у, э; otherwise, the preposition о is used.

In a Russian Apartment

In Russian cities, the great majority of people live in large apartment buildings. Although Soviet-built housing is still prevalent, the number of new, more spacious apartments is growing. When talking about an apartment, or квартира, Russians usually do not think in terms of number of bedrooms. Instead, a total number of rooms is mentioned, for example, однокомнатная квартира is a one-room apartment (a studio with a separate kitchen, bathroom, and hallway) and двухкомнатная квартира is a two-room apartment (with a separate kitchen, bathroom, and hallway). Note that kitchens, hallways, and bathrooms are not included in the total number of rooms. Because many apartments are small, rooms often serve several functions.

Another interesting feature of a typical Russian apartment is that a bathroom is often divided into two completely separate units. One, known as ванная, will have a sink and a bathtub, and the other, the туалет, will only have a toilet. The doors to both bathroom sections are generally kept closed: knock on the door or check if the light is on to see if you can use them.

ESSENTIAL

Don't be surprised if your Russian hosts ask you to take your shoes off after entering their apartment. Just think about all the bad weather, and you will understand the reasons behind this tradition. You will not be expected to walk around shoeless; your hosts will offer you a pair of slippers, or тапочки.

The following is a list of house-related vocabulary.

Table 9-3

At Home

Russian	English
квартира – на / в квартире	at / in the apartment
дом – в доме	in the house
пол – на полу	on the floor
стена – на стене	on the wall
потолок – на потолке	on the ceiling
дверь – на двери	on the door
окно – на окне	on the window
комната – в комнате	in the room
прихожая – в прихожей	in the hallway
столовая – в столовой	in the dining room
большая комната / гостиная	living room
спальня – в спальне	in the bedroom
кухня – на/в кухне	in the kitchen
ванная (комната) – в ванной	in the bathroom
гараж – в гараже	in the garage
мебель (fem.) - на мебели	on the furniture
диван – на диване	on the couch
стол – на / в столе	on/in the table
стул – на стуле	on/in the chair
кресло – в кресле	on/in the armchair
кровать (fem.) – на кровати	on the bed
шкаф – в /на шкафу	in the wardrobe
книжный шкаф – в книжном шкафу	in the bookcase
полка – на полке	on the shelf
тумбочка	stand
лампа	lamp
картина	picture
ковёр	carpet
плита	stove
холодильник	refrigerator
стиральная машина	washing machine

Russian	English
зеркало	mirror
телевизор	TV set
магнитофон	stereo
книга	book
журнал	magazine

Helpful Verbs to Remember

Below are several verbs that you will find helpful when talking about locations. Review the regular conjugation patterns in Chapter 8.

The verb "жить" ("to live") belongs to Group I Model 2. Its present tense stem contains an additional consonant –в (жить – жив-) that appears in all forms of the present tense:

Table 9-4

Жить (Group I, Model 2) – The Present Tense Stem Жив-

Person	Singular	Plural
I	живу	живём
II	живёшь	живёте
III	живёт	живут

The verbs лежать (to lie) (Group II, Model 2) and стоять (to stand) (Group II, Model 1) are frequently used in Russian not only to refer to the physical actions of people and animals, but also to describe locations of inanimate objects. Read below a description of an apartment to see how these verbs can be used in context.

Это моя квартира. Она маленькая, но удобная. В ней есть столовая, спальня, маленькая кухня, большая прихожая и ванная. В столовой стоит стол, стулья и два кресла. А ещё там есть телевизор и магнитофон. На кухне есть плита, холодильник и полки. Шкаф стоит в прихожей, а кровать, конечно, в спальне. Ковёр лежит на полу в столовой, а книги стоят на полках в спальне. На тумбочке в спальне лежат журналы. В ванной есть зеркало и стиральная машина.

This is my apartment. It is small but comfortable. In it, there is a dining room, a bedroom, a small kitchen, a big hallway, and a bathroom. In the dining room, there is a table, chairs, and two armchairs. And also there is a TV set and a stereo. In the kitchen, there is a stove, a refrigerator, and shelves. A wardrobe is in the hallway, and the bed is, of course, in the bedroom. A carpet is on the floor in the dining room, and books are on the shelves in the bedroom. Magazines are on the stand in the bedroom. In the bathroom, there is a mirror and a washing machine.

Note that the construction using есть that you learned in Chapter 7 can be also used to express location. In this sense, it is translated as "there is / there are." Although it is incorrect to use the adverb of place там (there) in the sentences where location is expressed through the prepositional case, it is acceptable to do so in constructions with есть.

Demonstrative Pronouns

Russian has a system of demonstrative pronouns that change their form to reflect the gender, number, and the case of the noun they modify. The most frequently used demonstrative pronoun is этот. It can be translated as this/that. If the speaker is trying to express a contrast between two objects or the conversation is about something that is out of reach and/or sight, the pronoun тот is used. Use the following table to study forms of demonstrative pronouns:

Table 9-5

Demonstrative Pronouns

Case	Masculine	Feminine	Neuter	Plural
Nominative	этот	эта	это	эти
Accusative	этот/этого	эту	это	эти/этих
Genitive	этого	этой	этого	этих
Prepositional	этом	этой	этом	этих
Dative	этому	этой	этому	этим
Instrumental	этим	этой	этим	этими

Note that for masculine pronouns and nouns denoting people and animals, the forms for the genitive and accusative cases overlap, both in singular and plural. On the other hand, for masculine and neuter pronouns and nouns denoting inanimate objects, the forms for the nominative and accusative cases are the same, in singular and plural.

Adjectives and Adverbs of Nationality

You already know some adjectives of nationality, for example, **русский**. In English, the same adjectives are used to describe nationality and to describe a corresponding language, as in English (a citizen of England) – to speak English. In Russian, on the other hand, an adverb is required to describe someone's language abilities, for example "**Мария Петровна говорит по-русски и по-английски**" (Maria Petrovna speaks Russian and English).

The following list contains the names of countries with appropriate adjectives and adverbs of nationality. Remember that Russian nouns have grammatical gender. This is why all nouns for nationalities have two forms: a feminine and a masculine form. Make sure that you know the difference between adjectives of nationality and corresponding nouns: in most cases, the forms of nouns and adjectives will be different, but in some cases they will completely overlap. Compare **американский** (American, adjective)–**американец / американка** (American, noun: masculine and feminine forms) and **русский** (Russian, adjective) – **русский / русская** (Russian, noun: masculine and feminine forms).

Neither nouns nor adjectives of nationality are capitalized in Russian. Finally, take notice that there are two forms of the noun/adjective "Russian:" **российский** and **русский**. The first one refers to Russian nationality and things that belong to the Russian Federation, whereas the second one refers to Russian ethnicity, one of many ethnicities in the Russian Federation.

Table 9-6

Countries, Nationalities, and Language Capabilities

TRACK 52

Country	Adjective	Noun	Adverb
Соединённые Штаты Америки (США) / Америка	американский	американец / американка	по-английски
Канада	канадский	канадец / канадка	по-английски / по-французски
Мексика	мексиканский	мексиканец / мексиканка	по-испански
Российская Федерация / Россия	российский / русский	россиянин / россиянка (русский/ русская)	по-русски
Англия	английский	англичанин / англичанка	по-английски
Франция	французский	француз / француженка	по-французски
Испания	испанский	испанец / испанка	по-испански
Италия	итальянский	итальянец / итальянка	по-итальянски
Германия	немецкий	немец / немка	по-немецки
Греция	греческий	грек / гречанка	по-гречески
Эфиопия	эфиопский	эфиоп / эфиопка	по-эфиопски
Египет	египетский	египтянин / египтянка	по-арабски
Австралия	австралийский	австралиец / австралийка	по-английски
Китай	китайский	китаец / китаянка	по-китайски
Япония	японский	японец / японка	по-японски

Note that plural forms of nouns denoting people of both genders belonging to the same nationality are formed from the masculine singular form, as in китаец – китайцы or египтянин – египтяне. Masculine nouns that end in -ец, omit the е vowel in their plural forms as in:

американец – американцы

канадец – канадцы

мексиканец – мексиканцы

Read the model dialogue below to learn how to ask someone about the languages they speak.

Дарья: Вы говорите по-английски?
Do you speak English?

Светлана: Да, говорю. А ещё я говорю по-русски и по-французски.
Yes, I do. I also speak Russian and French.

Russian adverbs that refer to language abilities are not capitalized. Also, Russians often skip the actual grammatical subject in a conversation if it is already clear from the context. For example, in the previous dialogue, **Светлана** omits the pronoun "I." This is possible because Russian verbs clearly identify the noun that they refer to. If in doubt, check the form of the verb; it will help you figure out the grammatical subject of the sentence.

Use adverbs to add an evaluative comment to your description of someone's language abilities, as in **чуть-чуть / плохо / неплохо / хорошо / свободно говорить по-русски** (to speak Russian a little / badly / okay / well / fluently).

Chapter Review

Review the material covered in this chapter and complete the following exercises.

Chapter Quiz

Answer the following questions and check your answers in Appendix A.

1. What is meant by the term "declension?"

_____

2. How can you tell which of the three major declension patterns a noun will follow?

_____

3. What is the main function of the prepositional case?

   _____

4. Which are typical endings of the prepositional case?

   _____

5. When the prepositional case is used to express the object of thought or speech, and which prepositions are used? _____

6. When Russians report of the number of rooms in an apartment, do they include kitchen, bathroom, and hallway in the total number of rooms?

   _____

Prepositional Case

Transform the following nouns from the nominative to the prepositional case, then translate the phrases expressing location into English:

1. дом – в   _____
2. завод – на   _____
3. теа́тр – в   _____
4. университе́т – в _____
5. рестора́н – в   _____
6. Росси́я – в   _____
7. Санкт-Петербу́рг – в _____

Adjectives and Nouns of Nationality

A. Match the adjectives of nationality with the most appropriate nouns from the following list. Some of the nouns in the list have cognates in English. Try to combine adjectives with the nouns with which they are typically associated. Make sure that adjectives and nouns agree in gender and number.

Nouns: чай, квас, футбо́л, самура́й, вино́, пирами́ды, парла́мент, пи́во, принце́сса

1. американский   _____
2. японский   _____
3. китайский   _____
4. французское   _____
5. немецкое   _____
6. английский   _____
7. испанская   _____
8. мексиканские   _____
9. русский   _____

B. Form proper sentences with the words provided. Remember that Russian nouns and adjectives agree in gender and number and that Russian verbs are conjugated.

10. Катя Иванова (русский)

_____

11. Хуан Карлос и Маркос Гарсия (испанец)

_____

12. Франсуа Лерош (говорить по-французски свободно)

_____

13. Генрих Манн (немецкий писатель)

_____

14. Марина Цветаева (русский поэт)

_____

Chapter 10

Transitive Verbs

This chapter introduces the notion of transitivity and discusses how it is expressed in Russian. Special attention is given to stem variation and irregularities in verbs. This chapter also focuses on the form and function of the accusative case in the Russian language. The cultural spotlight in this chapter is on shopping for clothes. You will study the vocabulary used to communicate with shop assistants and words and phrases helpful to describe clothing, colors, materials, and patterns.

The Verbal Category of Transivity

As in English, Russian verbs can be divided into two large groups: verbs that take a direct object (transitive), and verbs that do not take a direct object (intransitive). Compare the following sentences in English:

I read a book.
I swim in the sea.

The verb "to read" is transitive because it can take a direct object ("a book"). On the other hand, the verb "to swim" is intransitive because it can never take a direct object.

You already know several transitive verbs in Russian, including the verbs **читать** (to read), **смотреть** (to watch), **писать** (to write), and **любить** (to like/love). Below is a list of additional transitive verbs that belong to Group I Model 1:

слу**шать**	to listen
спра**шивать**	to ask
полу**чать**	to get
пока**зывать**	to show
поку**пать**	to buy
встре**чать**	to meet

The verb **учить** (to teach) belongs to Group II Model 2. To review major conjugation patterns of Russian verbs in the present tense, refer to Chapter 8.

Stem Variations and Conjugation Irregularities

In addition to verbs that consistently follow regular conjugation patterns, there are several transitive verbs that exhibit slight variation in their stems. In Chapter 8, we examined the verb **писать** (to write) and learned that it is prone to consonant variation in the present tense in all persons, as in я пиш**у** – ты пи**шешь** – он пи**шет**, etc. The verbs брать (to take), звать (to call), and ждать (to wait) are conjugated in a similar fashion. Review the following tables to practice their conjugations.

Table 10-1

Брать (Group I Model 2)

Person	Singular	Plural
I	бер**у**	бер**ём**
II	бер**ёшь**	бер**ёте**
III	бер**ёт**	бер**ут**

Table 10-2

Звать (Group I Model 2)

Person	Singular	Plural
I	зов**у**	зов**ём**
II	зов**ёшь**	зов**ёте**
III	зов**ёт**	зов**ут**

Table 10-3

Ждать (Group I Model 2)

Person	Singular	Plural
I	жд**у**	жд**ём**
II	жд**ёшь**	жд**ёте**
III	жд**ёт**	жд**ут**

These three verbs follow a variation of the Group I conjugation pattern, taking on the consonant ё in all the endings that typically take the consonant е.

Finally, let's take a look at the transitive verb хот**е**ть. This is a highly irregular verb that follows both conjugation patterns. In addition to its irregularities in the endings, pay close attention to the consonant variation in its stem (т-ч) and a shifting stress pattern.

Table 10-4

Хотеть (Irregular)

Person	Singular	Plural
I	хочу	хотим
II	хочешь	хотите
III	хочет	хотят

This verb is similar to the verb **любить** (to like/love) in that it can be used in infinitive constructions, such as **я хочу есть/пить/гулять/кататься на коньках** (I want to eat/drink/go for a walk/ice skate).

The Accusative Case

As mentioned previously, the Russian language relies on the case system to express different syntactic roles that nouns can perform in a sentence. The accusative case is used to indicate that a noun is a direct object in a sentence:

Я читаю книгу.
I am reading a book.

Они слушают музыку.
They are listening to music.

Катя покупает квартиру в Москве.
Katya is buying an apartment in Moscow.

Just like other cases in Russian, the accusative case is expressed through specific endings. Nouns that stand for people and animals, also known as animate nouns, and nouns that stand for objects and places, also known as inanimate nouns, have different accusative forms. Read the explanation below to learn the specific endings for each group of nouns:

- Animate nouns that belong to the first declension pattern take the ending –а or –я, as in **друг – ждать друга** (friend – to wait for a friend), тесть – ждать тестя (father-in-law – to wait for a father-in-law). It depends on whether the preceding consonant is hard (друг) or soft (тесть).

- The accusative case form for inanimate nouns that belong to the first declension pattern is identical to the nominative case form of these nouns, as in фильм – смотреть фильм (film – to see a film), письмо – писать письмо (letter – to write a letter).

- The nouns from the second declension pattern take the ending –у or –ю, regardless of whether they are animate or inanimate, as in музыка – слушать музыку (music – listen to the music), дядя - спрашивать дядю (uncle – to ask the uncle). Most—but not all—of these nouns are feminine.

- The accusative forms for both animate and inanimate nouns that follow the third declension pattern coincide with their nominative forms, as in шаль – покупать шаль (shawl – to buy a shawl).

- The accusative forms for inanimate nouns in plural are identical to the nominative plural forms of these nouns, as in книги – читать книги (books – to read books), фильмы – смотреть фильмы (films – to see films), шали – покупать шали (shawls – to buy shawls).

- The accusative forms for animate nouns in the plural are identical to the genitive plural, which you will study in the following chapters.

Revisit Chapter 6 to review the accusative forms of Russian personal pronouns.

The following is a list of verb and noun combinations that are frequently used in everyday conversations. All of the nouns are used in the accusative case.

TRACK 53

Читать книгу / газету / журнал
To read a book / newspaper / magazine

Смотреть фильм / шоу / концерт / спектакль / оперу / балет
To see a film / show / concert / play / opera / ballet

Писать письмо / книгу / заявление / жалобу
To write a letter / book / statement / complaint

Люб**и**ть м**у**жа / жен**у** / дет**е**й / м**а**му / п**а**пу / бр**а**та / сестр**у** / б**а**бушку / д**е**душку

To love a husband / wife / children / mother / father / brother / sister / grandmother / grandfather

Сл**у**шать м**у**зыку / р**а**дио / уч**и**теля

To listen to music / the radio / a teacher

Спр**а**шивать уч**и**теля / преподав**а**теля / врач**а**

To ask the teacher / university instructor / doctor

Получ**а**ть д**е**ньги / зарпл**а**ту

To receive money / a salary

Пок**а**зывать фильм / од**е**жду / дом / кварт**и**ру

To show a film / clothes / a house / an apartment

Покуп**а**ть прод**у**кты / од**е**жду / м**е**бель / маш**и**ну / кварт**и**ру / дом

To buy food products / clothes / furniture / a car / an apartment / a house

Possessive Pronouns: The Nominative, Accusative, and Prepositional Cases

Russian possessive pronouns also change to agree with the nouns they modify. Following is a table with the forms of possessive pronouns in the nominative, accusative, and prepositional cases.

Table 10-5

Possessive Pronouns: Accusative Case

Personal Pronouns	Masculine	Feminine	Neuter	Plural
я	мой (inanimate) / моег**о** (animate)	мо**ю**	моё	мо**и** (inanimate) / мо**и**х (animate)
ты	твой (inanimate) / твоег**о** (animate)	тво**ю**	твоё	тво**и** (inanimate) / тво**и**х (animate)

Personal Pronouns	Masculine	Feminine	Neuter	Plural
он	его	его	его	его
она	её	её	её	её
оно	его	его	его	его
мы	наш (inanimate) / нашего (animate)	нашу	наше	наши (inanimate) / наших (animate)
вы	ваш (inanimate) / вашего (animate)	вашу	ваше	ваши (inanimate) / ваших (animate)
они	их	их	их	их

The pronouns **моего** and **его** are pronounced with the "в" sound, instead of the "г" sound. Make sure you remember that the third person possessive pronouns **его**, **её**, and **их** keep the same form in all cases.

Shopping for Clothes

Buying clothes in a foreign country can be an interesting experience. Not only will you have to deal with potentially different fashion sensibilities, you will have to adapt to a new system of sizes and learn a culturally appropriate way of communicating with salespeople and other shoppers. During Soviet times when goods were few and far between, Russia was known for long lines of frustrated shoppers ready to buy just about anything. Fortunately, this has changed dramatically. Today, major Russian cities are jam-packed with fashionable stores and boutiques, all filled with expensive, trendy merchandise.

In Soviet times, goods that were in high demand and low supply were referred to as дефицит, or a deficit. Sadly, nearly anything a regular person wanted to buy fell within this category. Дефицит became excessively rampant during the late '70s and '80s and was particularly acute outside of Moscow. Many people made trips to stores in Moscow in hopes of buying food products (мясо, колбаса, сыр), clothes, and shoes.

A Russian proverb says "По одежде встречают, а по уму провожают." In English, it can be loosely interpreted as "People are met according to their dress, but sent off according to their intellect." Today the desire to follow the latest fashions is common, especially among young people who are willing to spend a considerable portion of their salary on brand name products. In general, looking fashionable is a way for people to show off themselves and their prosperity.

Russian Clothing

Sometimes young Russians spend more money on "keeping up appearances" than any other aspects of their lives. Women especially are prone to spend a lot of money on the way they look, often choosing feminine and sexy clothes as opposed to more relaxed styles. Don't be surprised to see a lot of people of both genders wearing furs in the winter. People for the Ethical Treatment of Animals has not yet made an impact on clothing choices in Russia. Long and cold Russian winters make a thick warm coat and a pair of well-insulated boots a necessity for everyone.

ALERT!

Russians use European sizes, both for clothing and shoes. Shop assistants might be able to help you "convert" your size; however, it might be easier to try on several sizes to see which one fits you best. You may also find it helpful to look up a conversion chart before you leave or keep a cheat sheet in your wallet.

Although Russians usually do not wear traditional national dress, for many people the Russian ушанка (a fur hat with ear flaps, worn either tied up on top of the hat or down protecting the ears), валенки (felt boots, worn outside with rubber galoshes to protect them from getting wet), and платок (a Russian wool headscarf often decorated with images of colorful flowers) constitute important elements of a traditional folk costume. See the list below to learn more vocabulary for clothing items and popular types of shoes.

Table 10-6

Shopping for Clothes

Russian	English
одежда	clothes
платье	dress
рубашка	shirt
блуза	blouse
брюки	pants
джинсы	jeans
юбка	skirt
костюм	suit
кофта	sweater, sweatshirt
свитер	sweater
пиджак	sports jacket (both for men and women)
галстук	tie
платок	kerchief, headscarf
шаль (fem.)	shawl
шапка	hat
шарф	scarf
пальто	coat
куртка	jacket or coat
шуба	fur coat
туфли (pl.)	women's shoes, pumps
ботинки (pl.)	boots
перчатки (pl.)	gloves

Russian Stores

Like Macy's in Manhattan, there are several Russian stores that are known nationwide, including ГУМ or Государственный универсальный магазин (State Universal Store), ЦУМ or Центральный универсальный магазин (Central Universal Store), and Детский мир (Children's World). All three are department stores located in the very heart of Moscow and have a long history.

ГУМ is perhaps more famous than others because it is located on Red Square and is housed in a gorgeous early-twentieth-century *art nouveau* building. Its layout concept is similar to that of a Parisian arcade. Today, more and more new chains are appearing in Russian cities, including stores such as **Метро** and **Седьмой континент**. These stores often sell clothes, household goods, and food products.

Many Russian clothing stores, or in Russian магазины одежды, that cater to women bear female names, such as Людмила or Наташа. Sometimes, the store's sign might have a subtitle, as in Людмила – магазин женской одежды. Other stores are named after the products that they carry, as in Молоко (Milk – diary products), Хлеб (Bread), Радио товары (Radio Products).

Remember that abbreviations act as regular nouns, for example, ГУМ (a store GUM) – в ГУМе (at the store GUM). ГУМ stands for **магазин**, which is a masculine noun belonging to the first declension pattern. This is why in the prepositional case, ГУМ acquires the ending –e, as in the following dialogue:

Вера :   Где ты покупаешь твою одежду?
(Where do you buy your clothes?)

Валя: В ГУМе. У них такая хорошая модная одежда. Это моё любимое синее шерстяное пальто. А это мой бежевый хлопчатобумажный свитер.
(At GUM. They have such good, fashionable clothes. Here's my favorite blue wool coat. And this is my beige cotton sweater.)

Shopping Phrases

Following are several expressions that are helpful to know in order to communicate with salespeople in stores as you are buying clothes:

TRACK 54

Чем я могу вам помочь?
How can I help you?

Я хочу купить
I'd like to buy . . .

Позвольте мне показать вам эту вещь.
Allow me to show you this item.

Сколько это стоит?
How much does it cost?

Это (стоит) дорого/дёшево.
This (costs/is) expensive/cheap.

Это вам (очень) к лицу.
This suits you (very much).

Это вам (очень) идёт.
This looks good on you.

Эта модель хорошо на вас сидит.
This model fits you well.

Где ваша касса?
Where is the checkout desk?

Я могу это померить?
Can I try this on?

Где у вас в магазине примерочная?
Where do you have a fitting room in the store?

Мне это мало/велико.
This is too small/big for me.

Какой это размер?
What size is this?

Colors, Materials, and Patterns

When buying clothes, it is important to be able to describe colors, patterns, and materials. Following is a list of adjectives for basic colors, popular patterns, and materials used for clothing. All adjectives are given in singular masculine, just as they would be in a dictionary. Remember that you must change the adjective's form so that it matches the grammatical gender, case, and number of the noun that it modifies. Adjectives are usually placed before nouns, with adjectives for colors in the initial position, as in **белая шёлковая блуза** (white silk blouse), unless there is a qualifying adjective that describes the quality of the item, as in **красивая белая шёлковая блуза** (pretty white silk blouse). Other qualifying adjectives that are helpful to know include **хороший** (good), **удобный** (comfortable), **новый** (new), **модный** (fashionable or trendy), **дорогой** (expensive), **дешёвый** (cheap), **любимый** (favorite), and **старый** (old).

Table 10-7

Colors, Patterns, and Materials for Clothes

Russian	English
белый	white
чёрный	black
красный	red
розовый	pink
зелёный	green
голубой	light blue
синий	dark blue
серый	grey
жёлтый	yellow
оранжевый	orange
коричневый	brown
бежевый	beige
кожаный	leather (adj.)
меховой	fur (adj.)
шерстяной	wool (adj.)
шёлковый	silk (adj.)
хлопчатобумажный	cotton (adj.)

Russian	English
кл**е**тчатый	checkered
в гор**о**шек	polka dotted
в пол**о**ску	striped
в цвет**о**чек	flower pattern

In Russian, adjectives are usually placed before nouns. However, expressions such as "в гор**о**шек" are placed after the nouns that they refer to.

As you already know, adjectives are also declined. Following are two tables that summarize adjectival endings for nominative, accusative, and prepositional forms. Remember that all Russian adjectives can be roughly divided into hard-stemmed (stems ending with hard consonants) and soft-stemmed (stems ending with a soft consonant). The endings for the accusative forms in the masculine, neuter, and plural forms are different depending on whether the noun defined is inanimate or animate.

Table 10-8

Hard-Stemmed Adjective Endings: Nominative, Accusative, Prepositional Cases

Case	Masculine	Feminine	Neuter	Plural
Nominative	-ый/-ий/-ой	-ая	-ое	-ые/-ие
Accusative	-ый/-ий/-ой (inanimate) -ого/-его (animate)	-ую	-ое	-ые/-ие (inanimate) -ых/-их (animate)
Prepositional	-ом/-ем	-ой/-ей	-ом/-ем	-ых/-их

Table 10-9

Soft-Stemmed Adjective Endings: Nominative, Accusative, Prepositional Cases

Case	Masculine	Feminine	Neuter	Plural
Nominative	-ий	-яя	-ее	-ие
Accusative	-ий (inanimate)/ -его (animate)	-юю	-ее	ие (inanimate) -их (animate)
Prepositional	-ем	-ей	-ем	-их

Chapter Review

Review the material covered in this chapter and complete the following exercises.

Chapter Quiz

Answer the following questions and check your answers in Appendix A.

1. What is the major difference between transitive and intransitive verbs?

   _____

2. Name the irregularities in the conjugation of the Russian verb хотеть.

   _____

3. What is the major function of the accusative case?

   _____

4. In addition to different declension patterns, what other variable is important to remember when you decide on the accusative form?

   _____

5. Give examples of clothing items that are considered by many to be staples of Russian national folk dress.

   _____

6. List two examples of Russian verbs that allow infinitive constructions.

   _____

7. What grammatical concepts define the ending that a noun and an adjective would take in the accusative case?

   _____

   _____

Grammar and Vocabulary Practice

A. Translate the following verb-noun expressions into Russian to practice forming accusative forms:

1. to buy a sweater   _____
2. to wait for a friend _____
3. to listen to music   _____
4. to read a book   _____
5. to love Moscow   _____
6. to buy a shirt   _____
7. to show a film   _____
8. to take a book   _____
9. to ask the mother   _____
10. to show a fur coat   _____

B. Translate the following sentences from Russian into English or from English into Russian. Make sure that you remember how to conjugate verbs and decline nouns, adjectives, and possessive pronouns:

11. Я читаю мою газету.

    _____

12. Вы слушаете их музыку.

    _____

13. Она покупает его одежду в ГУМе.

    _____

14. Мы любим вашу музыку.

    _____

15. Он покупает продукты.

    _____

16. I am buying a beautiful red suit.

    _____

17. He is meeting his good friend.

    _____

C. Listen to the corresponding track on the accompanying CD and translate the following sentences into English:

TRACK 55

18. Привет, Володя! Как дела в школе?

    _____

19. Спасибо, хорошо! А как ваши дела, Сергей Васильевич?

    _____

20. Тоже хорошо. Володя, ты встречаешь твою маму?

    _____

21. Нет, я жду моего друга. А Вы?

    _____

22. А я встречаю мою жену и дочь. Они покупают одежду в магазине.

    _____

Reading Practice

Read the following store names and write down in English what kind(s) of products these stores carry:

1. Детский мир _____
2. Наташа _____
3. Молоко _____
4. ГУМ _____
5. Оптика _____
6. Аптека _____
7. Радио товары _____
8. Электроника _____
9. Книги _____

Chapter 11

Happy Birthday in Russian

In this chapter, you will become familiar with the major function of the Russian dative case and learn dative forms for nouns, personal pronouns, and adjectives. Furthermore, you will become more aware of the connection between nouns and verbs by learning new verbal constructions that require nouns in the dative case. You will read about Russian birthday parties and gift-giving customs. Finally, you will be able to practice some new vocabulary and learn the basics of the Russian past tense.

Nouns and Pronouns in the Dative Case

The main function of the dative case is to indicate indirect objects, as in the following examples:

Кому ты пишешь письмо? — Я пишу письмо моей маме.
To whom are you writing a letter? — I am writing a letter to my mother.

Кому она читает книгу? — Она читает книгу её сыну.
To whom is she reading a book? — She is reading a book to her son.

Кому ваша жена покупает подарок? — Моя жена покупает подарок нашей внучке.
For whom is your wife buying a present? — My wife is buying a present for our granddaughter.

In the above sentences, the words моей маме (to my mother), её сыну (to her son), and нашей внучке (for our granddaughter) are indirect objects, and thus they are used in the dative case. Contrary to English, Russian indirect objects are identified by the dative case and do not always require the use of prepositions.

ESSENTIAL

Indirect objects are nouns that are indirectly impacted by verbs. When in doubt, remember that indirect objects answer the questions to whom, for whom (кому in Russian), to what, or for what (чему in Russian), immediately followed by a verb, as in to whom something is given.

The dative case shares some similarities with the nominative, accusative, and prepositional cases that you have already studied. The dative case is also expressed through specific ending added to the stem of a noun:

- The nouns from the first declension pattern take the ending -у if they are hard-stemmed or their stem ends with the letters ж, ш, ч, or щ, as in профессор – профессору (professor – to the professor), врач – врачу (doctor – to the doctor), окно – окну (window – to the window).

- The nouns from the first declension pattern take the ending -ю if they are soft-stemmed, as in писатель – писателю (writer – to the writer), словарь – словарю (dictionary – to the dictionary).
- The endings of the dative case for the nouns that follow the second and third declension patterns are identical to the endings that these nouns take in the prepositional case, as in женщина – женщине (woman – to the woman), аудитория – аудитории (lecture hall – to the lecture hall), тетрадь – тетради (notebook – to the notebook).
- Plural nouns in the dative case assume the ending -ам if they have a hard stem and the ending -ям if they have a soft stem, as in классы – классам (classrooms – in the classrooms), тетради – тетрадям (notebooks – in the notebooks).

The dative case forms for personal pronouns are grouped together with the nominative forms, which were presented initially: я – мне, ты — тебе, он — ему (masculine), она — ей (feminine), оно — ему (neuter), мы — нам, вы — вам, они — им. When learning these forms, remember that the third-person singular masculine and neuter forms are identical.

Adjectives in the Dative Case

Russian adjectives are declined, just like nouns. Hard-stemmed and soft-stemmed adjectives follow different declension patterns. The following tables summarize adjective endings for the nominative and dative cases for hard-stemmed and soft-stemmed adjectives.

Table 11-1

Hard-Stemmed Adjective Endings: Dative Case

Case	Masculine	Feminine	Neuter	Plural
Nominative	-ый/-ий/-ой	-ая	-ое	-ые/-ие
Dative	-ому/-ему	-ой/-ей	-ому/-ему	-ым/-им
Nominative	красивый	красивая	красивое	красивые
Dative	красивому	красивой	красивому	красивым

Table 11-2

Soft-Stemmed Adjective Endings: Dative Case

Case	Masculine	Feminine	Neuter	Plural
Nominative	-ий	-яя	-ее	-ие
Dative	-ему	-ей	-ему	-им
Nominative	лишний	лишняя	лишнее	лишние
Dative	лишнему	лишней	лишнему	лишним

Remember to apply Spelling Rule 1 when choosing the appropriate ending for adjectives: after Ж, Ш, Щ, Ч, К, Г, and Х always write И, not Ы. For example, холодный – горячий (cold – hot). This rule only applies to the adjectives with stressed stems. Compare: горячий – большой (hot – big).

Verbs in the Dative Case

There are several verbs that are commonly used with the indirect object, which requires the use of the dative case. These verbs include the following:

TRACK 56

давать	to give (Group I Model 1; present tense stem да-)
подарить	to give as a present (Group II Model I)
покупать	to buy (Group I Model I)
рассказывать	to tell a story (Group I Model I)
показывать	to show (Group I Model I)
помогать	to help (Group I Model I)
предлагать	to offer, suggest (Group I Model I)
советовать	to advise (Group I Model)

The present tense stem of the verb советовать is совет-, which results in the following conjugation pattern:

Table 11-3

Советовать – The Present Tense Stem Совет-

Person	Singular	Plural
I	советую	советуем
II	советуешь	советуете
III	советует	советуют

In addition, the verb нравиться (to appeal) also requires the use of the dative case, as presented in the following examples:

Мне нравится этот парк.
I like this park. (Literally: This park is appealing to me.)

Валентине нравятся испанские фильмы.
Valentina likes Spanish films. (Literally: Spanish films are appealing to Valentina.)

Let's look carefully at the structure of these sentences. The subjects of these sentences are парк and фильмы. How do we know this? Let's examine the forms of the verb нравиться. In the first example it is conjugated to agree with the word парк, and in the second example it is conjugated to agree with the word фильмы. In these sentences, the subjects are the things that are being liked and the person to whom they appeal is in the dative case.

Structurally, these verbs are very different; любить is followed by a noun in the accusative case (direct object), and нравиться is preceded by a noun or pronoun in the dative case (indirect object) and is followed by a noun in the nominative case (the nominal subject of the sentence, the thing that is appealing).

In previous chapters, you learned the verb любить, which has a similar meaning to the verb нравиться. However, the difference is that the verb любить has a more general meaning and denotes a strong feeling of love, whereas the verb нравиться usually refers to specific, isolated things or incidents and has a more subdued quality. Compare the following statements: Я люблю кино (I love cinema) and Мне нравится этот фильм (I like this movie).

At a Russian Birthday

Birthday celebrations are popular social occasions. In Russia, it is traditional for the person who is celebrating his or her birthday to organize a party, prepare food, and supply the drinks. The guests are responsible for presents and toasts. At children's parties, the parents of the birthday child are responsible for arranging entertainment, which may include a clown, games, and contests. Adults usually have a nice dinner with some singing and dancing afterwards.

FACT

"Dative" is derived from the Latin verb stem "da," meaning "to give." This is an appropriate name for the case that is used to indicate the giving of something, be it a gift, an answer, or some advice.

There is no traditional Russian version of the song "Happy Birthday." Often, the song is sung in English or sometimes it is substituted by a Russian song about birthdays from a classic children's cartoon. In addition to presents, guests often bring flowers, sweets, and cards. The person who is receiving presents is expected to be grateful and cheerful, because of the old saying: Дарёному коню в зубы не смотрят (Don't look a gift horse in the mouth). The following list contains useful words and expressions related to birthday celebrations:

TRACK 57

подарить (Group II Model I) подарок
to give a present to somebody (a noun in the dative case)

купить цветы / конфеты / торт
to buy flowers, sweets, a cake for somebody (a noun in the dative case)

день рождения
birthday (literally: the day of birth)

С днём рождения!
Happy Birthday! (a greeting to use in person or in writing on the birthday card)

поздравлять с днём рождения (Group I Model I)
to wish happy birthday

приглашать гостей (Group I Model I)
to invite guests

играть в прятки / в шахматы / в шарады (Group I Model I)
to play hide and seek / to play chess / to act out charades

печь пирог / торт
to bake a cake

готовить праздничный ужин
to prepare/cook a festive dinner

танцевать
to dance

разговаривать
to talk

петь
to sing

смеяться
to laugh

Be careful with the following verbs that exhibit irregularities in their conjugations:

Table 11-4

Печь (Group I Model II)

TRACK 58

Person	Singular	Plural
I	пеку	печём
II	печёшь	печёте
III	печёт	пекут

Table 11-5

Гот**о**вить (Group I Model I)

Person	Singular	Plural
I	гот**о**влю	гот**о**вим
II	гот**о**вишь	гот**о**вите
III	гот**о**вит	гот**о**вят

Table 11-6

Танцев**а**ть (Group I Model I)

Person	Singular	Plural
I	танц**у**ю	танц**у**ем
II	танц**у**ешь	танц**у**ете
III	танц**у**ет	танц**у**ют

Table 11-7

Петь (Group I Model I)

Person	Singular	Plural
I	по**ю**	поём
II	поёшь	поёте
III	поёт	по**ю**т

Table 11-8

Сме**я**ться (Group I Model I)

Person	Singular	Plural
I	сме**ю**сь	смеёмся
II	смеёшься	смеётесь
III	смеётся	сме**ю**тся

Read the following dialogue between two friends who came to celebrate another friend's birthday:

Вол**о**дя: Прив**е**т, Лар**и**са! Как дел**а** д**о**ма? (Hello, Larisa! How things are at home?)

Лариса: Всё нормально, спасибо. А как ваши дела? Как жена, дети? (Everything is fine, thank you. And how are you doing? How are the wife and children?)

Володя: Тоже всё хорошо. А что ты купила Ане в подарок на день рождения? (Also, everything is good. What did you buy for Anya as a birthday gift?)

Лариса: Мы купили две книги и путешествие на неделю в Африку. Но пока это секрет. (We bought two books and a one-week trip to Africa. But it's a secret for now.)

Володя: Здорово. Я знаю, что Аня любит путешествовать и ей нравится читать книги, когда она в пути. (Great. I know that Anya likes to travel and that she likes reading books when she is traveling.)

Аня: Лариса Петровна, Володя! Проходите, пожалуйста! Как хорошо, что вы здесь у нас. (Larisa Petrovna, Volodya! Please, come in! How nice it is that you are here with us.)

Лариса and Володя: Аня, поздравляем тебя с днём рождения! Ура! Желаем тебе всего прекрасного, хорошего настроения, побольше улыбок, счастья и исполнения всех твоих желаний! (Anya, happy birthday! Hooray! We wish you all the best, a good mood, more smiles, happiness, and may all of your wishes come true.)

Аня: Огромное спасибо! Пожалуйста, проходите в большую комнату и садитесь с нами за стол. (Thank you so much! Please, come into the living room and join us at the table.)

Two Irregular Verbs to Remember

There are several verbs that are sometimes referred to as isolated because they combine elements of both major patterns of conjugation. These verbs include хотеть (to want) and бежать (to run).

Table 11-9

Хотеть

Person	Singular	Plural
I	хочу	хотим
II	хочешь	хотите
III	хочет	хотят

Table 11-10

Бежать

Person	Singular	Plural
I	бегу	бежим
II	бежишь	бежите
III	бежит	бегут

Read the examples below to see how these two irregular verbs can be used in context:

Она хочет кошку себе в подарок. As a present, she wants a cat.

Они бегут домой. They are running home.

Мы бежали в магазин чтобы купить торт. We were running to the store to buy a cake.

Introduction to the Russian Past Tense

As you know, there are several past tenses in English. Compare the following sentences:

I went home yesterday.
By the time he arrived, I had gone home.
As I was going home, I saw him in the crowd in front of our office.

In Russian, there is only one past tense. The forms of the past tense are formed from the stem of the verb by adding the suffix –л and appropriate endings:

- Singular verbal forms that denote masculine persons and objects take on the suffix -л plus the zero ending, meaning they do not take on an additional ending. [-л]
- Singular verbal forms that refer to feminine persons and objects take on the suffix -л plus the ending -а.[-ла]
- Singular verbal forms that denote neutral objects take on the suffix -л plus the ending -о. [-ло]
- All plural forms irrespective of gender take on the suffix -л followed by the ending -и. [-ли]

See the following table to better understand the formation of the past tense verbal forms:

Table 11-11

Formation of Past Tense Forms

Infinitive	Stem	Masculine	Feminine	Neuter	Plural
Читать	Чита-	Я, ты, он читал	Я, ты, она читала	Оно читало	Мы, вы, они читали
Писать	Писа-	Я, ты, он писал	Я, ты, она писала	Оно писало	Мы, вы, они писали
Говорить	Говори-	Я, ты, он говорил	Я, ты, она говорила	Оно говорило	Мы, вы, они говорили

Remember that the pronoun вы always goes with either the plural verbal form, as in Девочки, вы читали эту книгу? (Girls, have you read this book?) or the formal form, as in Екатерина Владимировна, вы готовили ужин? (Yekaterina Vladimirovna, have you been preparing dinner?)

Remember that the Russian past tense is a simple tense that does not require the use of any auxiliary verbs. Compare the following statements and questions in English and Russian:

Ты писал письмо?
Were you writing a letter?

Нет, не писал.
No, I didn't.

The Past Tense and the Verb быть

We mentioned in the previous chapters that in the present tense, the Russian verb быть (to be) is always omitted. In the past tense, the verb быть (to be) is not omitted. Its past tense forms include the following:

- masculine singular – я, ты, он был
- feminine singular – я, ты, она была
- neutral singular – оно было
- plural – мы, вы, они были

In the feminine forms of the otherwise one-syllable verbs, the stress shifts onto the final -a ending, as in the following examples:

быть: Я был в магазине, а Люба была дома.　　I was at the store, and Lyuba was at home

брать: Я брал уроки музыки, а она брала уроки физики. I was taking music lessons, and she was taking physics classes.

In the negative forms of the verb быть, the stress is on the negative particle не (with the exception of the singular feminine form), as in не был, не была, не было, не были. For example:

Ты вчера был в гостях у Ларисы? – Нет, я не был.
Were you at Larisa's yesterday? – No, I wasn't.

У неё был день рождения. Было много гостей, но не было торта.
She had a birthday yesterday. There were many guests, but there was no cake.

Chapter Review

Review the material covered in this chapter and complete the following exercises.

Chapter Quiz

Answer the following questions and check your answers in Appendix A.

1. What is the main function of the dative case in the Russian language?
   _____

2. What is the connection between the dative case and such Russian verbs as покупать, советовать, дать?
   _____

3. What are the similarities and differences between the Russian verbs любить and нравиться?
   _____

4. When you need to add an indirect object to a sentence in Russian, should you use prepositions? _____

5. What is the meaning of the following saying: Дарёному коню в зубы не смотрят?
   _____

6. What is the suffix that you need to add to the stem of a verb to form any past tense form? _____

7. How many modes of the past tenses are there in the Russian language?
   _____

8. Which Russian verb is usually omitted in the present tense, but is present in the past tense? _____

Translation Exercise

A. Translate the following verb-noun expressions into Russian to practice forming dative forms.

1. to help Nina   _____
2. to give advice to a friend   _____
3. to suggest a plan to Helen   _____
4. to buy a gift for my mother   _____
5. to tell a story to your family   _____
6. to write a letter to Vladimir   _____
7. to give Misha a plate   _____
8. to help Vera   _____

B. Translate the following sentences from English into Russian. Make sure that you remember how to create questions and negative statements in Russian.

9. I like this small house.   _____
10. She likes beautiful clothes.   _____
11. He likes these magazines and newspapers.   _____
12. Do you like these books?   _____
13. They don't like this university.   _____

C. Translate the following expressions into Russian and conjugate the verbs in the present tense:

14. to want a present

_____

15. to cook dinner

_____

D: Translate the following sentences into Russian using what you know about the past tense:

16. I haven't been at home, but she was there.

_____

17. She was cooking dinner, and I was at the university.

_____

18. We wanted to write a letter to the senator.

_____

19. They were waiting for teachers in the classrooms.

   _____

20. You (formal) spoke the truth to Natasha.

   _____

   E. Translate the following sentences into English and then translate them into Russian using the past tense.

21. Я хочу поздравить тебя с днём рождения!

   _____

22. Он не понимает, что ты ему говоришь.

   _____

23. Павел, вы думаете, что это хорошая книга?

   _____

24. Марина любит читать газеты и журналы.

   _____

25. Тебе нравится русский язык?

   _____

Listening Comprehension

TRACK 59

Listen to the audio track. Transcribe and translate what you hear.

1. _____

2. _____

3. _____

4 _____

5. _____

6. _____

Chapter 12

Verbal Aspect and Verbs of Motion

This chapter provides a basic overview of how verbal aspect functions in the Russian language. English does not have aspects, but the concept is familiar. Verbal aspect in Russian demonstrates when the action of a verb occurred, either in the present or the past. This chapter focuses on recognizing the differences between the usage and formation of imperfective and perfective verbs. You will learn useful prefixes, suffixes, adverbs, temporal expressions, and basic verbs of motion. At the end of the chapter, you will apply your knowledge of verbs of motion to the accusative and dative cases.

Verbal Aspect in Russian

In addition to tenses, Russian verbs have two aspects: imperfective and perfective. The major function of the aspect is to show the speaker's attitude toward action in time. Russian uses the imperfective aspect to describe actions in process and the perfective aspect to express actions that have been accomplished.

> Most of the verbs that you have learned so far are imperfective. As your proficiency in Russian increases, you will acquire more verbs of both kinds and will be able to use them appropriately.

Imperfective Russian verbs can be used in the present tense, as in:

Я читаю эту книгу.
I read / I am reading this book.

Я рисую машину в тетради.
I draw / I am drawing a car in the notebook.

In the sentences below, observe the change of meaning when perfective verbs are used:

Я прочитал эту книгу.
I (have) read this book.

Я нарисовал машину в тетради.
I have drawn / drew a car in the notebook.

As we can see from the examples, a different verbal meaning is expressed by adding extra parts directly to the verb, the prefixes **про-** and **на-**. This way of forming perfective verbs is called prefixation. Often imperfective and perfective verbs form pairs that have a similar lexical meaning when translated into English, for example, **читать – прочитать** (to read, literally "to read" – "to have read"), рисовать – нарисовать (to draw, literally "to draw" – "to have drawn").

QUESTION?

Does English have the category of aspect?

No, English does not use the category of aspect in the same way as Russian. Actions are expressed as ongoing or as completed through complex verbal forms. In English, these take the form of the continuous and perfect tenses. Compare the following sentences: I am reading (continuous) – I have read (perfect), or I am drawing (continuous) – I have drawn (perfect).

Choosing Sides: Perfective or Imperfective?

Whenever you use a verb in Russian, you need to decide whether to use a perfective or an imperfective verb. The following are general guidelines to help you make the most appropriate selection. In general, remember that imperfective verbs describe actions as processes that have no temporal borders, whereas perfective verbs are concerned with actions limited in time.

Imperfective verbs are used to describe ongoing actions or repetitive actions. Use imperfective verbs in the following situations:

- To describe continuous actions that have not been completed: Я читаю книгу. (I am reading a book.)
- To underscore the length of an action: Вчера я долго читала эту книгу. (Yesterday I read this book for a long time.)
- To describe habitual and/or repetitive actions: В детстве я читала японские сказки. (In childhood, I used to like/liked reading Japanese fairy tales.)
- To describe the state of being of an object: На столе лежала книга. (A book was lying on the table.)
- To describe a quality, ability, or characteristic of a person: Мой брат хорошо плавает. (My brother swims well.)

Perfective verbs generally describe one-time actions. With perfective verbs, the focus is on the completion of the verb, not the process used to complete it. Use perfective verbs in the following situations:

- To describe one-time actions, as in Вчера я купила машину. (Yesterday, I bought a car.) Here is a partial list of perfective verbs that are frequently used to describe one-time actions: вспомнить (to remember), встретить (to meet), купить (to buy), ответить (to answer), открыть (to open), показать (to show), положить (to put), получить (to receive), понять (to understand), послать (to send), сказать (to say), спросить (to ask).
- To describe regular completed actions, as in Я написала письмо. (I have written a letter.) Here is a partial list of frequently used verbs to describe completed actions: выпить (to drink), вымыть (to wash), выучить (to learn), написать (to write), нарисовать (to draw), сделать (to do), позавтракать (to have breakfast), прочитать (to read).
- To denote quick, unexpected actions in conjunction with the adverb "вдруг" (suddenly), as in Вдруг он крикнул. (Suddenly he screamed.) Other verbs often used to express quick unexpected actions include: увидеть (to see), услышать (to hear), прыгнуть (to jump), крикнуть (to scream), свиснуть (to whistle), вздрогнуть (to shudder).

Many Russian verbs have both a perfective and an imperfective form, and both forms are used regularly.

Forming Perfective Verbs

Many perfective verbs are formed from imperfective verbs by adding an appropriate prefix. Unfortunately (or fortunately, depending on how you feel about the syntactical complexity of Russian), it is quite difficult to predict which prefix should be used with a particular verb, requiring students of Russian to practice their memorization skills.

The good news is that after you have learned a good deal of verbs, you will develop a better sense of the language (similar to that of a native speaker), which will help you make appropriate grammatical choices. Be patient and refer to the list below to learn some of the more frequently used prefixes and the perfective verbs they create. The first verb in each pair is imperfective and the second is perfective.

The prefix с-:

делать – сделать	to do
танцевать – станцевать	to dance
фотографировать – сфотографировать	to photograph

The prefix на-:

писать – написать	to write
рисовать – нарисовать	to draw
учить – научить	to teach
учиться – научиться	to learn

The prefix у-:

видеть – увидеть	to see
слышать – услышать	to hear

The prefix про-:

читать – прочитать	to read

The prefix под- (подо-):

ждать – подождать	to wait

The prefix вы-:

мыть – вымыть	to wash
пить – выпить	to drink

The prefix вы- is always stressed, as in пить – выпить (to drink).

The prefix при-:

готовить – приготовить	to prepare
готовиться – приготовиться	to prepare oneself, to study

The prefix за-:

платить – заплатить	to pay
плакать – заплакать	to cry

курить – закурить	to smoke

The prefix по-:

есть – поесть	to eat
завтракать – позавтракать	to have breakfast
обедать – пообедать	to have lunch/dinner
ужинать – поужинать	to have dinner
слушать – послушать	to listen
звать – позвать	to call
просить – попросить	to ask
думать – подумать	to think
играть – поиграть	to play
работать – поработать	to work
любить – полюбить	to love

The prefix за-:

говорить – заговорить	to talk
кричать – закричать	to scream
молчать – замолчать	to be/go silent
петь – запеть	to sing
смеяться – засмеяться	to laugh

Some pairs of perfective and imperfective verbs differ by one or two root vowels and/or a suffix. Again, the first verb in each pair is imperfective and the second is perfective:

отвечать – ответить	to answer
показывать – показать	to show
рассказывать – рассказать	to tell
спрашивать – спросить	to ask
вставать – встать	get up
открывать – открыть	to open
закрывать – закрыть	to close

Some pairs of perfective and imperfective verbs have completely different stems and must be memorized. As in the previous examples, the first verb in each pair is imperfective and the second is perfective:

отды**хать** – отдо**хнуть**	to rest
пони**мать** – по**нять**	to understand
поку**пать** – ку**пить**	to buy
гово**рить** – ска**зать**	to speak

Several Russian verbs that denote states of being, as opposed to actions, have no perfective forms. Some of these verbs include **лежать** (to lie), **сидеть** (to sit), **учиться** (to study at school), **иметь** (to own), **жить** (to live), and **существовать** (to exist).

Adding Prefixes and Suffixes

You already know that some Russian verbs rely on prefixes to modify their meaning. For example, **читать** (to read, imperfective) and **прочитать** (to read, perfective), **рисовать** (to draw, imperfective) and **нарисовать** (to draw, perfective). This way of forming perfective verbs is known as prefixation.

A more general term that is often applied to this word-formation strategy is suffixation. Suffixation includes the addition of grammatical and lexical word parts to the beginning and end of words to change their grammatical affiliations and/or to modify their lexical meanings.

QUESTION?

What is the difference between a prefix and a suffix?
A prefix is a word part that is added in front of the root, whereas a suffix is added to the end of the root. It is good to remember that usually Russian words can have only one prefix, but they might incorporate multiple suffixes. For example, the word "подпис**а**вшийся" (the one who signed the document) includes a prefix "под-", root "пис-" and several suffixes.

In brief, Russian uses two verbal aspects (perfective and imperfective) to show the speaker's attitude toward action in time.

As an example of how suffixation works in Russian verbs, let's look at the verb писать (to write, imperfective) together with a chain of closely related verbs.

With the help of the grammatical prefix "на-", we can form its perfective counterpart: написать (to write, perfective). Using various lexical prefixes, we can produce a series of perfective verbs based on the verb писать, yet each distinctly different in their meaning. These perfective verbs in turn form imperfective pairs, also known as secondary imperfectives. Secondary imperfectives are produced with the help of the imperfective grammatical suffixes "-ыва-/-ива-":

Table 12-1

Prefixation: The Verb "Писать" (To Write)

Perfective	Perfective Meaning	Secondary Imperfective
написать	to have written	
переписать	to copy	переписывать
подписать	to sign	подписывать
записать	to write down	записывать
вписать	to write in	вписывать
выписать	to write out	выписывать
описать	to describe	описывать
дописать	to finish writing	дописывать
приписать	to add in writing	приписывать

Take note of the regularly changing stress patterns in secondary imperfectives.

Russian verbs that have prefixes form imperfectives either by dropping their prefix, as in написать – писать (to write) or by adding an imperfective suffix while retaining their lexical prefix, as in подписать – подписывать (to sign). The following is a table of verbs and lexical prefixes that are frequently used in everyday speech in Russian:

Table 12-2

Lexical Prefixes and Verbs

Prefix	Meaning	Verb(s)
в-/во-	in, into, to: inward movement	вписать (to write in), внести (to carry in), войти (to enter)

Prefix	Meaning	Verb(s)
вы-	out: outward movement	**вы**писать (to write out), **вы**нести (to carry out), **вы**играть (to win)
до-	completion of the action	**до**пис**ать** (to finish writing), **до**рисов**ать** (to finish drawing), **до**нес**ти** (to deliver), **до**игр**ать** (to finish playing)
за-	action along the way	**за**беж**ать** (to run in), **за**нес**ти** (to drop off), **за**й**ти** (to drop in)
недо-	incomplete action	**недо**д**е**лать (to do incompletely), **недо****е**сть (not to finish eating), **недо**сп**ать** (not to finish sleeping)
от-/ото-	action away from	**от**ойт**и** (to walk off), **от**нес**ти** (to carry away/off)
пере-	action over, across or change in the direction	**пере**пис**ать** (to write over), **пере**нес**ти** (to carry over), **пере**д**у**мать (to rethink)
при-	action close by or adding to	**при**пис**ать** (to add in writing), **при**нес**ти** (to bring), **при**д**у**мать (to come up with)

Lexical Prefixes for Adjectives and Nouns

Nouns and adjectives also use lexical prefixes. See the following list to learn some key prefixes that will help you expand your Russian vocabulary:

- Prefix "не" (negative, similar to the English un-, im-, ir-, dis-, -less): **не**осто**ро**жный (careless), **не**осто**ро**жность (careless-ness) from осто**ро**жный (careful); **не**зав**и**симый (independent), **не**зав**и**симость (independence) from зав**и**симый (dependent).
- Prefix "без-" (negative, similar to the English im-, in-, un-): **без**оп**а**сный (safe), **без**оп**а**сность (safety) from оп**а**сный (dangerous).
- Prefix "под-" (under): **под**з**е**мный (underground, adjective), **под**зем**е**лье (underground, noun) from земл**я** (ground).
- Prefix "за-" (beyond): **за**граница (foreign land) – **за**гран**и**чный (foreign) from гран**и**ца (border).

- Prefix "со" (together, similar to English co-): собеседник (conversation partner) from беседа (conversation), сотрудник (co-worker) from труд (work, labor).
- Prefix "меж-/между" (between, similar to English inter-): международный (international) from народный (people, adjective), народ (people, noun), межпланетный (interplanetary) from планета (planet).
- Prefix "до" (before, similar to English pre-): довоенный (pre-war, adjective) from война (war, noun).
- Prefix "после" (after, similar to English post-): послевоенный (post-war, adjective) from война (war, noun).
- Prefix "анти-" (English anti-): антинаучный (unscientific) from научный (scientific) – наука (science), антигуманитарный (inhumane) from гуманитарный (humane).
- Prefix "ультра-" (English ultra-): ультраправый (ultra-right, adjective) from правый (right), ультрамодный (ultra-trendy) from модный (trendy) — мода (fashion).

The last two prefixes, анти- and ультра, are Latin-based prefixes that exist in both Russian and English. Although it is helpful to recognize them and look for similarities across the languages, remember that they might be applied to different words in each language.

Useful Adverbs and Temporal Expressions

TRACK 60

Adverbs are words that describe verbs, adjectives, or other adverbs. Although there are many types of adverbs, most of them indicate either manner, quality, quantity, time, place, or intensity of the action, as in:

Я мало читаю.
I read a little.

Он много знает.
He knows a lot.

Мы долго говорили.
We spoke for a long time.

Вы хорошо говорите по-русски.
You speak Russian well.

Я плохо понимаю по-испански.
I understand Spanish badly.

Russian adverbs do not change their form. The following is a list of common adverbs and expressions to describe quality, quantity, speed, and frequency:

TRACK 61

хорошо	good, well
плохо	badly
нормально	fine, OK
мало	a little
много	a lot
немного	not much
быстро	quickly
медленно	slowly
вдруг	suddenly
немедленно	at once
уже	already
обычно	usually
всегда	always
часто	often
каждый день	every day
каждое утро	every morning
каждый вечер	every evening
целый/весь день	whole/all day
целое/всё утро	whole/all morning
иногда	sometimes
редко	rarely
никогда	never

Notice that most Russian adverbs end in –o. Similarly, in English most adverbs end in –ly.

Three Verbs of Motion to Remember

As the name suggests, the verbs of motion express movement. Examples of verbs of motion in English include the verbs "to go," "to walk," "to drive," and "to fly." The following are conjugation tables of several useful Russian verbs of motion: гулять (to go for a walk, to stroll), идти (to walk, to go, to be going), and ехать (to go, to drive, to ride).

Table 12-3

Гулять (to go for a walk, to stroll)

Present Tense		
Person	Singular	Plural
I	гуляю	гуляем
II	гуляешь	гуляете
III	гуляет	гуляют

Past Tense: гулял/а/о, гуляли

Table 12-4

Идти (To walk, to go, to be going)

Present Tense		
Person	Singular	Plural
I	иду	идём
II	идёшь	идёте
III	идёт	идут

Past Tense: шёл/шла/шло, шли

Table 12-5

Ехать (to go, to move, to drive, to ride)

Present Tense		
Person	Singular	Plural
I	еду	едем
II	едешь	едете
III	едет	едут

Past Tense: ехал/а/о, ехали

Although the verbs гулять, идти, and ехать in some cases can be translated with the same English verb "to go", they have distinctive semantic differences in Russian.

- The verb гулять is associated with leisure and strolling.
- The verb идти denotes either walking on foot, as in "Я иду домой" (I am going home) or can refer to the movement of particular means of transport, as in "Поезд идёт" (The train is coming).
- Finally, the verb ехать refers to the movement by transport, as in "Они долго ехали на поезде." The type of transportation is expressed through an appropriate noun in the prepositional case with the preposition "на", which is the equivalent of the English word "by": ехать на поезде, на метро, на автобусе, на трамвае, на такси (to go, ride by train, metro, bus, tram, taxi).

Read the following dialogue between two friends, Маша and Витя, at the bus station. Pay special attention to how the verbs of motion are used, and practice your understanding of Russian perfective and imperfective verbs.

Маша: Привет, Витя! Как дела?
Hello, Vitya! How's it going?

Витя: Спасибо, Маша, всё хорошо. Куда ты идёшь?
Thanks, Masha! Everything is fine. Where are you going?

Маша: В продуктовый магазин. Моя мама попросила меня купить продукты и цветы. Завтра у моего папы день рождения и моя мама готовит праздничный обед.
To the grocery store. My mom asked me to buy some food and flowers. Tomorrow is my dad's birthday and my mom is making a celebratory dinner.

Витя: А, понятно. А я еду в институт. Сегодня у нас экзамены по истории.
Oh, okay (gotcha). I am going to the institute. Today we have a history exam.

Маша: Ты в**ы**учила весь матери**а**л?
Have you learned all of the material?

В**и**тя: По-м**о**ему, да. Вчер**а** я гот**о**вилась ц**е**лый день.
I think so. Yesterday I studied all day long.

Маша: Молод**е**ц! Я ув**е**рена, что ты прекр**а**сно пригот**о**вился к экз**а**мену. А вот и мой авт**о**бус идёт. Я обяз**а**тельно позвон**ю** теб**е** сег**о**дня в**е**чером, л**а**дно?
Well done! I am sure that you have beautifully prepared for the exam. Here's my bus. I will definitely call you tonight, okay?

В**и**тя: Хорош**о**. Пок**а**!
Alright. Bye!

How can you praise someone in Russian?
In informal situations when addressing someone of equal or lesser status, it is customary to praise someone by using the word "молод**е**ц" (literally fine fellow). Although grammatically it is a masculine noun, it can be applied in reference to both men and women. In English, this expression of praise is usually translated as "Well done!" or "Good job!" If you need to praise a group of people, use the plural form "Молодц**ы**!"

Unidirectional and Multidirectional Verbs of Motion

Russian differentiates between the verbs that describe motion in one direction and the verbs that describe motion in more than one direction. Compare the following sentences:

Я ид**у** в шк**о**лу.
I am going to school. (Meaning: I am on the way to school.)

Я хожу в шк**о**лу.

I go to school (Meaning: I attend school and come back home when school is over.)

The verbs **идти** and **ехать** are unidirectional. The multidirectional verb that corresponds to the verb **идти** is **ходить**, and the multidirectional verb that corresponds to the verb **ехать** is **ездить**. In other words, these four verbs form the following pairs: **идти** – **ходить** and **ехать** – **ездить**. You already know how to conjugate the verbs **идти** and **ехать**. Following are the conjugations for the verbs **ходить** and **ездить**.

Table 12-6

Ходить (to go on foot and to come back; to go back and forth: multidirectional)

Present Tense		
Person	Singular	Plural
I	хож**у**	х**о**дим
II	х**о**дишь	х**о**дите
III	х**о**дит	х**о**дят

Past Tense: ходил/а/о, ходили

Table 12-7

Ездить (to make round-trips by vehicle: multidirectional)

Present Tense		
Person	Singular	Plural
I	**е**зжу	**е**здим
II	**е**здишь	**е**здите
III	**е**здит	**е**здят

*Past Tense: **е**здил/а/о, **е**здили*

The verbs **ходить** and **ездить** can be used in the following contexts:

- The verb **ходить** implies a round trip to a particular location and back, as in Я хож**у** в шк**о**лу к**а**ждый день. – I go to school (and come back) every day.

- The verb "ходить" is typically limited to describing only movement on foot. In order to express multidirectional movement that covers longer distances (and thus requires transportation) use the verb "ездить." Similar to the construction used with the verb "ехать," the exact type of transportation is specified by an appropriate noun in the prepositional case together with the preposition "на," as in "ездить на машине, на автобусе, на метро, на велосипеде"—to go by car, by bus, by metro, or by bike. However, sometimes the manner of transportation is omitted altogether, as in "Она ездит на работу каждый день," i.e., she goes (by some means of transportation) to work every day.

- A special note should be made about expressing the process of making round trips in the past. In addition to ходить and ездить, you can also use the verb to be (быть) in its past tense forms to indicate going places, as in "Вчера я была дома, а ты где был?" - Yesterday I was at home, and where were you?

Perfective Verbs of Motion

Imperfective multidirectional verbs of motion (ходить and ездить) do not have perfective counterparts. The unidirectional verbs of motion (идти and ехать) have corresponding perfective verbs of motion, which are formed with the help of the prefix по-, as in идти – пойти (to go, to walk), ехать – поехать (to go, to ride, to drive). Both пойти and поехать indicate the initial stage of movement or trip, as in to start walking, to set off, to begin the journey. Compare the examples below:

Он пошёл домой. He has gone/left for home. (Meaning: the beginning of the trip has been initiated by foot)

Она шла домой.   She was walking/walked home. (Meaning: the process of walking is being described)

Мы поехали на машине.   We have set off (on our trip) by car. (Meaning: the beginning of the trip has been initiated by car)

Мы ехали на машине.   We were riding in a car. (Meaning: the process of riding is being described)

Verbs of Motion and the Dative and Accusative Cases

In the previous chapters, you learned the basics uses of the dative and accusative cases. The dative and accusative cases are also used with the verbs of motion. Compare the following examples:

TRACK 62

Я иду к музею (dative).
I am going to/toward the museum (direction toward).

Я иду в музей (accusative).
I am going to/into the museum (direction inside).

Куда идёт этот трамвай? – Он идёт к вокзалу (dative).
Where does this tram go? – It goes to the railway station (direction toward).

Куда идёт этот поезд? – Он идёт в Москву (accusative).
Where does this train go? – It goes to Moscow (direction into).

Ты куда едешь? – Я еду на почту (accusative). А ты? – Я еду в театр (accusative).
Where are you going? – I'm going to the post office. And you? – I'm going to the theater (direction inside).

Автобус идёт к музею (dative)? Нет, он идёт к кинотеатру (dative).
 Does this bus go toward the museum? – No, it goes toward the movie theater (direction toward).

The dative case with the preposition "к" is used to indicate the movement toward a place or a person with a goal of being near, as in "идти к дому, музею, школе, брату, врачу" (to go toward the house, to the museum, to the school, to the brother, to the doctor). The accusative case is used with the prepositions "в" or "на" to express the movement with the goal of being inside a specific place or space, as in "идти в школу, на почту, на работу" (to go to school, to the post office, and to work).

Use the prepositional case to indicate the location, as in "Я живу в Москве" (I live in Moscow) or "Он встретил её в театре" (He met her in the theater).

Chapter Review

Review the material in this chapter and complete the following exercises.

Chapter Quiz

Answer the following questions and check your answers in Appendix A.

1. How many aspects does Russian have? _____

2. What is main function of the verbal aspect?

   _____

3. Can Russian perfective verbs form present tense forms?

   _____

4. What is the most common method of forming perfective verbs?

   _____

5. Which aspect would you use when describing one-time actions in the past tense?

   _____

6. Which aspect would you use when describing habitual actions in the past tense?

   _____

7. What is suffixation?

   _____

8. Which two types of prefixes are common in Russian?

   _____

9. What are two models of forming imperfective verbs from Russian perfective verbs that have prefixes?

   _____

10. Which aspect do you need to use with the Russian adverb "вдруг"?

    _____

11. Name as many Russian verbs of motion as you can.

    _____

Translation Exercises

A. Translate the following sentences into English:

1. Она написала книгу.

   _____

2. Вдруг он закричал.

   _____

3. Моя сестра хорошо рисует.

   _____

4. Мы долго говорили и пили чай.

   _____

5. Иногда они отдыхали в деревне.

   _____

B. Translate the following sentences into Russian:

6. He has shown us his school.

   _____

7. They usually had breakfast at home.

   _____

8. She has done it.

   _____

9. My younger brother can read very well.

   _____

10. Have you (informal) finished writing this letter?

    _____

Reading Comprehension

Re-read the dialogue on page 172. Write down in the spaces below all the following verbs in the infinitive form:

1. Verbs of motion used in the dialogue:

   _____

2. Imperfective verbs used in the dialogue:

   _____

3. Perfective verbs used in the dialogue:

_____

4. List all conversational formulas used in the dialogue in Russian and then translate them into English:

_____

Translation Practice

A. Translate the following verbs from English into Russian. Make sure that all the Russian verbs are imperfective.

1. to describe _____
2. to copy _____
3. to finish writing _____
4. to write down _____
5. Which suffix is used to mark these verbs as imperfective verbs?

_____

B. Translate the following words from Russian into English or from English into Russian. Indicate whether these words are nouns or adjectives.

6. независимость _____
7. послевоенный _____
8. unscientific _____
9. заграничный _____
10. безопасность _____
11. conversation partner _____
12. международный _____

C. Translate the following mini-dialogues into English.

13. Ты куда идёшь? – На почту.

_____

14. Автобус идёт в центр? – Нет, он идёт к стадиону.

_____

15. М**а**ша **е**здит на раб**о**ту на маш**и**не **и**ли на велосип**е**де? – Иногд**а** на маш**и**не, а иногд**а** на велосип**е**де.

_____

16. Где **О**ля?– Он**а** пошл**а** к своем**у** бр**а**ту.

_____

D. Translate the following mini-dialogues into Russian.

17. Does this train go to Moscow? – No, it's going to St. Petersburg.

_____

18. Do you (formal) take the train or the bus to work? – The bus.

_____

19. I usually go to my mother's house to have lunch. – Every day? – Yes.

_____

Listening Comprehension

Listen to the corresponding CD track and write down the missing words in the spaces below.

TRACK 63

1 Вы _____ говор**и**те по-р**у**сски.

2. Вдруг он _____.

3. На стол**е** леж**а**л _____.

4. Вчер**а** мы д**о**лго _____.

5. Ты _____ **э**ту кн**и**гу?

6. Он**а** б**ы**стро _____ ур**о**ки, а пот**о**м пригот**о**вила об**е**д.

Chapter 13

Daily Life and Impersonal Constructions

This chapter introduces impersonal constructions that are often used in Russian to describe various daily occurrences. You will also learn about two forms of the future tense and expand your overall understanding of how grammatical notions of tense and aspect operate in the Russian language. Finally, you'll add several helpful expressions to your lexicon in Russian and will have an opportunity to explore the meanings and uses of popular Russian sayings and proverbs.

13

Impersonal Constructions

We express our thoughts in phrases that become complete sentences in writing. A typical sentence usually has a subject and a verb. However, in Russian there are many sentences in which there is no grammatical subject and adverbs are used as predicates (verbs). Such constructions are often referred to as impersonal because the identity of the subject who is performing the described action or instigating a particular state or mood is unclear or irrelevant to the meaning of the sentence. Compare the following sentences in Russian with the corresponding constructions in English:

На улице тепло.
It is warm outside.

Володе плохо.
Volodya is feeling sick.

In the first example, the English sentence has a grammatical subject expressed by the pronoun "it," and the predicate consists of the verb "to be" and the adjective "warm." The corresponding Russian sentence does not have a subject, and the adverb alone serves the predicate function. In the second example, the English sentence has a clear subject (Volodya) and a predicate (is feeling sick). The Russian sentence, on the other hand, lacks a grammatical subject, the adverb "**плохо**" is used as a predicate, and the dative case "**Володе**" of the name "**Володя**" indicates the logical subject of the sentence.

Russian often uses impersonal constructions with adverbs as predicates to describe weather and to refer to a person's immediate physical state or emotional condition, as in:

Сегодня холодно / тепло / жарко.
Today it is cold / warm / hot.

TRACK 64

Ему плохо / хорошо.
He is feeling bad / sick / well.

Нам весело / скучно / грустно.
We are having fun / feeling bored / feeling sad.

Борису холодно / жарко / тепло.
Boris is feeling cold / hot / warm.

На улице очень хорошо.
It is very nice outside (literally on the street).

Тебе душно?
Do you feel like it's stuffy?

Russian often relies on impersonal constructions to express needs, permissions, and restrictions. Similarly to the impersonal constructions that we described in the previous section, nouns and pronouns in the dative case express the logical subject of the sentence.

Impersonal constructions with "**нужно**" and "**надо**" are used to express needs, as in:

TRACK 65

Им нужно ехать домой.
They need to go home.

Ему нужно бежать в аптеку.
He needs to run to the drugstore.

Тебе надо идти в школу?
Do you need / must you go to school?

Impersonal constructions with "**можно**" express permissions and abilities, as in:

TRACK 66

Вам можно гулять в парке?
Are you allowed to walk in the park?

Где можно купить газеты?
Where can one buy newspapers?

Тебе можно кататься на коньках?
Are you allowed to skate?

Здесь мо**ж**но кур**и**ть?
Is smoking permitted here?

   Impersonal constructions with "**нельзя**" are used to express restrictions and prohibitions, as in

TRACK 67

Теб**е** нель**зя** пить алког**о**льные нап**и**тки.
You should not drink alcoholic drinks.

Здесь нель**зя** кур**и**ть.
Smoking is prohibited here.

Мне нель**зя** есть мор**о**женое.
I can't (am not allowed to) eat ice cream.

> Folk remedies for common ailments vary from culture to culture. For example, Russians believe that it is detrimental to your health to eat ice cream when you are suffering from a sore throat. Instead, you are expected to drink hot milk with mixed-in melted butter and eat honey or homemade raspberry jam.

   As you can see from the previous examples, Russian impersonal constructions expressing needs, wants, permissions, and restrictions are often used in conjunction with the infinitive of the verb that carries the major semantic meaning. This is similar to English constructions such as "can do," "must read," and "should not cry."

The Future Tense and the Verb Быть

You have already learned how to form the present and past tenses in Russian. In this section, we will look at Russian future tenses. We will begin by looking into the use of the verb "**быть**" (to be). As you might remember, this verb is always omitted in the present tense, but its present tense conjugation forms are used to express future.

Table 13-1

The Verb "Быть": Group I Pattern II

Person	Singular	Plural
I	бу́ду (I will be)	бу́дем (we will be)
II	бу́дешь (you (fam.) will be)	бу́дете (you [plural/formal] will be)
III	бу́дет (he/she/it will be)	бу́дут (they will be)

Compare the following Russian sentences in the present and future tenses. Notice how the verb "быть" is used to express future in Russian impersonal constructions and in Russian sentences that lack the linking verb to be in the present tense.

TRACK 68

Сего́дня тепло́.
Today it is warm outside.

За́втра бу́дет тепло́.
Tomorrow it will be warm outside.

Сего́дня ему́ на́до идти́ в шко́лу.
Today he should go to school.

За́втра ему́ на́до бу́дет идти́ в шко́лу.
Tomorrow he will have to go to school.

Мари́на в библиоте́ке.
Marina is at the library.

Мари́на бу́дет в библиоте́ке за́втра.
Marina will be at the library tomorrow.

Remember that the verb "быть" is not omitted in the past tense either, as in "Вчера́ бы́ло тепло́." (Yesterday it was warm outside). In impersonal constructions in the past and future tenses, the verb "быть" is used in the third person singular, respectively as in "бы́ло" (it was) and "бу́дет" (it will be).

Imperfective and Perfective Future Forms

In Russian, there are two forms of the future tense: imperfective and perfective. The major difference between them is that imperfective future expresses unfinished, continuous actions or actions that will be repeated in the future. On the other hand, perfective future describes single, one-time actions that will be completed in the future:

Я куплю газету.

I will buy a newspaper. (Perfective future: a completed action in the future.)

Я буду покупать дом летом.

I will be buying a house in the summer. (Imperfective future: a process in the future.)

Сначала я куплю квартиру, а потом я буду делать в ней ремонт.

First I will buy an apartment, and then I will renovate it. (Perfective future in the first clause: a completed action in the future; imperfective future in the second clause: a process in the future.)

As you can see from the examples above, imperfective future forms consist of the conjugated form of the verb "быть" plus the infinitive of the imperfective verb, as in

TRACK 69

Я буду говорить.	I will speak.
Ты будешь говорить.	You (informal) will speak.
Он/она/оно будет говорить.	He/she/it will speak.
Мы будем говорить.	We will speak.
Вы будете говорить.	You (plural/formal) will speak.
Они будут говорить.	They will speak.

To review the definitions of perfective and imperfective verbs, please refer to Chapter 12. In brief, imperfective verbs express actions as continuous processes (e.g. писать – to write), and perfective verbs describe completed actions (e.g. написать – to write, meaning to have written.

Russian imperfective future forms are identical to the simple English future forms "shall/will be." However, in contrast to English, in negative sentences the negative particle "не" (not) is placed in front of the verb "быть", as in the following examples:

Я буду рисовать.	I will draw.
Я не буду рисовать.	I will not draw.
Ей будет весело.	It will be fun for her.
Ей не будет весело.	It will not be fun for her.

Russian perfective future forms only exist for perfective verbs. These forms are produced by conjugating a perfective verb following the rules you studied for Group I and Group II of Russian verbs in the present tense. Look at the following examples to learn the conjugation of the perfective verb "прочитать" (to read, meaning "to have read:"

TRACK 70

Я прочитаю эту книгу.
I will read this book.

Ты прочитаешь эту статью.
You (informal) will read this article.

Он/она прочитает эту инструкцию.
He/she will read this instruction manual.

Мы прочитаем эту сказку.
We will read this fairy tale.

Вы прочитаете этот рассказ в школе.
You (plural/formal) will read this short story at school.

Они прочитают эту газету завтра.
They will read this newspaper tomorrow.

Reading is one of the most beloved Russian pastime activities, it is good to know the terms for different kinds of reading materials. Study the list below to learn what your Russian friends might be reading.

Table 13-2

Reading Materials in Russian

Russian	English
книга	book
роман	novel
повесть	short story
рассказ	story
пьеса	play
сказка	fairy tale
басня	fable
стихотворение	poem
текст	text
газета	newspaper
журнал	journal/magazine
статья	article (in a magazine/newspaper)
инструкция	instructions
дневник	diary/journal

Russian books are different from books in English, not only because they are in a different languages, but also because of the way they are put together. For example, don't look for the table of contents at the beginning of a Russian book. It is usually located at the very end of the book.

Tenses and Aspects in Russian

Congratulations! You have now covered the entire system of Russian tenses and aspects. It is one of the most challenging parts of Russian grammar, and it usually requires a lot of practice to get it right. As you continue improving your Russian language skills, always remember the connection between tenses and aspect. See the table below to review what you have learned so far and to solidify your understanding of these important grammatical concepts:

Table 13-3

Correlation of Tenses and Aspect in Russian

Aspect	Infinitive	Present	Past	Future Tense
Imperfective	чит**а**ть	я чит**а**ю	я чит**а**л(а)	я б**у**ду чит**а**ть
In English	to read	I read/am reading	I read/was reading/have been reading	I will read/will be reading
Perfective	прочит**а**ть		я прочит**а**л(а)	я прочит**а**ю
In English	to read/ have read		I read/ have read	I will read/will finish reading

Because there is no exact correspondence between Russian and English verbal forms, take a close look at the context in to order to choose appropriate verbs. Read the following dialogues to practice recognizing Russian tenses and aspects within a particular conversational context.

Dialogue 1: Conversation about a Daily Routine

Серг**е**й: Влад**и**мир, как ты начин**а**ешь твой день?
Vladimir, how do you begin your day?

Влад**и**мир: Я р**а**но вста**ю**, д**е**лаю зар**я**дку, м**о**ю г**о**лову, ч**и**щу з**у**бы и гот**о**влю з**а**втрак.
I get up early, do exercises, wash my hair, brush my teeth, and make breakfast.

Серг**е**й: А что ты д**е**лаешь днём?
And what do you do in the afternoon?

Влад**и**мир: Днём я раб**о**таю.
In the afternoon, I work.

Серг**е**й: А в**е**чером?
And in the evening?

Влад**и**мир: В**е**чером об**ы**чно я смотр**ю** телев**и**зор и чит**а**ю.
In the evening, I usually watch TV and read.

Сергей: А чем ты занимаешься в субботу и воскресенье?
And what do you do on Saturday and Sunday?

Владимир: По выходным я убираю квартиру, хожу в магазин и гуляю в парке.
On weekends I clean my apartment, go to the store, and walk in the park.

Dialogue 2: An Early Morning Dialogue

Mother: Ваня, ты уже сделал зарядку?
(Vanya, have you already done your exercises?)

Son: Нет, но я уже почистил зубы и вымыл голову.
(No, but I already have brushed my teeth and washed my hair.)

Mother: Хорошо. Я уже приготовила завтрак. Ты вчера сделал домашнюю работу по математике?
(Good. I have already made breakfast. Yesterday did you do your math homework?)

Son: Нет, но это не проблема. Урок по математике будет завтра, так что у меня есть время.
(No, I didn't, but it's not a problem. The math lesson is tomorrow, so I have time.)

In Russian, many of the expressions we use to describe our daily activities contain imperfective or perfective verbs coupled with nouns. Grammatically these nouns are objects, so remember to use the accusative case. The following table provides a brief compilation of phrases for daily activities, both in the imperfective and perfective aspect.

Table 13-4

Daily Activities

Imperfective	Perfective	English
чистить зубы	почистить зубы	to brush one's teeth
мыть голову	вымыть голову	to wash one's hair
принимать душ	принять душ	to take a shower
делать зарядку	сделать зарядку	to exercise

Imperfective	Perfective	English
готовить завтрак	приготовить завтрак	to make breakfast
смотреть телевизор	посмотреть телевизор	to watch television
слушать радио	послушать радио	to listen to the radio
делать домашнюю работу	сделать домашнюю работу	to do homework
убирать квартиру	убрать квартиру	to clean up the apartment
встречать друзей	встретить друзей	to meet friends
выгуливать собаку	выгулять собаку	to walk the dog
мыть посуду	вымыть посуду	to wash dishes
гладить одежду	выгладить одежду	to iron clothes

Multiple Negative Constructions

In English, double negatives are considered grammatically incorrect: only one negative is permitted. In Russian, multiple negatives are possible. In fact, Russian puts no limit on how many negatives can be included in a sentence. Compare the following sentences in Russian and English:

Я ничего не вижу.
I don't see anything.

Я никого не знаю в этой комнате.
I don't know anyone in this room.

Я никогда здесь не был.
I have never been here.

Он никак не может понять ничего из того, что я говорю.
He can't understand anything that I am saying.

To form a basic negative construction in Russian, use the particle "не" to negate a verb. Use the prefix "ни," as in никто (nobody), ничто (nothing), никогда (never), and никуда (nowhere) to include additional negatives. Pronouns are declined in Russian, but adverbs are not. Below is a table summarizing the declension of the interrogative pronouns кто (who) and что (what). Negative pronouns are declined in a similar fashion.

Declension of Interrogative Pronouns Кто (Somebody) and Что (Nothing)

Case	кто	что
Nominative	кто	что
Accusative	кого	что
Genitive	кого	чего
Prepositional	ком	чём
Dative	кому	чему
Instrumental	кем	чем

Russian Proverbs

Proverbs say a lot about the culture they come from. Some proverbs translate well, others don't. The following is a selection of frequently used Russian proverbs that you might hear in everyday conversations. These proverbs represent a typical commentary on everyday activities. Don't be surprised to hear some variation in the wording of these proverbs in live speech; people adapt them to suit a particular situation or to represent a particular version that they learned from their family and friends.

TRACK 71

Худой мир лучше доброй ссоры.
A bad peace is better than a good quarrel. (An old adage used to keep peace in the family.)

Правда хорошо, а счастье лучше.
The truth is good, but happiness is better. (Used to defend a white lie.)

На охоту ездить – собак кормить.
Don't feed the dogs right before you go on a hunt. (Used to indicate that someone is doing something at a very late and inconvenient time, "haste makes waste.")

Выше головы не прыгнёшь.
You can't jump over your own head. (Used to explain the futility of trying to do too much.)

Рыба тухнет с головы.
A fish rots from the head down. (Used to explain corruption in high places.)

Доверяй, но проверяй!

Be trustful but be sure to double check! (Used to caution against being too trusting.)

Слово не воробей – вылетит, не поймаешь!

A word is not a sparrow: you can't catch it when it flies away! (Used to justify careful, deliberate speech.)

Ешь пока рот свеж.

Literally, "eat while your mouth is still fresh." (Enjoy your life while you are still young: "Eat, drink, and be merry, for tomorrow we die.")

Chapter Review

Review the material covered in this chapter and complete the following exercises.

Chapter Quiz

Answer the following questions and check your answers in Appendix A.

1. What is the term for Russian sentences with no clear grammatical subject? _____

2. Which case should you use to express a logical subject in impersonal constructions in Russian? _____

3. Is the verb "быть" omitted in the future tense?

   _____

4. What are two major differences between perfective and imperfective future forms? _____

5. Where will you most likely find a contents page in a Russian book?

   _____

6. Explain why a word by word approach will not work when translating verbal forms from English to Russian and vice versa?

   _____

7. How many negatives can be included in a grammatically correct Russian sentence? _____

Translation Practice

A. Translate the following sentences into English:

1. Тебе нельзя есть шоколад.

   _____

2. Ему надо идти домой.

   _____

3. Вам можно смотреть телевизор?

   _____

4. Где можно купить коньки?

   _____

5. Мне нужно прочитать эту книгу.

   _____

B. Translate the following sentences into Russian:

6. Is smoking permitted here? – Yes, it is.

   _____

7. Where can one buy a good car? – I don't know.

   _____

8. I need to be going to work.

   _____

9. They need to write a letter.

   _____

10. Are you allowed to play in the park?

C. Translate the following Russian sentences into English and convert them to the future and past tenses.

11. Ей плохо.

_____

12. Здесь нельзя играть.

_____

13. Мне можно кататься на лыжах.

_____

14. Вам надо домой.

_____

15. Сегодня на улице холодно.

_____

Conversational Practice

Answer the following questions in Russian to the best of your ability.

1. What do you usually do in the morning?

_____

2. What do you usually do on weekends?

_____

3. What did you do yesterday in the morning?

_____

4. What did you do yesterday in the evening?

_____

5. What daily activities do you usually avoid doing in the morning?

_____

Chapter 14

Reflexive Verbs and the Instrumental Case

14

It's a traveler's worst nightmare: something breaks or gets lost in an unfamiliar foreign country. Fortunately, if you know how to communicate in the native language, this does not have to be a traumatic experience. This chapter focuses on the reflexive verbs you might need to report different kinds of accidents, losses, and repairs. We will then focus on the basics of the instrumental case, paying special attention to its main functions and forms in nouns and pronouns. Finally, you will learn about two word formation strategies in Russian that will help you expand your vocabulary and see more connections between English and Russian.

Breaking Things and Making Repairs

In Chapter 8, you learned that some Russian verbs are reflexive, or in other words, they express actions that reflect back to the performer. In this chapter, we will learn a new subgroup of reflexive verbs that deal with breaking things and making repairs. In the following table, you will find pairs of perfective verbs that are similar in meaning but different grammatically: the first column contains transitive non-reflexive verbs, and the third column lists reflexive intransitive verbs.

QUESTION?

What are the key categories used to describe Russian verbs?
Aspect, transitivity, reflexivity, conjugation type, and tense are the key categories you need to know to use Russian verbs correctly. At this point, it might seem like a daunting task, but the more you practice your Russian, the better you will become at making appropriate choices about verbs and other grammatical and lexical options.

First person singular forms in the future tense are provided to help you conjugate these verbs. Refer to Chapter 8 for more information about conjugation patterns. All of the verbs except for the verb найти (to find), are regular in the past tense.

Table 14-1

Breaking Things and Making Repairs: Verbs to Remember

Transitive Verb	English	Reflexive Intransitive Verb	English
сломать (future: сломаю)	to break	сломаться	to break oneself
разбить (future: разобью/ ёшь/ёт/ём/ёте)	to shatter	разбиться	to shatter oneself
разорвать (future: разорву)	to tear up	разорваться	to tear oneself up

Transitive Verb	English	Reflexive Intransitive Verb	English
потер**я**ть (future: потер**я**ю)	to lose	потер**я**ться	to lose oneself
разр**у**шить (future: разр**у**шу)	to destroy	разр**у**шиться	to destroy oneself
почин**и**ть (future: почин**ю**)	to fix	почин**и**ться	to fix oneself
постр**о**ить (future: постр**о**ю)	to build	постр**о**иться	to build oneself
найт**и** (future: найд**у**, past: наш**ё**л, нашл**а**, нашл**и**)	to find	найт**и**сь	to find oneself

Remember that not all verbs can be reflexive and not all verbs keep the same meaning if they do become reflexive, as in заш**и**ть (future: заш**ью**) - to sew up, заш**и**ться (colloquial) - to be wiped out, and приш**и**ть (future: при-ш**ью**) - to sew onto, приш**и**ться (colloquial) - to bother someone.

What Broke and Who Did It?

The beauty of the reflexive verbs introduced in the previous section is that they allow Russian speakers to report an accident or a problem without necessarily having to acknowledge exactly who the culprit is. Compare the following sentences in English and Russian:

Маш**и**на слом**а**лась.
The car broke down.

Мо**я** маш**и**на слом**а**лась.
My car broke down. (It is unknown who broke my car.)

У мен**я** слом**а**лась маш**и**на.
My car broke down. (Although there is some ambiguity as to who exactly broke the car, it is most likely that I did it.)

Ваш сын слом**а**л мо**ю** маш**и**ну.
Your son broke my car. (There is no ambiguity: we know who broke my car.)

Документы потерялись.

The documents got lost.

Их документы потерялись.

Their documents got lost. (It is unknown who lost their documents.)

У них потерялись документы.

Their documents got lost. (Although there is some ambiguity as to who exactly lost the documents, it is most likely that they did it.)

Вы потеряли их документы.

You lost their documents. (There is no ambiguity: we know who lost their documents.)

As you can see from the above sentences, whenever reflexive verbs are used to report an accident, a loss, or a problem, a certain level of ambiguity is preserved as to who the real culprit or the source of the issue is. It is often said that the two greatest enduring questions of Russian social life and literature have been "Кто виноват?" (Who is to blame?) and "Что делать?" (What is to be done?). Russian grammar allows space for multiple interpretations rather than promoting only one way of seeing things.

In the sentences where the construction with the preposition "у" plus a noun/pronoun in the accusative case is used, the word order is different than in English. Grammatically, these sentences are similar to the impersonal constructions that you studied in Chapter 13; there is no grammatical subject and the logical subject is expressed through a prepositional phrase.

So what else can be broken? Refer to the following list for a variety of things that can be broken and, hopefully, repaired.

Ваза / тарелка / чашка разбилась.

A vase / plate / cup is broken.

Машина / компьютер / стиральная машина / пылесос / кофеварка / плита / телевизор / микроволновая печь сломалась / сломался.

A car / computer / washing machine / vacuum cleaner / coffee maker / stove / television set / microwave is broken.

Паспорт / виза / сумка / фотоаппарат / куртка / шапка / ключи потерялся / потерялась / потерялись.
A passport / visa / bag / camera / coat / hat / keys is / are lost.

Дом / здание / дача разрушился / разрушилось / разрушилась.
A house / building / country cottage is destroyed.

The following are three mini dialogues that illustrate the use of these reflexive verbs and corresponding nouns and pronouns.

Dialogue 1

Катя: Витя, что случилось? Почему ты такой печальный?
What happened? Why are you so sad?

Витя: Ничего страшного. Просто моя любимая книга потерялась.
Nothing terrible. It's just that my favorite book got lost.

Катя: Ты не помнишь куда ты её положил?
Don't you remember where you put it?

Витя: Нет. Да, и моя мама могла положить её куда-нибудь в другое место.
No. But also my mom could have put it somewhere in a different place.

Dialogue 2

Саша: Мария Петровна, ваша хрустальная ваза разбилась.
Maria Petrovna, your crystal vase got broken.

Мария Петровна: Ах, как жалко! Саша, ты её разбила?
Oh, what a pity! Sasha, did you break it?

Саша: Нет, я только нашла осколки на полу на кухне.
No, I only just found the broken pieces on the floor in the kitchen.

Мария Петровна: Наверное, это Вася. Он такой неуклюжий. Ну, что с ним делать? Я просила его быть осторожней.
It was probably Vasya. He is so clumsy. But what can you do with him? I asked him to be more careful.

Dialogue 3

Коля, у мен**я** к теб**е** пр**о**сьба. Ты м**о**жешь мне пом**о**чь?
Kolya, I have a favor to ask. Can you help me?

Кон**е**чно, что случ**и**лось?
Of course. What happened?

У мен**я** слом**а**лся компь**ю**тер. Возм**о**жно, **э**то в**и**рус. У теб**я** есть вр**е**мя его пров**е**рить?
My computer broke. It's possible it's a virus. Do you have to time to check it?

Да, сад**и**сь, пож**а**луйста. Дав**а**й посм**о**трим, что происх**о**дит с тво**и**м компь**ю**тером.
Yes, sit down please. Let's see what's happening with your computer.

Useful Phrases

Learn the following phrases that are often used to express a feeling of pity, irritation, or embarrassment when something is missing or broken. These phrases consist of the Russian word "как" (how) plus an adverb. Note the difference between English and Russian: corresponding English phrases use adjectives, not adverbs.

TRACK 72

Как ж**а**лко!	What a shame!
Как об**и**дно!	How frustrating!
Как непри**я**тно!	How unpleasant!
Как неуд**о**бно!	How inconvenient! / How embarrassing!
Как неож**и**данно!	How unexpected!
Как оп**а**сно!	How dangerous!
Как стр**а**шно!	How terrifying!
Как уж**а**сно!	How terrible!

TRACK 73

Learn the following phrases to ask for help and express your gratitude:

Вы м**о**жете мне пом**о**чь?   Can you (formal/plural) help me?

Как хорош**о**!
How nice/good!

Мне н**у**жно найт**и** америк**а**нское пос**о**льство.
I need to find the American embassy.

Спас**и**бо за п**о**мощь!
Thank you for your help!

Вы мне так помогл**и**!
You (formal/plural) helped me so much!

TRACK 74

If someone asks you for help, remember the following phrases:

Что случ**и**лось?
What happened?

Чем я мог**у** вам/теб**е** пом**о**чь?
How can I help you?

The Basics of the Instrumental Case

The main function of the instrumental case is to indicate the means, manner, or agent of an action, as in the following examples.

TRACK 75

Чем ты п**и**шешь? – Я пиш**у** р**у**чкой.
What are you writing with? - I'm writing with a pen.

Чем ты почин**и**шь **э**ту маш**и**ну? – Я д**у**маю, что я почин**ю** её **э**тим инструм**е**нтом.
What are you going to fix this car with? – I think I will fix it with this tool.

Кем ты б**у**дешь, когд**а в**ырастешь? – Я б**у**ду врач**о**м, а ты? What are you going to be when you grow up? – I will be a doctor, and you?

The instrumental case is expressed through specific endings.

- Add the ending –ом/-ем to singular nouns that follow the first declension pattern: masculine nouns ending in a consonant, a soft sign, or "й" as well as neuter nouns ending in –о or -е. For example, хлеб (bread) – хлеб**ом**, словарь (dictionary) – словар**ём**, муз**ей** (museum) – муз**еем**, окн**о** (window) - окн**ом**.

- Plural nouns of the first declension pattern take the endings –ами/-ями, as in хлеб**ами**, словар**ями**, музе**ями**, **о**кнами.
- Feminine and masculine nouns ending in –а/-я that belong to the second declension take the endings of –ой/-ей, as in вод**а** (water) – вод**ой**, нед**е**ля (week) – нед**е**лей, п**а**па (dad)– п**а**пой, д**я**дя (uncle) – д**я**дей.
- Plural nouns from the second declension pattern take the endings –ами/ями, as in п**а**пами and нед**е**лями.
- Feminine nouns ending in a soft sign from the third declension pattern take the ending –ю, as in морк**о**вь (carrot) – морк**о**вью, пл**о**щадь (square) – пл**о**щадью.
- Plural feminine nouns from the third declension pattern take the ending –ями in the instrumental case, as in площад**я**ми.

After ж, ш, щ, ц, write the vowel "о" in stressed singular endings in the instrumental case, and the vowel "е" in unstressed singular endings, as in нож (knife) – нож**ом**, ключ (key) – ключ**ом**, каранд**а**ш (pencil) – каран-даш**ом**, госпож**а** (Mrs.) – госпож**ой**, but муж (husband) – м**у**жем, к**а**ша (kasha)– к**а**шей.

Prepositions and the Instrumental Case

The instrumental case is sometimes used with several prepositions. With the preposition "с" (with) to express a joint action, as in Я гул**я**ю в п**а**рке с мо**ей** м**а**мой. (I am walking in the park with my mom.) In addition to the verb "гул**я**ть," the verbs "жить" (to live), "друж**и**ть" (to be friends), and "раб**о**тать" (to work) often express a mutual action (as in to live with, to be friends with, and to work with) and are used with the preposition "с" followed by a noun in the instrumental case.

The following prepositions are used in the circumstances outlined here:

- Use the preposition "с" to indicate a combination of two substances, as in the following set expressions: "хлеб с маслом" (bread and butter), "кофе с молоком" (coffee and milk), "пирог с капустой" (cabbage pie).
- Use the preposition "рядом с" (near to) to indicate proximity, as in the following expressions: "рядом с домом" (close to home), "рядом со школой" (next to school).
- Use the preposition "между" (between), as in the following expressions: "между небом и землёй" (between sky and earth; in a suspended, uncertain condition), "между людьми" (among people).
- Use the preposition "с" and the pronoun "мы" (we) to indicate either a group of people that includes the speaker or only the speaker and the person expressed by the noun or pronoun in the instrumental case, as in "мы с Ваней" (we and Vanya) and "мы с Ваней" (Vanya and I). The exact meaning is usually clear within the specific communicative context.
- Use the preposition "с" in several set expressions to denote two people, as in "мы с тобой" (you (informal) and I), "мы с вами" (you (formal) and I), "он / она со мной / тобой" (he / she and I / you), "мы с сестрой / братом" (my sister / brother and I), "мы с женой / мужем" (my wife / husband and I).

The instrumental case forms for personal pronouns are grouped with the nominative forms, which were presented in the earlier chapters: я – мной, ты — тобой, он — им (masculine), она — ей (feminine), оно — им (neuter), мы — нами, вы — вами, они — ими. When learning these forms, remember that the third person singular masculine and neutral forms are identical.

The Instrumental Case: Professions and Family Relations

The instrumental case is also used after the verbs "быть" (to be), "становиться" (to become, imperfective), "стать" (to become, perfective), and "работать" (to work). Compare the following examples in Russian and English:

TRACK 76

Ты кем бу́дешь, когда́ зако́нчишь шко́лу? – Я бу́ду студе́нтом в университе́те.

What are you going to be when you finish high school? – I will be a student at the university.

Ты не зна́ешь, кем она́ рабо́тает? – Да, зна́ю. Она́ мне сказа́ла, что она́ рабо́тает врачо́м в больни́це.

Do you know what her profession is? – Yes, I do. She told me that she is a doctor at a hospital.

Во вре́мя войны́ он был лётчиком.

During the war, he was a pilot.

Вы не зна́ете, где рабо́тала А́нна Миха́йловна? - По́сле институ́та она́ до́лго рабо́тала инжене́ром, а пото́м ста́ла дире́ктором заво́да.

Do you know where Anna Mikhailovna worked? - After the institute [meaning: after graduating from the institute], she worked for a long time as an engineer, and then became the director of a factory.

Note that Russian speakers often use negation in questions for courtesy, as in "Вы не зна́ете, где здесь кинотеа́тр?" (You don't know where the movie theatre is here, do you?) or "Ты не зна́ешь, кем он рабо́тал в Аме́рике?" (Do you know what his profession was in America, do you?)

There are several nouns that form irregular plural endings in the nominative and in the instrumental case. These nouns are often used in sentences with the verbs "быть" (to be) and "станови́ться" - "стать" (to become).

Table 14-2

Irregular Endings in the Instrumental Case

Nominative Singular	English	Nominative Plural	Instrumental Singular	Instrumental Plural
брат	brother	братья	братом	братьями
друг	friend	друзья	другом	друзьями
муж	husband	мужья	мужем	мужьями
сын	son	сыновья	сыном	сыновьями
ребёнок	child	дети	ребёнком	детьми
человек	human being	люди	человеком	людьми

Read the dialogue below to practice the use of the instrumental case and learn some new colloquial expressions that Russians often use to share news with each other.

Маша: Ты знаешь новость о Сергее?
Do you know the news about Sergei?

Таня: Нет. А что?
No. What is it?

Маша: Марина мне сказала по секрету, что он скоро станет отцом.
Marina told me in confidence that he'll soon be a father.

Таня: Да ты что! Вот это новость! Значит Ольга Петровна будет бабушкой.
It can't be! Now that's news! That means Olga Petrovna will be a grandmother.

Маша: Да, но будет ли она рада?
Yes, but will she be happy?

Таня: А почему нет? Она мне много раз говорила, как ей нравится играть с детьми.
Why not? She told me many times she likes to play with children.

Маша: Да, но Марине и Сергею нужно будет помогать. С детьми всегда много хлопот.
Yes, but Marina and Sergei will need help. There are always many worries with children.

Таня: **Э**то пр**а**вда. Но и мн**о**го р**а**дости. Серг**е**й и Мар**и**на так**и**е молод**ы**е. У них всё пол**у**чится.

That's true. But lots of joy, too. Also, Sergei and Marina are so young. It will all go fine for them.

Common Roots and Loan Words

How can you improve your vocabulary in Russian? One of the techniques is to try to learn frequently used roots and combine these roots with different prefixes and suffixes to form additional words. You might also want to look more carefully into the history of some Russian words to discover their connections to the words that you already know in English or other languages.

Word Building: Recognizing Common Roots

You have probably noticed that several of the verbs included in this chapter have common roots, for example, the verbs "заш**и**ть" (to sew up) and "приш**и**ть" (to sew onto) share the same root "ш**и**ть" (to sew). The semantic link between these two words is expressed through the use of the same root. This type of word formation is called suffixation, and it is common both in English and Russian. The following are examples of commonly used roots with several words derived from them. It is possible that you already know some of these words, while others might be new to you.

The root крас (red/beauty)	
крас**а**	beauty (dated)
кр**а**сный	red
красот**а**	beauty
крас**и**вый	beautiful
крас**а**вец	a handsome man
крас**а**вица	a female beauty
кр**а**ситься	to put on makeup
красов**а**ться	to show off

The root боль (pain)	
боль	pain
больно́й	an ill/sick person
боле́знь	illness/sickness
больни́ца	hospital
заболе́ть	to fall ill
заболева́ние	an ailment

The root лекар	cure, treat
ле́карь	doctor (dated)
лека́рство	medicine, cure
лечи́ть	to treat medically
лече́ние	(medical) treatment
вы́лечить	to cure

The root здрав (health)	
здра́вие	well-being
здоро́вье	health
здра́вствовать	to be well and healthy
здра́вствуй(те)	a greeting formula (formal/informal)
вы́здороветь	to get better

The root игр	play, game
игра́	game
игра́ть	to play
игро́к	player
игру́шка	toy
вы́игрыш	prize, winning
вы́играть	to win
про́игрыш	loss, losing
проигра́ть	to lose

Etymology is a field of linguistics that deals with the history of words. In addition to scientific etymology based on thorough research, lay people often create folk etymologies for various words. The best way to learn the etymology of a word is to refer to "этимологи́ческий слова́рь" (an etymological dictionary).

Loan Words

You already know that languages borrow words from each other. Some borrowings are hard to pinpoint because they are formed with the help of native words. These are called loan words. In Russian there are several loan words from English, for example, "небоскрёб" (from English 'skyscraper'), "телохранитель" (from English 'bodyguard'), and "картина" (from English 'picture', meaning 'movie'). More recent additions to Russian lexicon that have roots in English and are gaining popularity both in Russian press and in everyday conversational language are "деловая женщина" (business woman), "говорящая голова" (talking head), "вотум недоверия" (no confidence vote), and "отмывание денег" (money laundering).

Chapter Review

Review the material covered in this chapter and complete the following exercises.

Chapter Quiz

Answer the following questions and check your answers in Appendix A.

1. What are reflexive verbs?
   _____

2. Can reflexive verbs be transitive?
   _____

3. Give at least three examples of frequently used word roots with several examples illustrating their usage.
   _____

4. What strategies can you employ to expand your vocabulary in Russian?
   _____

5. What is the main function of the instrumental case?
   _____

Translation Practice

A. Translate the following sentences into Russian and use an appropriate expression of frustration:

1. My computer broke.

   _____

2. My keys got lost.

   _____

3. Our washing machine is not working.

   _____

4. Her new bag got lost.

   _____

B. Translate the following dialogue into Russian:

5. What happened?

   _____

6. My passport got lost.

   _____

7. How can I help?

   _____

8. I need to find the American Embassy.

   _____

C. Translate the following Russian colloquial expressions into English:

9. По секрету _____

10. А почему нет? _____

11. Да ты что! _____

12. Мы с мужем _____

13. Между небом и землёй _____

14. Мы с Мариной _____

Grammar and Vocabulary Drill

Answer the following questions in Russian to the best of your ability.

1. Вы не знаете где здесь телефон?

   _____

2. Мы будем друзьями?

   _____

3. Кем ты будешь, когда закончишь школу?

   _____

Listening Comprehension

Listen to the corresponding CD track and write down the missing words in the spaces below.

TRACK 77

1. У меня _____ машина.

2. Наши документы _____.

3. Он _____ наш телевизор.

4. У меня сломался компьютер. Как _____!

5. Мне нужно _____ американское посольство.

6. После института она долго работала _____!.

Chapter 15

The Genitive Case

In this chapter, we will explore the basics of the genitive case, paying special attention to the system of endings that mark this case in nouns, adjectives, and possessive and demonstrative pronouns. The genitive case is used to express possession, quantity, and negation. To expand your understanding of Russian culture, read about the history and current state of private property and learn more about Russian higher education. Useful vocabulary is introduced and reinforced through dialogues and exercises.

The Basics of the Genitive Case

The main function of the genitive case is to show possession. You already know how to describe possession with the help of possessive pronouns and/or special sentence structures. Compare the following examples:

TRACK 78

Это мой брат. **Э**то е**го** маш**и**на.
This is my brother. This is his car.

Это мой брат. У н**его** есть маш**и**на.
This is my brother. He has a car.

Это маш**и**на мо**его** бр**а**та.
This is my brother's car.

Это мо**я** сестр**а**. **Э**то её кварт**и**ра.
This is my sister. This is her apartment.

Это мо**я** сестр**а**. У неё есть кварт**и**ра.
This is my sister. She has an apartment.

Это кварт**и**ра мо**ей** сестр**ы**.
This is my sister's apartment.

Это маш**и**на мо**его** бр**а**та and **Э**то кварт**и**ра мо**ей** сестр**ы** are examples of the genitive case. As you can see, the genitive case is the most succinct way of describing possessions belonging to people other than the speaker. English, too, has a similar construction, sometimes referred to as the possessive case. However, it is important to note a major difference in the word order: in Russian the word that expresses the owner is always put after the word that stands for the property, as in **кварт**и**ра сестр**ы**. In English we use the reverse word order, as in "my sister's apartment".

To remember the correct word order in genitive constructions, it might be useful to consider a similar English construction that we sometimes use to express possession, that is, "an apartment of my sister." In this prepositional phrase, the word order is identical to Russian genitive constructions.

Forming the Genitive Case

As with the other cases, the genitive case is expressed through specific endings.

- Add -**a** to masculine nouns that end in consonants and neuter nouns that end in -**о**.

друг – квартира друга
friend – apartment of a friend

окно   окна

- Add -**я** to masculine nouns that end in -**й** and -**ь** and neuter nouns that end in -**е** and -**ие**.

преподаватель – книга преподавателя   university instructor – book of a university instructor

море – рыбы моря
sea – fish of the sea

- Add -**и** to feminine nouns that end in -**я** and -**ь**.

тетрадь – страница тетради
notebook – page of a notebook

- Add -**ы** to feminine nouns that end in -**а**.

машина – водитель машины
car – driver of a car

Remember that some nouns in the accusative case also take the endings -**a** or -**я**. The only way to tell which case is being used is to pay attention to the context.

Plural Nouns in the Genitive Case

Plural nouns in the genitive case are used to indicate the quantity or absence of objects. A special note needs to be made about the formation of the genitive case of plural nouns. Plural nouns in the genitive case are rather complex and depend not only on the declension of a particular noun, but also take into consideration whether the noun is hard- or soft-stemmed and what grammatical gender it belongs to. To make the matter more complex, there are exceptions. The following are several common patterns in the formation of the genitive case for plural nouns.

- Hard-stemmed masculine plural nouns, except for ч, щ, ш, and ж, take the ending of -ов.

ресторан – рестораны – владелец ресторанов
restaurant – restaurants – owner of restaurants

- Plural nouns that end in the consonants ч, щ, ш, and ж in the singular nominative case take the ending of -ей in the genitive case.

мяч – мячи – покупатель мячей
ball – balls – buyer of balls

карандаш – карандаши – покупатель карандашей
pencil – pencils – buyer of pencils

- Soft-stemmed masculine plural nouns take the ending of –ев.

словарь – словари – владелец словарей
dictionary – dictionaries – owner of dictionaries

- Hard-stemmed feminine and neuter plural nouns take the zero ending, meaning only the noun's stem is used without the addition of a suffix.

школа – школы – директор школ
school – schools – principal of schools

слово – слова – недостаток слов
word – words – lack of words

- Soft-stemmed feminine plural nouns take the ending of –ь or –ей.

неде́ля – неде́ли – дни неде́ль
week – weeks – days of weeks

- Feminine plural nouns that already end in -ь take the -ей ending

тетра́дь – тетра́ди – страни́цы тетра́дей
notebook – notebooks – pages of notebooks

This may look like an awfully long list of rules, but most masculine nouns in the plural generative case end in –ов, and most feminine nouns in the plural generative case take the zero ending.

Private and Public Property in Russia

During the communist era, all property in Russia was proclaimed to be public. In Soviet lingo, everything belonged to the people. Private property was restricted to a very limited list of necessities, such as one's clothes, furniture, and other very personal necessities. Apartments and houses were leased from the state and were officially under municipal ownership.

All of this changed dramatically after the fall of the Soviet Union, making it possible for people to exercise their rights of ownership unrestrained by the government. A "quick and dirty" and often rigged system of privatization resulted in the concentration of financial and political power in the hands of very few, often referred to in Russian media as **олига́рхи** (oligarchs). Overall, **власть олига́рхов** (the power of the oligarchs) has been greatly diminished by the Putin government. The Russian government's technique of digging into the oligarchs' shady past and prosecuting them for illegal activities has been effective in suppressing the oligarchy.

The following is a vocabulary list that will help you discuss private and public property in Russia in Russian.

Table 15-1

Vocabulary Dealing with Property

TRACK 79

Russian	English
собственность	property
частная собственность	private property
общественная собственность	public property
подарок	gift
завещание	will
владелец(а) / владельцы	owner (fem)/ owners
покупать в кредит	to buy using credit
платить наличными деньгами	to pay with cash
продавать/покупать по аукциону	to buy / sell in an auction
недвижимость (fem)	real estate
рынок недвижимости	real estate market
продавец недвижимости	real estate seller
заём	loan
процентная ставка	interest rate
налоги на недвижимость	property taxes
банкротство	bankruptcy

Adjectives and Pronouns in the Genitive Case

As you remember, adjectives and pronouns agree with nouns in number, gender, and case. Generally, masculine and neuter singular nouns take the endings of -ого / -его, while feminine singular nouns in the genitive case end in -ой / -ей, as in "дом известного писателя" (a famous writer's house) and "книга младшей сестры" (a younger sister's book). Remember that the consonant "г" in the endings of the adjectives and pronouns is always pronounced as the Russian consonant "в."

Review the genitive forms and usage of Russian personal pronouns: меня, тебя, его/её/его, нас, вас, их in Chapter 7. Remember that these pronouns are often used with the preposition "у" (by) to indicate either possession (У меня есть кот. - I have a cat.) or close proximity (Я у него. – I (am) at his place.) Now that you know how to form the genitive case of nouns, note that both of these constructions can be applied to animate nouns, as in У врача есть лекарство – The doctor has medicine. or Я живу у дядяи – I live at my uncle's.

The following table summaries the genitive forms of the possessive and demonstrative pronouns in singular and plural. The first two columns include corresponding masculine forms in the nominative case and the English translation. Note that the pronouns его (his), её (her), and их (their) are not declined and retain their form in the genitive case.

Table 15-2

Genitive Forms of Personal, Possessive and Demonstrative Pronouns

Nominative	English	Masculine	Feminine	Neuter	Plural
мой/твой	my/yours (informal, singular)	моего/ твоего	моей/ твоей	моего/ твоего	моих/ твоих
наш/ваш	our/your (formal, plural)	нашего/ вашего	нашей/ вашей	нашего/ вашего	наших/ ваших
этот/тот	this/that	этого/того	этой/той	этого/того	этих/ тех

Some Russian family names in their form are identical to Russian adjectives. For example, think about famous Russian writers (Достоевский, Толстой, and Некрасов) and composers (Чайковский and Мусоргский). These and other grammatically similar names are declined as adjectives: роман Достоевского (Dostoevsky's novel), повесть Толстого (Tolstoy's short story), поэма Некрасова (Nekrasov's poem), балет Чайковского (Tchaikovsky's ballet), опера Мусоргского (Musorgsky's opera).

The Genitive Case in Noun Phrases

The genitive case is also used to modify a noun with another noun or noun phrase, as in the following examples.

Моя сестра – учитель русского языка.
My sister is a Russian language teacher.

Это учебник математики.
This is a math textbook.

This is a useful model, often used to describe academic disciplines, known in Russian as **предметы**. Consult the following table to learn new vocabulary that will help you discuss your academic interests. Also consider this as a side-note on the Russian system of higher education. All the disciplines mentioned in the table below represent popular majors in Russian universities and colleges. A college degree in Russia usually means a five-year degree, with the fifth year spent on writing a thesis in the major. Students have to defend their thesis and if successful, are granted a **диплом** (diploma) that certifies their degree.

In the past, all education was free for qualified candidates; all you needed to do was pass a series of exams held in each institution. Today, there is a complex system in place. There are still many institutions of higher learning that are sponsored by the state and are free for students; however, the competition for admission is extremely high.

On the other hand, there are many private colleges and universities that charge tuition fees. These colleges and universities are less highly regarded. However, if you really want to attend one of the top-notch institutions, you can still do it even if you didn't score too well on the entrance exams. Nearly of them now admit "paying" students in an effort to improve their financial situation. Another important factor that determines the popularity of higher education is that Russia still has a draft, or **призыв**, and one of the reasons for delaying service in the armed forces is enrollment in a program of higher learning.

Table 15-3

Academic Disciplines: Popular Majors

Russian	English
высшее образование	higher education
предмет	subject, discipline
наука	science
биология	biology
медицина	medicine
математика	mathematics
право/юриспруденция	law / jurisprudence
культура	culture
антропология	anthropology
лингвистика	linguistics
архитектура	architecture
искусство	arts
физика	physics
химия	chemistry
литература	literature
история	history
география	geography
психология	psychology
педагогика	pedagogy

Now that you know the names of several academic disciplines and have a good understanding of the formation of the genitive case, let's explore several standard descriptive phrases related to the academic world. As you will see from the following table, many of the terms used in the academy have Latin and Greek roots in Russian and English.

Table 15-4

Describing the Academic World

Lead Noun	Descriptive Noun	Phrase	English
студент/ка	первый/второй/третий/четвёртый/пятый курс	студент/ка первого/второго/третьего/четвёртого/пятого курса	first-/second-/third-/forth-/fith-year student
учебник	физика	учебник физики	physics textbook
преподаватель	математика	преподаватель математики	math instructor
профессор	лингвистика	профессор лингвистики	linguistics professor
кафедра	иностранные языки	кафедра иностранных языков	foreign languages department
факультет	право	факультет права	law school
институт	биология	институт биологии	biology institute
клуб	международные отношения	клуб международных отношений	international relations club

The genitive construction is not used with the following nouns: **лекция** (lecture), **занятие** (class), **задание** (assignment), **курсовая работа** (term paper), and **диплом** (diploma). Instead, use the dative case in the prepositional construction with the preposition "**по**": **лекция по истории** (lecture in history), **занятие по русскому языку** (a class in Russian), and **диплом по физике** (diploma/degree in physics).

"Нет" *and the Genitive Case*

The final use of the genitive case that we will analyze is in negative constructions with the word "**нет**." Compare the following English and Russian sentences:

В парке есть/был/будет фонтан.
In the park there is/was/will be a fountain.

В парке нет/не было/не будет фонтана.
In the park there is no fountain.

Он дома /он был/будет дома.
He is/was/will be at home.

Его нет/не было/не будет дома.
He is not at home.

У него есть/была/будет квартира.
He has an apartment.

У него нет/не было/не будет квартиры.
He doesn't have/didn't have/will not have an apartment.

To express negation, Russian uses a construction with "нет" in the present tense plus a noun in the genitive case. The construction "нет" is transformed into "не было" in the past and "не будет" in the future, plus a noun in the genitive case. Note that in the last sentence in the example, the genitive case is used twice: first to express the person who doesn't/didn't/won't have an apartment ("у него"), and second to indicate what this person is lacking ("квартиры").

The negative construction of the past and future tenses of verb "to be" do not seem to be conjugated because the deep structure of such sentences is impersonal, and thus, the linking verb "to be" (which only is physically apparent in the past and future tenses) has to be in the third person singular.

The Genitive Case in Context

Read the following dialogues to practice recognizing and using the genitive case in context. Remember that some of the words and expressions might be new to you. In this case, read the translations and try to memorize them.

Dialogue 1

Оля: Что это у тебя в сумке?
What do you have in your bag?

Света: Это подарок Маше на день рождения. Это книга.
This is a present for Masha for her birthday. It is a book.

Оля: Книга?
A book?

Света: Да, это роман Толстого "Война и мир". Ты думаешь, ей это понравится?
Yes, it's Tolstoy's novel *War and Peace*. Do you think she will like it?

Оля: Конечно. Какая прекрасная идея! Ты знаешь, это моя любимая книга.
Of course. It is a wonderful idea. You know, this is my favorite book.

Dialogue 2

Юля: Привет, как дела?
Hi, how's everything?

Ира: Хорошо. Я еду на квартиру моего старшего брата.
Good. I'm going to my older brother's apartment.

Юля: Это далеко?
Is it far away?

Ира: Да, но мне надо с ним встретиться и вернуть его учебник математики.
Yes, but I need to meet with him to return his math textbook.

Юля: Да, а ведь завтра у нас контрольная работа. Ты готова?
Yes, but tomorrow we have a test. Are you ready?

Ира: Не совсем. А ты?
Not completely. And you?

Юля: К сожалению, я тоже. Математика - это так трудно!
Unfortunately, me either. Math is so hard!

Ира: Да, но это любимый предмет моего брата. Он преподаватель математики в институте. Может быть, он сможет нам помочь? У меня так много вопросов! Хочешь поехать со мной?

Yes, but it's my brother's favorite subject. He is a math instructor at an institute. Perhaps he can help us? I have so many questions. Would you like to go with me?

Юля: Это прекрасная идея. Спасибо!

That is a wonderful idea. Thanks!

As you noticed from these dialogues, the genitive case is used quite frequently in everyday conversation.

Chapter Review

Review the material covered in this chapter and complete the following exercises.

Chapter Quiz

Answer the following questions and check your answers in Appendix A.

1. What is the main function of the genitive case? _____

2. What are the additional uses of the genitive case?

   _____

3. In addition to nouns, what other parts of speech follow the declension system? _____

4. What is the correct pronunciation of the ending -ого / -его?

   _____

5. Why does the form of the verb "to be" in the past and future tenses in the negative constructions with the genitive case remain in the third person singular? _____

Translation Practice

A. Translate the following expressions into Russian.

1. my sister's car _____
2. his brother's house _____
3. their grandmother's gift _____
4. a writer's notebook _____
5. your (informal; singular) mother's letter _____
6. students' assignment _____
7. an owner of the restaurants _____
8. a buyer of real estate _____
9. a lack of pencils _____
10. a lack of schools _____

B. Translate the following sentences into English.

11. У меня есть брат и сестра. _____
12. У врача есть лекарство. _____
13. Я живу у него в доме. _____
14. У меня в комнате есть компьютер и телевизор.

_____
15. У них нет кота, но есть собака. _____
16. У моей сестры нет диплома. _____
17. Сегодня у него нет лекции. _____
18. У неё не было дома. _____
19. Марины нет дома. _____
20. У нас не будет контрольной работы. _____

Vocabulary Practice

Use the prompts below to create phrases describing professions, buildings, and objects found in the academic world.

1. факультет (international relations) _____
2. преподаватель (anthropology) _____
3. лекция (arts) _____
4. клуб (Russian language) _____

5. занятие (geography) _____

6. профессор (physics) _____

7. учебник (mathematics) _____

8. студент (literature) _____

9. задание (chemistry) _____

Comprehension Practice

Answer the following questions by writing down your answers in Russian.

1. If you are a homeowner, in Russia you will be referred to as _____.

2. When Russian newspapers are writing about the very few who were able to build financial empires during the privatization of public property after the fall of the Soviet Union, they usually refer to _____.

3. You could lose your house if you don't pay _____ to the state.

4. If you would like to ensure that your children inherit your house, you should write a _____.

5. In addition to the quest for knowledge, higher education is so popular among young Russian men because it allows them to avoid _____.

Listening Comprehension

Listen to the corresponding CD track and write down the sentences exactly as you hear them. Some of the sentences are statements, and some are questions.

TRACK 81

1. _____

2. _____

3. _____

4. _____

5. _____

6. _____

7. _____

Chapter 16

Sentence Structure and the Imperative

In this chapter, you will learn about differences and similarities in English and Russian sentence structure. Now that you've learned the basics of Russian grammar, you can learn how to form complex sentences using several subordinate conjunctions. This chapter will also discuss the notion of grammatical mood and briefly analyze major uses and formation patterns of the Imperative mood in Russian. In addition, you'll be able to explore Russian sensibilities about time.

Simple, Compound, and Complex Sentences

Now that you are familiar with major topics in Russian grammar, including cases, verb conjugations, and the system of pronouns, let's examine Russian sentence structure. All Russian sentences can be divided into three major groups: simple, compound, and complex sentences.

Simple Sentences

Simple sentences usually consist of at least a subject and a verb. In addition, depending on the type of the verb used, a sentence can have a direct and/or indirect object as well as various types of modifiers (adjectives, adverbs, prepositional and participle phrases). The structure of Russian simple sentences is similar to that of English sentences with two exceptions: Russian features flexible word order, and some Russian sentences might lack a grammatical subject or verb. Compare the following examples of simple sentences in English and Russian:

TRACK 82

Я (subject) **рисую** (verb).
I am painting.

Я (subject) **рисую** (verb) **картину** (direct object).
I am painting a picture.

Я (subject) **рисую** (verb) **картину** (direct object) **моей маме** (indirect object).
I am painting a picture for my mother.

Я (subject) **рисую** (verb) **хорошую** (modifier) **картину** (direct object) **моей дорогой** (modifier) **маме** (indirect object).
I am painting a good picture for my dear mother.

На улице тепло (the verb "есть" is missing; no grammatical subject).
It is warm outside.

Although Russian is famous for its flexible word order, its preferred word order is the same as in English: subject – verb – object.

Compound Sentences

Simple sentences, both in English and Russian, can combine to form compound sentences. Compound sentences are sentences that consist of two or more simple sentences, also known as clauses, connected by a coordinating conjunction. Clauses in a compound sentence are fully functional and can stand on their own. These clauses are also known as independent clauses.

Simple sentence: Я иду пешком.
I am walking / going by foot.

Simple sentence: Он едет на трамвае.
He is taking the tram.

Compound sentence: Я иду пешком, а он едет на трамвае.
I am walking, but he is taking the tram.

The three most commonly used coordinating conjunctions in Russian are: и (and), а (and/but), and но (but). Please refer to Chapter 7 to review the difference between "и" and "а."

Complex Sentences

Complex sentences include two or more simple clauses connected by a subordinating conjunction. In a complex sentence, one of the clauses is independent, and the other is dependent. The independent clause contains key information, while the dependent clause modifies it in some way. The dependent clause cannot stand on its own and must include a subordinating conjunction:

Simple sentence: Я иду пешком.
I am walking.

Complex sentence: Когда он едет на трамвае (subordinate clause), я иду пешком (independent clause).
When he is taking the tram, I am walking.

In contrast to English writing conventions, Russian writers prefer longer sentences with multiple clauses, which might be confusing to someone unfamiliar with this style of writing. For example, in *War and Peace*, Tolstoy is said to have written one of the longest sentences in literature; it continues for several pages. What should you do? Just be careful and use your understanding of sentence structure to figure out logical connection between different clauses.

Subordinating Conjunctions

Subordinating conjunctions let us qualify ideas by introducing additional information in dependent clauses. In a way, they are the markers of "fine print"; main ideas are communicated in independent clauses, but the details can only be found in subordinate clauses. What use is it to know that "Мы будем есть" (We will eat) if you don't know the information in the subordinate clause: "когда ты приготовишь завтрак" (when you make breakfast)? Knowledge of major subordinating conjunctions in Russian will allow you to recognize logical hierarchy in the sentences produced by other speakers and to form your own complex sentences. See the following table to learn more subordinate conjunctions in Russian:

Table 16-1

TRACK 83

Subordinate Conjunctions in Russian

Russian	English	Example
что	that	Он сказал, что завтра он будет дома. (He said that tomorrow he will be at home.)
когда	when	Лена всегда звонит домой, когда она задерживается на работе. (Lena always calls home when she is delayed at work.)
если	If	Если она любит танцевать, она обязательно придёт на дискотеку. (If she likes to dance, she will surely come to the night club.)
даже если	even if	Мы вас встретим, даже если вы приедете очень поздно. (We will meet you, even if you arrive very late.)
потому, что	because	Я не пойду гулять в парк потому, что на улице очень холодно. (I will not go for a walk in the park because it is very cold outside.)

Russian	English	Example
чт**о**бы	so that / in order to	Мы ждём н**а**шу сестр**у**, чт**о**бы мы вм**е**сте по**е**хали на д**а**чу. (We are waiting for our sister so that we all can go to the dacha.)
хот**я**	although	Хот**я** у мен**я** нет твоег**о** телеф**о**на, я теб**е** напиш**у** по Интерн**е**ту. (Although I don't have your number, I will write to you online.)
п**о**сле тог**о**, как	after	Он приглас**и**т их в г**о**сти п**о**сле тог**о**, как он зак**о**нчит рем**о**нт. (He will invite them to his house after he finishes the renovation.)
п**е**ред тем, как	before	П**е**ред тем как вы позавтр**а**каете, вам принес**у**т газ**е**ту. (Before you have breakfast, they will deliver a newspaper.)
в то вр**е**мя, как	while	**О**ля сл**у**шала м**у**зыку в то вр**е**мя, как Н**а**стя гот**о**вила об**е**д. (Olya listened to the music while Nastya was making dinner.)

*The pronoun "*тог**о***" is pronounced with the Russian consonant "*в*".*

Subordinating conjunctions include clauses that indicate three different situations: cause. (I came because you called), purpose (I came in order to talk), and condition (I will come if you call me).

Common Attitudes Toward Time

You probably know that cultures differ in their attitudes toward time. Some value time as a commodity that has to be saved and used wisely, whereas others see it more as a free-flowing river with a current far too strong to control and manipulate. If we were to place Russian and American cultures on a continuum to compare their respective attitudes toward time, they would end up on opposite ends.

In contrast to many Americans, Russians have a very relaxed attitude toward time. Usually being late, or in Russian "оп**а**здывать" is not considered to be a huge *faux pas*, and many Russians will wait patiently for their friends for half an hour or so after the agreed upon time has come and gone. Dinner parties never start on time, and it is better to arrive late than to show up early and catch your host unprepared. If you are traveling by public transportation, you might experience some delays. Exercise your patience in advance; trains and commuter rail rarely arrive on time. The train time schedule, "график прибытия и отбытия поездов" will have signs that read "Поезд задерживается" (The train is delayed) or "Поезд опаздывает" (The train is late).

However, you should know that even in Russia there are several occasions when you are expected to be on time. These include coming to class (even though professors can be five minutes late); boarding a plane; arriving to the theater or a concert; keeping your appointment with a doctor, a lawyer, or a clergy member (they, in turn, might be late); and, alas, arriving for a funeral. The following is a list of verbs, related nouns, and conversational phrases that will help you navigate Russian time sensibilities and explain your own view of time.

Table 16-2

TRACK 84

Subordinate Conjunctions in Russian

Russian	English
время (neuter)	time
опаздывать (Group I)	to be late (imperfective)
опоздать (Group I)	to be late (perfective)
опоздание	delay
задерживаться (Group I)	to be late (imperfective)
задержаться (Group I)	to be late (perfective)
задержка	delay
успевать (Group I)	to be on time (imperfective)
успеть (Group I)	to make it/ to be on time (perfective)
объяснять (Group I)	to explain (imperfective)
объяснить (Group II)	to explain (perfective)
объяснение	explanation
извиняться (Group I)	to apologize (imperfective)
извиниться (Group II)	to apologize (perfective)
ждать час/полчаса/двадцать/пятнадцать/десять минут	to wait for an hour/half hour/twenty/fifteen/ten minutes
Так получилось.	That's just the way it happened.
Я скоро буду.	I will be in soon.
Не спеши(те).	Don't rush. (informal/formal).

Russian	English
Извини(те) меня за задержку/опоздание.	Forgive me for being late (informal/formal).
Вовремя	At the proper time; on time.
Ладно.	Okay
Ничего.	It's all right.
На это ушло/уйдёт много времени.	This took/will take a long time.
У нас много/мало времени.	We have a lot of/little time.
У нас ещё есть пять/десять минут/ час, чтобы добраться до . . .	We have five/ten minutes/ an hour to get to . . .
Наконец-то ты/вы здесь! Мы тебя/вас заждались.	At last you (informal/formal) are here! We've been waiting and waiting for you (informal/formal).

Although time is less valued, Russian culture puts a lot of emphasis on patience, industriousness, and attention to details, as illustrated in the following popular Russian proverbs:

Тише едешь – дальше будешь.
Slow and steady wins the race.

Поспешишь – людей насмешишь.
Literally, "if you rush you'll make people laugh." Similar to "haste makes waste."

Делали наспех, а сделали насмех.
Literally, "they did it in a rush and it turned out to be a joke." Also similar to "haste makes waste."

Играть играй, да дело знай!
Work as hard as you play.

And of course, "Не трать время даром!" (Don't waste time!) translates across cultures and time.

The Grammatical Concept of Mood

When you refer to "mood" in everyday conversation, you describe your attitude toward the events you are experiencing at the moment. The grammatical notion of mood applies to verbs, and it transmits the speakers' attitudes toward what they are saying. In other words, your everyday mood and the grammatical notion of mood are similar in that they express your personal attitude toward what you are describing. In English and Russian, there are three grammatical moods: the indicative, the imperative, and the subjunctive/conditional.

Instead of using the subjunctive mood, Russian relies exclusively on conditional forms. In this book, we will explain the main functions of the English subjunctive and explore how these forms can be translated into appropriate Russian conditional forms.

So far nearly all of the verbs you have studied in this book have been in the indicative mood. This is because the main function of the indicative mood is to describe facts and events that are occurring now, will happen in the present, or took place in the past. Note in the following conversation that verbs in the indicative mood can be used in statements, questions, and exclamatory remarks with clear tense markers to indicate present, past, and future.

Что ты сейчас делаешь? - Я читаю книгу.
What are you doing now? – I am reading a book.

Что ты делала вчера вечером? – Сначала я делала домашнюю работу, а потом смотрела телевизор.
What were you doing yesterday? – First, I did homework and then I watched TV.

Что ты будешь делать завтра? - Я пойду в библиотеку и буду готовиться к экзамену по истории. – Какая ты трудолюбивая!
What will you do tomorrow? – I will go to the library and prepare for the history exam. - What a hardworking person you are!

TRACK 85

The function of the imperative mood in English and in Russian is to express commands. Compare the following examples in Russian and English:

Не кричи!
Don't scream!

Иди домой!
Go home!

Пожалуйста, говорите громче!
Speak louder, please, !

Беги скорей домой – тебя ищет твоя мама!   Quick, run home – your mom is looking for you!

In Russian the direct object expressed through a personal pronoun in the accusative case (меня, тебя, его/её/его, нас, вас, их) is often placed before the verb, as illustrated in the previous example.

The subjunctive mood in English is used to describe hypothetical, unreal events. It is the mood of "wishful thinking" that is often used in conjunction with English conditional forms ("if I had money," and "if he had told me in advance"). Refer to the following examples in English with their Russian translation to get a better understanding of how the subjunctive/conditional forms function in English and how they are rendered in Russian:

If I had money (conditional), I would have traveled to Brazil (subjunctive).
Если бы у меня были деньги (conditional), **я бы поехал в Бразилию** (conditional).

I wish (indicative) you were here (subjunctive).
Мне так хочется (indicative), **чтобы вы были здесь** (conditional). / **Жаль, что вас здесь нет** (indicative).

If he had told me about his problem (conditional), I would have helped him (subjunctive). But he didn't (indicative).

Если бы он мне рассказ**а**л о ег**о** пробл**е**ме (conditional), я бы ем**у** помогл**а** (conditional). Но он **э**того не сд**е**лал (indicative).

The Formation and Meaning of the Russian Imperative

The Russian imperative is used to express commands, direct requests, invitations, and warnings. Let's briefly examine three types of imperative forms that are common both in English and Russian.

The imperative is used for commands and warnings directed at "you," as in "Говор**и**те гр**о**мче!" (Speak louder!). Russian has two 'you' forms (informal singular "you" and formal "you," which also overlaps with the plural "you"), so there are two imperative forms.

Formal "you" and plural "you" imperatives end with –**айте**, -**ите**, or –**ьте**. Study the following examples.

чит**а**й – чит**а**йте	to read
раб**о**тать – раб**о**тайте	to work
оп**а**здывать – оп**а**здывайте	to be late
пис**а**ть – пиш**и**те	to write
спеш**и**ть – спеш**и**те	to be in a hurry
идт**и** – ид**и**те	to go
гот**о**вить – гот**о**вьте	to cook/prepare

Informal singular forms end either in –**ай**, -**и**, or –**ь**, as in the following examples.

чит**а**й	to read
раб**о**тай	to work
пиш**и**	to write
спеш**и**	to be in a hurry
ид**и**	to go
гот**о**вь	to cook/prepare

Imperatives directed at oneself and groups that include ourselves (e.g., let us), also known as inclusive commands, can be formed with **давайте** (let us) plus an infinitive, as in "**Давайте танцевать**" (Let's dance). There are other construction models for this type of command, but they are beyond the scope of this book.

Imperatives that express permission, suggestions, or commands directed at third person singular or plural (let him/her/it/them) are formed by **пусть** (let) plus the third person singular or plural form of the present tense of imperfective verbs or the future tense of the perfective verbs, as in "**Пусть мама отдыхает**" (Let Mom take a break) or "**Пусть студенты читают**" (Let the students read).

> Remember that 'you' imperatives are often used to express warnings. To form negative imperatives, add the negative particle "**не**" in front of the warning, as in the following examples: Не пей воду из-под крана! (Don't drink the tap water!); Не злись! (Don't be angry!); Не говори глупости! (Don't say silly things!).

It is important to realize that there are major cultural differences in the way Russian and American English speakers use "you" imperatives. In English, imperative forms are often considered to be too direct and can only be interpreted as commands or orders given by the authority or someone trying to assume the authoritative stanza. Russians, on the other hand, often use "you" imperatives to form direct requests, which when in combination with **пожалуйста** (please) are considered culturally appropriate and polite. Also, consider the common expressions that you already know: the greeting **Здравствуй(те)**! – the imperative from the verb "**здравствовать**" (to be in good health) and the apology **Извини(те)**! – the imperative from the verb "**извинить**" (to excuse).

Chapter Review

Review the material covered in this chapter and complete the following exercises.

Chapter Quiz

Answer the following questions and check your answers in Appendix A.

1. Name three major types of sentences in Russian and English.

    _____

    _____

    _____

2. What types of conjunctions are used in compound and complex sentences? _____

3. Although the structure of a simple Russian sentence is similar to that of an English one, there can be at least two differences. What are they?

    _____

4. Is being on time a big priority for most Russians?

    _____

5. What is the main function of the grammatical notion of mood?

    _____

6. How many moods do Russian verbs have?

    _____

7. What do we express through the imperative?

    _____

Translation Practice

Translate the following commands, requests, suggestions, and warnings. Make sure the imperative forms match the people at whom these statements are directed.

1. Don't rush (informal)! _____
2. Vera, go home! _____
3. Excuse me (formal)! _____
4. Volodya, don't say silly things! _____
5. Don't drink tap water! (informal) _____
6. Let the children play. _____

Comprehension Exercise

Read the following dialogue, then answer the questions in Russian.

Виктор: Привет, Максим! Наконец-то ты здесь! Ты знаешь, я жду тебя уже целых полчаса.

Максим: Виктор, извини. Так получилось. Мне надо было встретиться с моим профессором по биологии, и на это ушло много времени. А потом долго не было автобуса, и мне пришлось идти пешком.

Виктор: Ладно, ничего. У нас ещё есть десять минут, чтобы вовремя добраться до стадиона и найти наши места.

Максим: Хорошо. Хотя у нас есть время, давай поймаем такси. Я так хочу увидеть начало матча.

1. Как их зовут? _____

2. Кто опоздал на встречу? _____

3. Куда они идут? _____

4. У них есть время, чтобы туда добраться?
   _____

Chapter 17

The Conditional Mood and Complex Sentences

This chapter offers more information on the mood system in Russian, with a specific focus on the conditional mood and its formation and semantic functions. In addition, you will learn several new conjunctions that are frequently used in complex sentences, including sentences expressing wishes, regrets, and requests.

Real and Unreal Conditions

When we comment on our surroundings, we often discuss conditions under which certain things are possible or impossible, probable or improbable. In order to be able to do this, we have to be able to differentiate between two types of conditional statements: those that express real conditions that can be met and those that describe improbable conditions. Both types are illustrated in the following examples:

TRACK 86

Если у нег**о** б**у**дут д**е**ньги, он к**у**пит ей под**а**рок.
If he has the money, he will buy her a present.

Если бы у нег**о** б**ы**ли д**е**ньги, он бы куп**и**л ей под**а**рок.
If he had the money, he would buy her a present. / If he had had money, he would have bought her a present.

The first sentence describes a plausible situation: there is a great certainty that as soon as he gets the money, he will buy her a present. This is why the indicative mood is used. The second sentence, on the other hand, contains a highly hypothetical idea: there is no certainty that he will ever have the money, and, thus, the situation described is improbable. To describe such improbable situations English uses the subjunctive mood, and Russian uses the conditional mood.

Be aware of the differences in tense usage in English and Russian to describe real life conditions in the indicative mood. In English, the future tense is not permitted in subordinate conditional clauses, whereas in Russian there is no such limitation, and all three tenses, including the future tense, are used, depending on the context.

The Subjunctive/Conditional Mood

The functions of the conditional mood in Russian generally correspond to those of the subjunctive in English. However, in contrast to English, the same Russian conditional verbal forms are used both in the main and subordinate conditional clauses, as the following examples illustrate. The conditional mood is formed with the particle "бы" plus the verb in the past tense.

Если бы у него **б**ы**ли д**е**ньги** (conditional), **он бы куп**и**л ей под**а**рок** (conditional).
If he had had the money, he would have bought her a present.

Если бы мы не спеш**и**ли (conditional), мы бы опозд**а**ли (conditional).
If we had not hurried, we would have been late.

In the first example, the implication is that he didn't have the money to buy a present for her, and, thus, no present was bought. In the second example, the implication is that they had to hurry so they would not be late. Thus, both sentences describe hypothetical situations that could have happened but did not.

Wishful thinking is admittedly one of Russia's national vices. It's known in Russia as "ман**и**ловщина", which is derived from the "Ман**и**лов" character in Nikolai Gogol's "Dead Souls." Ман**и**лов idly spends his time fantasizing about doing things and achieving great results, whereas in reality nothing is being done. The name "Ман**и**лов" comes from the verb "ман**и**ть" that can be loosely translated as "to attract, pull toward, magnetize."

The Russian conditional mood does not make references to time, and the past tense forms used to form conditional constructions are not past in their meaning. References to present, past, and future are not achieved through verbal forms but via the context. Also note that negative conditional forms are constructed by adding the particle "не" in front of the verb. At the same time, the place of the particle "бы" that marks the sentence as conditional is relatively flexible; it can either go before the verb or after the verb without any change in the meaning of the sentence. Compare the following sentences in Russian and English:

Table 17-1

Conditional Forms: Positive and Negative

Positive	Negative	English
Он рассказ**а**л бы	Он не рассказ**а**л бы	He would (not) tell
Он бы рассказ**а**л	Он бы не рассказ**а**л	He would (not) have told

Positive	Negative	English
Он бы вчера рассказал	Он бы вчера не рассказал	He would (not) have told yesterday
Он бы завтра рассказал	Он бы завтра не рассказал	He would (not) tell tomorrow

"Чтобы" *Clauses*

In Chapter 16, you learned several subordinate conjunctions used in Russian to build subordinate clauses. One of the most commonly used subordinate conjunctions is the conjunction "чтобы," which can be roughly translated as "so that." It is possible to produce at least two types of subordinate clauses with the help of this conjunction. Using the indicative mood, we can create clauses with "чтобы" to express a purpose or a goal; by relying on the conditional mood, we can make clauses that express a desire for someone else to do something that is unreal, improbable or contrary to fact.

Sentences that describe hypothetical situations are conditional by definition, and thus should require the presence of the particle "бы." However, because "бы" is already present within the subordinate conjunction "чтобы," no additional "бы" is necessary. Don't forget to use the past tense form of the verb; this marker is consistent with the regular pattern of forming the conditional mood.

Compare the following examples to see the differences between two types of subordinate clauses formed with the conjunction "чтобы." Notice that subordinate clauses with "чтобы" that express a purpose use the infinitive form of the verb.

Expressing a purpose: Я буду заниматься биологией, чтобы хорошо сдать экзамен.
I will study biology so that I pass the exam.

TRACK 87

Expressing a purpose: Я прочит**а**ю **э**ту кн**и**гу, чт**о**бы найт**и** отв**е**т на **э**тот вопр**о**с.

I will read this book to find an answer to this question.

Expressing a wish: Я хоч**у**, чт**о**бы ты пригот**о**вил мне об**е**д.

I want you to make me dinner. (Literally: "I want that you should make me dinner.")

Expressing a wish: Я хоч**у**, чт**о**бы я был**а** д**о**ма.

I wish I were at home.

Examples 1 and 2 illustrate the use of the conjunction "чт**о**бы" followed by the infinitive of the verb to express a purpose or a goal. Examples 3 and 4 show how the same conjunction can be used with the conditional construction to express a command or an unrealistic desire. In both types of constructions, tense references are expressed exclusively through the verb in the main clause, and whenever possible, through context. Verb forms in the subordinate clauses are left unchanged.

"Why" and "Because" Sentences

Now that you know how to use the construction with the conjunction "чт**о**бы" to report on a purpose or goal, let's learn how to ask someone to explain their behavior or give reasons for the choices they made. In this section, you will look into the construction of "why," "because," "so that," and "in order" statements in Russian:

TRACK 88

Почем**у** ты идёшь дом**о**й? – Я ид**у** дом**о**й потом**у**, что мне **на**до д**е**лать ур**о**ки.

Why are you going home? – I am going home because I need to do homework.

Почем**у** ты идёшь дом**о**й? – Я ид**у** дом**о**й, чт**о**бы д**е**лать ур**о**ки.

Why are you going home? – I am going home (in order) to do homework.

Почем**у** ты опозд**а**л на л**е**кцию? – Я опозд**а**л на л**е**кцию потом**у**, что мой буд**и**льник слом**а**лся.

Why were you late for the lecture? – I was late for the lecture because my alarm clock broke.

Examples 1 and 2 illustrate how you can ask someone to explain the goal or purpose of their behavior. Example 3 demonstrates how you can ask someone to explain the underlying reason for their behavior. To form your questions, use the question word "почему" ("why").

When you answer, the most universally used construction, regardless of whether you are reporting on goals or reasons, is "потому, что" ("because") plus a dependent clause. In addition, you may use "чтобы" ("in order to") plus a clause with an infinitive of the verb to explain the goal or purpose, or use "из-за того, что" ("because of") plus a clause to give your reason. Finally, remember you don't have to give a full answer unless, of course, you are practicing your Russian grammar! Just like in English, Russians also often choose brief answers, as in the following examples.

TRACK 89

Почему ты идёшь домой? – Потому, что мне надо делать уроки.
Why are you going home? – Because I need to do homework.

Почему ты идёшь домой? – Чтобы делать уроки.
Why are you going home? – (In order) to do homework.

Почему ты опоздал на лекцию? – Мой будильник сломался.
Why were you late for the lecture? – My alarm clock didn't work.

Using Conditional Phrases to Make and Decline Requests

Now it's time to look into some useful vocabulary for making polite requests, expressing your regrets, asking for help, and/or asking for an explanation. In order to achieve all these goals, the most useful verb to remember is мочь (can, be able to, imperfective). It follows Group I conjugation pattern, but has a changing consonant in its root: я могу, ты можешь, он/она/оно может, мы можем, вы можете, они могут. Its past tense forms are мог, могла, and могли.

Other verbs and phrases that you should know include:

помог**а**ть	to help (Group I Model 1)
п**о**мощь	(feminine; noun) help
перест**а**ть	to stop (Group I Model 2; there is an additional consonant in the root: я перест**а**ну, ты перест**а**нешь, etc.)
над**е**ется	to hope (Group I Model 1)
над**е**жда	hope (noun)
пл**а**кать	to cry (Group I Model 2; there is a changing consonant in the root: я пл**а**чу, ты пл**а**чешь, etc.)
плач	crying, weeping (noun)
в**е**рить	to believe (Group II Model 1)
в**е**ра	faith (noun)

Russians often use imperative forms together with politeness formulas (e.g. "пожалуйста" please) to make polite requests. However, conditional forms with "бы" are considered more polite. Examine the following examples to see how the same request can be articulated in two different ways:

Позов**и**те, пож**а**луйста, мо**ю** м**а**му к телеф**о**ну. – Пож**а**луйста, не могл**и** бы вы позв**а**ть мо**ю** м**а**му к телеф**о**ну?
Please call my mom to the telephone. – Could you please call my mom to the telephone?

Пож**а**луйста, помог**и**те мне. – Пож**а**луйста, не могл**и** бы вы мне пом**о**чь?
Please help me. – Could you please help me?

Notice that the second version of this request is structurally more complex. It contains the phrase "не могл**и** бы вы" followed by the infinitive phrase that indicates the actual request. This request model is very formal. In fact, its conditional nature makes it so polite that in some contexts it might border on sarcasm or snobbery. Remember that requests made with the imperative must include the politeness formula "пожалуйста," while its inclusion is optional in conditional requests that use "не могли бы вы."

Remember to be consistent in your usage of personal pronouns when addressing people. Russians rarely switch from "вы" to "ты," especially in the same conversation. Such a switch could indicate either an intended insult or a profoundly intimate change in the relationship. If neither is your goal, stick with the formal address.

Now imagine that you are unable to fulfill a request. The following are some ways of politely declining requests using conditional phrases:

TRACK 90

Я бы с удовольствием, но . . .
It would be a pleasure, but . . .

Я бы с радостью, но . . .
I would be happy to, but . . .

Мне бы хотелось вам/тебе помочь, но я не могу.
I would like to help you (formal/informal), but I can't.

Если бы я мог/могла, я бы вам помог помогла.
If I could help, I would help /would have helped you.

Конечно, мне бы хотелось вам/тебе помочь, но к сожалению я не могу.
Certainly, I would like / would have liked to help you (formal/informal), but unfortunately I can't.

Cultural Notes

Russia has some unique cultural notions that you must know if you are to function well among Russians. Let's begin with an examination of Russian family values. Although things are changing, Russians still put tremendous value on their immediate community, which consists of their extended family and close friends.

Russian Attitudes Toward Family and Community

The community, your sense of where you come from, plays in a key role in how you define yourself. A famous Russian proverb declares: "Не имей сто рублей, а имей сто друзей!" (It's better to have a hundred friends than a hundred rubles!) The notion of "мы и они" (them and us) or "свои и чужие" (ours and theirs) has a tight hold on Russian society, cementing and fragmenting it at the same time.

Family is at the center of one's social circle, and nepotism often becomes an inevitable evil. The frequently heard Russian expressions "по блату" and "по знакомству" refer to getting something not through work or merit, but because of one's connections. Perhaps not exclusively Russian, "блат" is a system of mutual favors that wards off outsiders by distributing power and opportunity within a closely-knit group. The opposite of a meritocracy, "блат" promulgates social injustice, while continuously recreating itself through an ever-extending web of connections and favors.

Personal Space

Everyone knows about tiny Soviet apartments and the lack of privacy in the so-called "коммуналки" (communal apartments). However, what is not widely known outside of Russia is that personal space is culturally of less significance in Russia than in American and Western European cultures. For example, in a conversation Russians have a tendency to lean closer to their counterparts than Americans do, creating a more intimate atmosphere.

Being in closer proximity to your conversation partner in Russia does not have sexual undertones and in most cases is expected as a culturally appropriate communication strategy. If you need more personal space to feel comfortable, make sure to indicate this to your Russian friend. It is almost always better to address the issue directly rather than avoid it. Most likely, you will have to find a balance between protecting your personal space and making your Russian friends comfortable while interacting with you.

Reading Practice: Dialogues

Read the dialogues below to practice recognizing new vocabulary and grammatical notions that you learned in this chapter.

Dialogue A

Лидия : Не могли бы вы мне помочь с моими сумками? Они такие тяжёлые. Could you please help me with my bags? They are so heavy.

Николай : Мне бы хотелось вам помочь, но я не могу. У меня проблемы с позвоночником и я не могу поднимать тяжести. Но мой брат вам, конечно, поможет. Семён, помоги этой женщине! I would like to help you, but I can't. I have problems with my back, and I can't lift heavy things. But my brother, Semyon, will, of course, help. Semyon, help this woman!

Лидия : Огромное там спасибо! Thank you very much!

Dialogue B

Нина: Почему ты плачешь?
Why are you crying?

Саша : Потому, что я не могу найти мою любимую книгу.
Because I can't find my favorite book.

Нина: Перестань плакать и давай искать вместе.
Stop crying and let's look for it together.

Саша : Я бы с удовольствием, но у меня так болит голова.
I'd do it with pleasure, but I have such a headache. (My head is hurting so much.)

Нина: Тогда иди отдохни, а я буду искать.
Then go rest, and I will look for it.

Саша: Большое тебе спасибо. Как бы я была без тебя – я не знаю.
Thank you so much. I don't know what I would do without you.

Chapter Review

Review the material covered in this chapter and complete the following exercises.

Chapter Quiz

Answer the following questions and check your answers in Appendix A.

1. Which mood do we use to describe true-to-life conditions?
   _____

2. Which mood do we use to describe hypothetical situations in Russian?
   _____

3. Are there any restrictions on tense usage in subordinate conditional clauses in Russian? _____

4. How are the conditional forms constructed in Russian?
   _____

5. Can the conditional forms in Russian refer to present, past, or future tenses? _____

6. How many and which types of subordinate clauses can be constructed with the conjunction "чтобы"?
   _____

7. How do you make tense references in complex sentences containing subordinate clauses with the conjunction "чтобы"?
   _____

8. What is "маниловщина"?
   _____

9. What is the meaning of the expression "по блату"?

_____

10. What are "коммуналки"?

_____

Translation Practice

Translate the following exchanges from Russian into English.

1. Почему ты сегодня дома? – Потому, что сегодня у нас праздники.

_____

2. Почему вы опоздали на работу? – Потому, что моя машина сломалась.

_____

3. Почему ты кричишь? – Из-за того, что ты меня не понимаешь.

_____

4. Почему ты идёшь домой? – Я иду домой потому, что мне надо поговорить с моими родителями.

_____

5. Почему вы живёшь в Москве? – Я живу в Москве, чтобы быть рядом с моей семьёй.

_____

Conversational Practice

Use your imagination to create responses to the following statements:

1. Вы не могли бы мне помочь с работой?

_____

2. Почему ты смеёшься?

_____

3. Почему ты не в школе?

_____

Listening Comprehension

TRACK 91

Listen to the corresponding CD track and write down the missing words in the spaces below.

1 Я прочит**а**ю **э**ту кн**и**гу, чт**о**бы найт**и** отв**е**т на **э**тот

_____

2. **Е**сли бы у нег**о** б**ы**ли д**е**ньги, он _____
ей под**а**рок.

3. Мне бы хот**е**лось вам пом**о**чь, но я не

_____

4. Я ид**у** дом**о**й _____, что мне н**а**до
д**е**лать ур**о**ки.

5. Я хоч**у**, _____ ты напис**а**л мне письм**о**.

Chapter 18

Origins of Russian Cultural Traditions

In this chapter, we will shift our attention from grammar and word formation to Russian cultural traditions. Understanding cultural notions and the history that shaped them is important. It gives you a broad view of the country and the people who speak the language you are learning, and it will be valuable if your travels take you to Russia. This chapter also focuses on ancient Russia and its religious and cultural traditions. You may begin to see the strong connection between Russia's distant past and its current cultural practices.

The Beginnings of Russian Cultural Traditions

As you have already learned, the development of the Cyrillic alphabet was tied to the influx of Christian missionaries. However, you may also know that most Russians worship a branch of Christianity that is different from any of the Western European faiths. In this chapter, we will also explore Russian traditions, celebrations, and art forms.

Before you begin reading the cultural notes, make sure that you go over the new vocabulary list below. To help you remember the list, pay attention to the cognates and word endings that identify different parts of speech.

TRACK 92

Table 18-1

Vocabulary on Russian Cultural Traditions

Russian	English
культура	culture
традиция	tradition
обычай – обычаи	custom(s)
начало	beginning
развитие	development
территория	territory
язычество	paganism
христианство	Christianity
православие	Russian Orthodoxy
православный/ая/ые	Russian Orthodox (masculine, feminine, plural)
Русская Православная Церковь	Russian Orthodox Church
святой/ая/ые	saint (masculine, feminine, plural); sacred (adjective)
князь	prince, a sovereign ruler of a principality
княгиня	wife of a prince, princess
княжна	unmarried daughter of a prince
княжество	principality
царь	tsar
царица	tsarina

Russian	English
цар**е**вич	son of a tsar
цар**е**вна	daughter of a tsar
ц**а**рство	country ruled by a tsar
ц**е**рковь	church (feminine)
соб**о**р	cathedral
к**у**пол – купол**а**	dome/s (in a church)
алт**а**рь	altar (masculine)
ик**о**на	icon
пр**а**здник/и	holiday(s)
гул**я**ние/я	community celebration(s)
кост**ё**р	bonfire
Вел**и**кий Пост	Lent

Rus and the Advent of Christianity

Русь, or Rus, is the name traditionally used for the land where the Russian culture originated. The eastern Slavic tribes, sometimes referred to as **рус**ячи, populated some of the territory of modern-day Ukraine, parts of Belarus, and parts of today's European Russia. These tribes are considered to be the direct ancestors of modern Russians, Belorussians, and Ukrainians. In the early days, **рус**ячи were pagans, worshipping idols such as Perun, the Slavic god of thunder and lightning. Their land was eventually divided into several principalities, all ruled by a sovereign leader, known as "князь." Each principality, or "княжество," was governed from a town that was recognized as its political center.

Киевская Русь

The principality that united Русь into an empire known as Киевская Русь was the principality built around the Slavic city of Киев in the ninth century A.D. For the first time, something resembling a modern state appeared. Citizens paid taxes and obeyed laws. In return, they were protected from outside enemies.

Christianity was adopted as the state's religion by Prince Vladimir in 988. As a sign of breaking away from the pagan past, Vladimir ordered the wooden statues of Perun and other gods to be burned and tossed into the Dnepr River. The Christianity that was adopted in Rus was based on the teachings of the Greek Orthodox Church, which at that time had a tremendous influence all over Eastern Europe from its seat in Byzantium.

ALERT!

Киев is an ancient Slavic city located on the river Dnepr. It was founded around the fifth century a.d. and has played a central role in the development of Киевская Русь. For many Russians, Ukrainians, and Belorussians, it symbolizes their joint history. Today, it is the capital of Ukraine with a population of 2.5 million people.

Unified Киевская Русь flourished for three centuries until 1054 when it was torn apart by unending fratricidal wars. Rus's fragmentation left it vulnerable to outside invaders, and the Mongols launched devastating raids from the east in the following centuries.

Russian Literature

Out of tsarist Russia came some of the world's best known literary figures—Tolstoy, Dostoevsky, Chekhov, Gogol, and, of course, Pushkin. Their works embody a host of common Russian themes.

In *Anna Karenina*, Leo Tolstoy ponders sin and morality. The title character is a woman in an unhappy marriage who falls in love with another man. Is it better, Tolstoy wonders, to maintain a miserable existence simply because it is the right thing to do, or is it acceptable to behave immorally if the result is happiness?

Fyodor Dostoevsky's *Crime and Punishment* uses a prevalent theme in Russian literature, perseverance through suffering, to tell the story of a man who goes mad after killing an evil pawnbroker. Christian symbolism is a dominant presence in all of Dostoevsky's works.

FACT

Anton Chekhov (1860-1904) was the grandson of a serf who started writing to earn money while he studied medicine. Chekhov practiced medicine, but he is best remembered for his plays, which used humor and satire to explore the quintessential Russian themes of loneliness and desperation. *The Seagull, The Three Sisters,* and *The Cherry Orchard* are among his best known works.

"I resolved to gather into one heap everything that was bad in Russia which I was aware of at that time," Nikolai Gogol wrote of *The Government Inspector*, a satire of nineteenth century Russian bureaucracy. The government is often a menacing figure in Russian literature, but this play attempts to make it comic. The suspicion of the government which so many Russian authors captured was a reflection of public sentiment in the nineteenth and early twentieth century—and it did not disappear during Communist rule.

The Cultural Impact of Christianity

Russian history has influenced the Russian people, and so has their faith. Orthodox Christianity originally arrived from Byzantium, introducing literacy, new secular music, decorative arts, and architecture. Its cultural impact was felt in all areas of life. Even today when you go into a Russian church, you can easily spot the Byzantine influence in the elaborate decorations used in various forms of worship. Especially spectacular are the screens that separate the altar from the worshippers. These screens are known in Russian as "иконостас."

ESSENTIAL

When discussing the painting of icons, Russians always use the verb "писать" as in Андрей Рублёв писал иконы. – Andrei Rublyov painted icons. One of the possible explanations of this usage is that icons are considered to be the Gospel in paint, and those who paint them recreate the word of the Gospel by "writing" it in holy images.

Traditionally, "иконостас" will have several images of the Holy Family and other Saints, painted as icons, or "иконы." Russian icons trace their lineage to the religious images of the Byzantium, but Russians were able to reinterpret what was brought from the outside and created a distinctive and varied style of icons. Icons are usually painted on wood and are often intricately decorated in gold, silver, and semi-precious stones. Иконы are used as images for worship and are not only found in churches, but are often kept in private homes as objects of worship. At home, icons are placed on the wall in "красный угол," a "red" or "beautiful" corner of worship. It is traditional to place an oil candle, known as "лампадка" in front of the holy image.

Icons contain a complex system of symbols that were originally designed to tell stories to worshippers who couldn't read. Several icons with the images of the Blessed Virgin are said to be miraculous and are credited with saving cities from destruction and protecting the young and the weak. These icons are known by the names of the towns with which they are associated, for example, икона Владимирской Богоматери (the icon of Blessed Virgin of Vladimir) and икона Казанской Богоматери (the icon of the Blessed Virgin of Kazan).

QUESTION?

What language is used in Russian Orthodox Church?
The Russian Orthodox Church still relies on the use of Old Church Slavonic for its liturgy, which poses a considerable challenge to many Russians who have to learn it from scratch. This situation is similar to the Catholic Church's use of Latin.

Russian secular architecture is famous for its onion-shaped domes, known as "купола," and its vibrant colors. Some of the best examples of traditional Russian architecture are Saint Sophia in Kiev, the Assumption Cathedral in the Kremlin, and St. Basil's in Red Square in Moscow. Borrowing both from the east and the west, the Russians created their own distinctive architectural style that is widely celebrated and reflects their cultural identity. This centuries-old identity is passed from generation to generation, and the Russian Orthodox Church provides an important link between past and present. Many of the rituals that can be witnessed in Russian churches today are still the same as they were centuries ago.

Russian Spring Festival: Масленица

Many Russian traditional celebrations are dualistic nature: on the surface, they are Christian, but deep inside they have retained a core essence of paganism. When the Church was not able to get rid of pagan rituals, it decided to co-opt and incorporate them in celebrating Christian values. One of the best examples is the traditional Russian spring festival known as масленица. Масленица is a week-long festival similar in spirit to Mardi Gras or Carnival. Also called the pancake festival, it was originally celebrated at the very beginning of spring, but with the advent of Christianity it was moved in an effort to coordinate it with the end of Christmas celebrations and the beginning of Lent.

ESSENTIAL

The name itself comes from the Russian word "масло" (butter) and refers to the abundant use of butter in the preparation and consumption of pancakes, or "блины," a staple during this celebration. In old times, their round shape and golden color symbolized the return of the sun and the increasing warmth and longer days it brought.

Масленица is a celebration of good food and revelry that occurs just before Lent, or in Russian "Великий Пост" ("the Great Fast"). Its Christian interpretation is that it marks a final run of hedonistic pleasures before the somber period of Lent. However, in reality масленица is a folk tradition with deep roots in old pagan times. Its original meaning is to celebrate the end of the long, cold winter and the beginning of spring.

In the past, масленица was one of the most popular folk celebrations. For the whole week, communities celebrated with гуляния, or community parties, that culminated in the burning of an effigy of the past winter. Young people showed their courage and vigor by jumping over the bonfire. More dancing, singing, and drinking ensured that the coming spring would bring fertile crops and a busy fall. With the arrival of Christianity, the last of day of масленица became connected with the ritual asking for forgiveness, charity work, and remembrance of the dead. This was the time when people prepared for the trials of Lent. Finally, at the very end of **масленица** many people went through the purification of the Russian "**баня**," or bathhouse.

Although many of the **масленица** traditions, pagan and Christian alike, were lost during Communist times, many communities today are trying to revive the festival by organizing **гуляния** and educating people about the meaning of many rituals still associated with **масленица**. In fact, the cultural significance of this celebration cannot be underestimated. The following old Russian sayings were collected by Vladimir Dal more than 100 years ago but are still used today, even by Russians who have never participated in **масленица** festivities:

Не житьё, а **масленица**.
"Living the good life. "

Хоть с себя всё заложить, а **масленицу проводить**.
"Everyone should celebrate maslenitsa, even if it means giving away your very last penny." (Used to encourage the spirit of celebration.)

Не всё коту масленица, будет и великий пост.
"From feast to famine." (Used to warn someone who is not prepared for hardships.)

Traditional Folk Art

Folk pictures—"**лубки**" or "**народные картинки**"—represent an art form that is not well known outside of Russia despite their important role in sustaining and developing Russian folk traditions.

Лубки were cheap mass-produced pictures for the eyes of the masses with low levels of literacy. These pictures or engravings were printed from about 1668 to 1917. Their simple form is deceptive; artists often used the art form to comment on social and religious issues. Many pictures contain satirical details and often incorporate both images and text. Usually printed on a press and quickly hand-colored with daubs of watercolors, **лубки** were a popular way to quickly transmit current information (and jokes) to people.

ESSENTIAL

The origin of the name is uncertain; it may stem from the cheap, woven wooden baskets that the prints were sold from by street, or it could be from the paper they were printed on, the inner bark of the linden tree.

The role of **лубки** in the development of folk culture is quite notable, as they offered an outlet for sharing folk wisdom, announcing news, and dealing with commonly held fears. If an elephant, rhino, or a giant came to town, a **лубок** was printed and sold on the streets to give people who couldn't afford a chance to see whatever was being exhibited. They were also sent to neighboring towns and villages to announce the upcoming arrival of such wonderful beasts and unusual people. If an unpopular law was passed, such as Peter the Great's law requiring old believers to cut their beards, **лубки** appeared on the streets and were dispatched quickly into the houses of the villagers to be pored over and discussed.

With the advent of the mechanical press and better means of disseminating information, **лубки** dwindled in popularity. Interestingly, during World War I and the ensuring Civil War, the form of **лубки** was resurrected for the war effort with notable artists using this folk tradition to inspire Russian troops and the civilian population.

Chapter Review

Review the material in this chapter and complete the following exercises.

Chapter Quiz

Answer the following questions and check your answers in Appendix A.

1. What is suffixation? _____
2. Which two types of prefixes are common in Russian?

   _____

3. What are two models of forming imperfective verbs from Russian perfective verbs that have prefixes? _____

4. What is the name of old Russia? _____

5. When was the Orthodox Christianity adopted in Russia? _____

6. What language is used for liturgy in the Russian Orthodox Church? _____

Cultural Exercise

Define the following cultural and historic notions:

1. масленица _____
2. икона _____
3. лубок _____
4. православие _____

Chapter 19

Putting It All Together

This chapter describes ways to practice your Russian language skills both outside and inside Russia. Suggestions are made about some of the sites to visit in two of Russia's most important cities, Moscow and Saint Petersburg. Keep in mind that these are just a few of many interesting places to explore while you are in Russia. Finally, this chapter offers advice about effective strategies to use as you continue to learn Russian.

Places to Practice Russian

Now that we have covered major topics in Russian grammar and vocabulary, let's discuss places where you can practice your Russian language skills outside of Russia.

Immigrant Communities

Practically every major city in the United States and Canada has a sizeable Russian community. In any large city, you are bound to find districts where first-wave immigrants live in a close-knit community and still speak Russian as a primary means of communication.

Please be advised that many of the people who reside or associate with these communities might not necessarily be ethnically Russian. Some may be Jewish, Ukrainian, or Belorussian. However, all of these diverse communities have the Russian language in common.

If you live in a city with a Russian immigrant community, figure out if there is a district famous for a high concentration of Russian-language stores and services. Be prepared to use your Russian skills; sometimes even a little bit of effort will make a good impression. Definitely ask around to learn if there is a Russian-language bookstore. Often bookstores sell not only books, but also tickets to concerts and performances as well as a selection of CDs and DVDs with the latest Russian music hits, video, and TV releases.

Volunteering

Another way to learn about your local Russian-language community is to volunteer in local English as a Second Language programs. Many ESL programs offer conversation partner programs and other opportunities for second language learners to make connections with English-speaking communities.

Remember that if you are volunteering as a conversation partner, you are expected to focus on the development of your partner's English language skills. However, it is a great opportunity for you to learn about cross-cultural differences and ask questions about Russian culture, history, and current politics.

To volunteer for an ESL program, look up local programs and call or visit their Web sites to find out if they need volunteers. Most programs will provide any training and resources you need. Time commitments vary depending on the program, but you should plan to set aside at least two hours one day a week.

The Russian Internet

Another good way to practice your Russian skills without leaving your home is by visiting Russian Web sites. There are virtually thousands of Web sites available at your fingertips. Addresses of Russian Web pages usually end in .ru.

You can find Russian newspapers and radio stations online. Pravda, one of Russia's most well-known newspapers, has both a Russian site and a site with English translations.

Meeting Russian Tourists

If your travel plans do not include going to Russia quite yet, consider spending your vacation time in a place where you might encounter Russian-speaking tourists. In the United States, you might see some Russian tourists in Florida, Hawaii, New York, and California.

Many major world-class museums, such as the Metropolitan, the Louvre, and the British Museum, carry guides in Russian. Practice your Russian by picking up two guides: one in Russian and one in English. Try to navigate through the museum using the Russian guide, and compare the two as a language exercise.

When and Where to Go in Russia

If you feel ready to venture across the ocean and explore Russian culture in situ, you should carefully consider the time of your visit and your itinerary.

If it is your first visit to Russia, you will probably spend some time in Moscow and Saint Petersburg. If so, the best time to visit these Russian cities is between May and September. Whatever time you choose as the time to visit Russia, make sure that you have a well-developed itinerary that offers opportunities to visit places of interest, interact with locals, and practice your language skills.

Consider renting an apartment instead of staying at a hotel when you visit Russia. This will allow you to experience life in a Russian neighborhood, and you will be more likely to use your Russian language skills.

Suggested Activities in Moscow

Take some time to learn the Moscow metro system. This extensive subway connects nearly the entire city, and it is the most efficient way to get around. Subway cards can be purchased at any metro station, and you pay a flat fee for each journey regardless of how far you travel.

The Moscow metro launched operations in 1935, making it one of the oldest subway systems in the world. Today it's one of the busiest anywhere, accommodating an estimated eight million people a day on twelve lines. The central ring line is the oldest, and its stations feature ornate chandeliers, mosaics, and sculptures.

The Kremlin and Red Square

The Kremlin is the heart and soul of Russia, the historic site of the tsars' coronations and the current official residence of the Russian president. The Kremlin complex contains palaces and cathedrals, all surrounded by the original fifteenth-century walls. Red Square is adjacent to the Kremlin; walk by the Lenin Mausoleum and see the famous onion-shaped domes of St. Basil's Cathedral.

Along one side of Red Square, visit one of the oldest department stores, ГУМ, to purchase souvenirs and people-watch. If you are lucky, you will see newlyweds visiting the Alexander Gardens and the Tomb of the Unknown Soldier with its eternal flame and the changing of the guards. It's customary for a newly married couple to stop by the tomb and leave flowers.

Tverskaya Street

Tverskaya Street, formerly known as Gorky Street, is Moscow's main street. It is very close to the Kremlin and is one of the busiest streets in town. Be prepared to see lots of advertisements, street vendors, and street performers. And, yes, be aware of your surroundings and watch your belongings.

Stop by Pushkin Square to see the statue to the revered Russian poet and watch young couples wait for each other at the base before their date. If you are so inclined, check out the first Russian McDonald's. When it first opened in 1990, there was always a long line up front.

FACT

More than 27,000 people applied for 630 available jobs at McDonald's before the Pushkin Square restaurant opened on January 31, 1990. On opening day, more than 30,000 people ate there, breaking the chain's record for busiest first day ever. It was Russia's first introduction to the Western fast food phenomenon.

Gorky Park

Picturesque Gorky Park on the Moskva River provides great opportunities for visitors no matter what the season. In the winter, you can go ice skating in the park. In the summer, be sure to try Russian ice cream and go for a spin on the old Ferris wheel. If you have several hours to kill, buy a ticket for a boat ride down the Moskva River.

Tretyakov Gallery

Built from the private collection of Pavel Tretyakov, a nineteenth-century art collector, this museum features an extensive collection of Russian art dating back 1,000 years. The museum boasts a fine sampling of Russian iconic paintings and masterpieces from the nineteenth and twentieth centuries, including works by Kandinsky and Chagall.

Suggested Activities in Saint Petersburg

There is no lack of places to visit in Russia's second capital, a cultural powerhouse in its own right. The city has a unique literary history, evident to the tourists who prowl its streets and squares. It is also a city with awe-inspiring architecture and unrivaled museums.

The Hermitage

This enormous, sprawling museum combines a rich collection of world-class art and dramatic history. The building, the Romanovs' Winter Palace, is a work of art in itself. Start with a guided tour that covers the museum's highlights and history. After the tour, you can go back and explore on your own, focusing on the art or time period that intrigues you most.

The Hermitage collection comprises more than 3 million items kept in six buildings on the River Neva. Visit the Web site at *www.hermitagemuseum.org* for specifics on hours, entrance fees, and special exhibits.

St. Isaac's Cathedral

The cathedral's stately grandeur is sure to leave an impression. Erected in 1703 as a small church, it was finished in 1859 as an enormous house of worship. Climb to the balcony in the dome for a stunning view of the city.

The Neva River

A wonderful experience in Saint Petersburg is to take a boat ride along the Neva River and its canals. Experience the charm of the stately capital of the Russian empire.

Nevsky Prospect

A visit to Saint Petersburg is not complete without a stroll along Nevsky Prospect. Visit a couple of small plazas off the main thoroughfare; these are the dark and dingy courtyards that are omnipresent in Dostoevsky's novels.

Walking Tour

Saint Petersburg is often called the Russian Venice. At night, you can stroll along the embankment and see several of the city's drawbridges open to let water traffic through. If you have an opportunity to visit the city in June, you will most likely arrive there in time to experience its white nights. There are many cultural events scheduled for white nights, but it is also a great time to just walk around and experience the magic of this great city.

A Final Note

Now that you have learned the basics of Russian language and culture, it is time for you to consider how you can apply and expand your language skills. It is ultimately your initiative that will make the difference. Learning a new language is all about practice and consistency.

FACT

Joseph Brodsky, the noted poet, was fluent in both English and Russian. He once remarked, "A language is a more ancient and inevitable thing than any state."

Take some classes at a local college, continue studying the language on your own, and, if at all possible, make plans to visit Russia. When speaking with native speakers of Russian, don't be afraid to try difficult words or phrases or ask for help. What really counts is your interest in the language and culture and your ability to navigate the complexities of cross-cultural differences without losing your own cultural identity. Most importantly, stay motivated and focused, and you will begin to reap the rewards of seeing the world through the of the eyes of two different languages and cultures.

Appendix A

Answer Key

Chapter 1

Chapter Quiz

1. b. at least 145 million
2. d. French
3. a. Pushkin
4. a. or d. (World War II is known as The Great Patriotic War in Russia)

Chapter 2

Chapter Quiz

1. 33 letters.
2. The Cyrillic alphabet is named after Saint Cyril, a monk from Byzantium.
3. The alphabet was created in order to facilitate the spread of Christianity among the Slavs.
4. Transliteration.
5. 21 letters.
6. One.
7. Азбука.
8. Russians spell foreign names the way they are pronounced in Russian.

Writing Practice

1. George Washington
2. Emily Dickenson
3. Charlie Chaplin
4. Mark Twain
5. Kobe Bryant
6. Nicholas Cage
7. Detroit
8. New Orleans
9. Cincinnati
10. Boston
11. California
12. San Francisco
13. Seattle
14. Colorado
15. Texas
16. Vicksburg
17. Oregon

Chapter 3

Chapter Quiz

1. Four.
2. Vowel reduction.
3. The hard and the soft sign.
4. The soft sign, the vowel sounds Я, Е, Ё, Ю, И signal that the consonant preceding them is soft, and palatalized consonants can make neighboring consonants soft.
5. At the end of words, voiced consonants are pronounced like their voiceless counterparts.
6. Consonant assimilation.
7. Российская Федерация.
8. Новгород, Владимир, Владивосток, Санкт-Петербург.

Pronunciation Practice

1. р
2. л
3. л
4. л
5. с
6. л and д
7. л and т
8. д
9. н

10. с and г
11. г and н
12. с and м
13. к and р
14. с

Practicing Russian Greetings

1. Здравствуйте! Доброе утро!
2. Спокойной ночи! Пока!
3. Добрый день! Здравствуйте!
4. Спокойной ночи!
5. Прощай!

Chapter 4
Chapter Quiz

1. Cognates
2. Мат
3. Спасибо
4. Извините or Простите.
5. Пожалуйста, говорите помедленней.
6. Повторите, пожалуйста, по-английски.
7. Спасибо за вашу помощь.
8. Где здесь туалет?
9. «Ж» stands for Женский туалет and «М» stand for Мужской туалет.
10. Спасибо за приглашение.
11. Entrance is Вход, and Exit is Выход.
12. Следующая станция…
13. Yes is Да, and No is Нет.
14. Осторожно.
15. Fire.

Vocabulary Building Exercise

1. Такси
2. Отель or Гостиница
3. Инспекция
4. Паспорт
5. Школа
6. Университет
7. Виза

8. Ресторан
9. Центр (города)
10. Стоп

Reading, Listening, and Pronunciation Practice

1. Excuse me, where around here is the bus stop?
2. It's over there.
3. Is it far from here?
4. No, it's a five minute walk from here. Go straight, then turn left.
5. Thank you for your help.
6. You're welcome.
7. I would like to invite you to a restaurant.
8. Thank you for inviting me.
9. I would like to invite you to a café.
10. Thanks, but I don't have time now. Perhaps next time.

Translation Practice

1. Извините, где мужской туалет?
2. Извините or Простите, я не знаю.
3. Вызовите скорую помощь
4. Пожалуйста, подождите здесь.
5. Пожалуйста, приходите в гости.

Chapter 5
Chapter Quiz

1. Potatoes, wheat, cabbage, and various kinds of meats
2. By examining their endings
3. Six
4. To name and to indicate that the noun is utilized as a subject of the sentence
5. Masculine, feminine, or neuter
6. А, Я, Ь
7. завтрак, полдник, обед, ужин
8. Small dishes served all at once as an accompaniment to a pre-meal shot of vodka or a glass of wine

9. Answers will vary, but can include блины, щи, борщ, закуски, икра, пельмени, квас
10. Приятного аппетита!
11. **О**чень в**к**усно!
12. Metaphor for friendship and trust
13. Gender, number, and case
14. Adjectives with hard and soft stems have different endings.

Grammar Drill

1. Lunch (masculine)
2. Jam (neuter)
3. Caviar (feminine)
4. Juice (masculine)
5. Bread (masculine)
6. Strawberry (feminine)
7. Potato (masculine)
8. Sausage (feminine)
9. Meat (neuter)
10. Wine (neuter)
11. Restaurant (masculine)
12. Menu (neuter)
13. Bill (masculine)
14. Dessert (masculine).

Translation Drill

1 хор**о**шее вин**о**
2. н**о**вое меню
3. сол**ё**ная колбас**а**
4. г**о**рький шокол**а**д
5. вк**у**сный **у**жин
6. м**я**гкий хлеб
7. сол**ё**ные огурц**ы**
8. св**е**жие помид**о**ры
9. хор**о**ший суп
10. плох**и**е р**у**сские пельм**е**ни

Reading, Listening, and Pronunciation Practice

1. Starters: pickles and tomatoes, caviar, cheese and sausage.

2. First dishes: soup (cabbage soup and beet soup).
3. Main dishes: mushrooms and potatoes, beef and macaroni, pelmeni, pork and vegetables.
4. Dessert: cake, ice cream.
5. Drinks: tea, coffee, water, kvas, diet coke.
6. Answers will vary.

Chapter 6
Chapter Quiz

1. Grandparents
2. Wrong stress
3. Conceptualizations of in-law relationships.
4. Mother - **м**ама, мать; father - **о**тец, п**а**па.
5. Three: a first name, a patronymic, and a last name.
6. No, all Russian full first names are either masculine or feminine.
7. Ник**и**та or Дан**и**ла.
8. The literal translation of a patronymic name is 'the son of' or 'the daughter of'.
9. To form a patronymic for men use -**о**вич/**е**вич and for women –**о**вна/**е**вна.
10. No, foreigners do not have patronymics.
11. Usually, Russian names have a feminine and a masculine form.
12. Address a Russian doctor or teacher by their first name and patronymic.
13. Ты, вы, вы.
14. By the ending –ть.
15. Answers will vary, but may include the question «Кто это?» and this is / these are sentences (Это…).

Name Recognition and Vocabulary Drill

1. Мар**и**я Петр**о**вна Серг**е**ева – daughter of #2, sister of #8, sister of #10 (сестр**а**, дочь)
2. П**ё**тр Никол**а**евич Серг**е**ев – father of #1 and #8, husband of #4 (отец, муж)
3. Влад**и**мир Серг**е**евич Никан**о**ров – brother of #6, son of #9 (брат, сын)
4. Кс**е**ния Бор**и**совна Серг**е**ева – mother of #1 and #8, wife of #2 (м**а**ма, жен**а**)

5. **Николай Дмитриевич Сергеев** – father of #2, grandfather of #1 and #8 (**отец, дедушка**)
6. **Станислав Сергеевич Никаноров** – brother of #3, son of #9 (**брат, сын**)
7. **Борис Алексеевич Никаноров** – father of #4, father-in-law of #2, grandfather of #1 and #8 (**отец, тесть, дедушка**)
8. **Александр Петрович Сергеев** – son of #2, brother of #1 (**сын, брат**)
9. **Сергей Матвеевич Никаноров** – father of #3 (**отец**)
10. **Наталья Петровна Сергеева** - daughter of #2, sister of #8, sister of #1 (**дочь, сестра**)

Grammar Drill

1. Меня зовут Иван.
2. Как его зовут?
3. Его зовут Владимир. / Это Владимир.
4. Кто это?
5. Это Марина. Она – мама и жена.
6. Как их зовут?
7. Их зовут Александр и Мария. / Это Александр и Мария.

Listening Comprehension

1. Петровна
2. Петрович
3. Николаевна
4. Николаевич
5. Викторвна

Chapter 7
Chapter Quiz

1. Russian nouns, adjectives, and pronouns agree in gender, case, and number.
2. Third person singular and plural: **его, её, их**.
3. **Вы / ваш** refers either to second person singular (formal you) or second person plural (you all).
4. Masculine, singular, and in the nominative case

5. Answers will vary, but may include the following: **У тебя такая умная и красивая сестра!** or **Какая у тебя умная и красивая сестра!**
6. Вы
7. Господин / госпожа / господа
8. Есть
9. By using different intonation: a statement has a falling pitch, and a question has a rising pitch.
10. By adding the particle 'не' in front of the word that is being negated.
11. Use the word 'нет' (no) for a negative answer and the word 'да' or the construction 'да, у меня есть…' for a positive answer.
12. No, some have distinctive forms, and others use the masculine form to indicate both females and males.
13. И, а, and но.
14. Not bad; moderately good or acceptable. It's an adjective that expresses modest praise.

Grammar and Vocabulary Drill

1. Твоя/ваша красивая сестра
2. Его симпатичный сын
3. Моя талантливая дочь
4. Его тёща и тесть
5. Её старый дедушка
6. Ваш умный муж
7. Вы/ты такая красивая!
8. Вы/ты такой симпатичный!
9. У вас такой хороший муж!
10. У тебя/вас такая талантливая и красивая дочь!
11. Это моя младшая сестра. Её зовут Лена. Она – студентка.
12. Кто это? – Это моя жена, Вера. Она – талантливый учёный и хороший преподаватель.

Reading Practice

1. Is this your car?
2. No, it is his car. Is this your motorcycle?
3. Yes. It's old, but very good. Is this your house?
4. Yes, it's small, but comfortable.

5. This is my apartment. I have a telephone, a nice TV set, and an old computer. Do you have an apartment?
6. No, I have a small house. There I have a small TV set and telephone.
7. Who is this?
8. This is my husband, Nikolai Fyodorovich. He is a very good engineer. This is my daughter, Masha. She is a student. And this is her fiancée, Vasya.
9. Vasya is very good-looking. Is he a student?

Listening Comprehension

1. Is this Moscow? - Да, это Москва.
2. Do you have time? - Да, у меня есть время.
3. Is this your dog? - Да, это наша/моя собака.
4. Do you have money? – Да, у меня есть деньги.

Chapter 8
Chapter Quiz

1. Two: Group I (the Е Group) and Group II (the И Group).
2. You must remember the present tense stem of the verb. Conjugation endings of the present tense are added to this stem.
3. The particle -сь/-ся at the end of the verb.
4. Three: present, past, and future.
5. No, the вы form should be used.
6. Вы.
7. Check the form of the verb.
8. Думать: я думаю, ты думаешь, он/она думает, мы думаем, вы думаете, они думают.
9. Заниматься: я занимаюсь, ты занимаешься, он/она занимается, мы занимаемся, вы занимаетесь, они занимаются.
10. Смотреть: я смотрю, ты смотришь, он/она смотрит, мы смотрим, вы смотрите, они смотрят.
11. Любить: я люблю, ты любишь, он/она любит, мы любим, вы любите, они любят.
12. Летом я люблю плавать в бассейне.
13. Зимой я люблю кататься на лыжах и коньках.
14. Я люблю читать книги, играть на пианино и заниматься спортом.

Writing Dates

Write the following dates in Russian:
1. понедельник, первое ноября
2. воскресенье, семнадцатое мая
3. четверг, четвёртое сентября
4. суббота, седьмое февраля
5. вторник, девятое марта
6. среда, одиннадцатое октября
7. пятница, двадцать второе января
8. Answers will vary.

Chapter 9
Chapter Quiz

1. A combination of all possible endings for any particular noun.
2. By considering the noun's final letter in the nominative case and its grammatical gender.
3. To express location.
4. Е, И, and sometimes У.
5. О or Об.
6. No, the kitchen, bathroom, and hallway are not counted toward the total number of rooms in a Russian apartment.

Prepositional Case

1. дом – в доме
2. завод – на заводе
3. театр – в театре
4. университет – в университете
5. ресторан – в ресторане
6. Россия – в России
7. Санкт-Петербург – в Санкт-Петербурге

Adjectives and Nouns of Nationality

1. американский футбол (American football)
2. японский самурай (Japanese samurai)
3. китайский чай (Chinese tea)
4. французское вино (French wine)

5. немецкое пиво (German beer)
6. английский парламент (English parliament)
7. испанская принцесса (Spanish princess)
8. мексиканские пирамиды (Mexican pyramids)
9. русский квас (Russian kvas)
10. Катя Иванова – русская. (Katya Ivanova is Russian.)
11. Хуан Карлос и Маркос Гарсия – испанцы. (Juan Carlos and Marcos Garcia are Spanish.)
12. Франсуа Лерош говорит по-французски свободно. (Francois Leroch speaks French fluently.)
13. Генрих Манн—немецкий писатель. (Henrich Mann is a German writer.)
14. Марина Цветаева—русский поэт / русская поэтесса. (Marina Tsvetaeva is a Russian poet.)

Chapter 10
Chapter Quiz

1. Transitive verbs can take a direct object, and intransitive verbs cannot.
2. The verb хотеть follows both conjugation patterns. It also has a consonant variation in the stem (т-ч) and a shifting stress pattern.
3. To indicate the direct object.
4. Animate versus inanimate.
5. Ушанка, валенки, and платок.
6. Любить (to like/love) and хотеть (to want).
7. Grammatical gender, inanimate/animate category, declension pattern.

Grammar and Vocabulary Practice

1. Покупать свитер
2. Ждать друга
3. Слушать музыку
4. Читать книгу
5. Любить Москву
6. Покупать рубашку
7. Показывать фильм
8. Брать книгу
9. Спрашивать маму
10. Показывать шубу

11. I read my newspaper.
12. You listen to their music.
13. She is buying his clothes at GUM.
14. We like your music.
15. He buys groceries / food products.
16. Я покупаю красивый красный костюм.
17. Он встречает его хорошего друга.
18. Hello Volodya! How are things going at school?
19. Thank you, well. And, how are you, Sergei Vasilyevich?
20. Well, too. Volodya, are you meeting your mother?
21. No, I am waiting for my friend. And you?
22. I am meeting my wife and daughter. They are buying clothes at the department store.

Reading Practice

1. Children's World: toys, clothes, shoes, and other products for children
2. Natasha: women's clothes and shoes
3. Milk: Milk and dairy products
4. GUM: State Universal Store: a big department store
5. Eye Wear: glasses, contacts, and other eyewear products
6. Drugstore: medicine and other pharmaceutical products
7. Radio Products: radio-related products
8. Electronics: home electronics and appliances
9. Books: books, newspapers, and magazines

Chapter 11
Chapter Quiz

1. To express indirect objects
2. These and several other verbs are often used with an indirect object, which is always in the dative case.
3. The two verbs have similar meanings, but любить has a more general meaning and describes more intense emotions, whereas нравиться has a more specific meaning focused on a particular object, idea, person. They are also different syntactically.
4. No.
5. Don't look a gift horse in the mouth.
6. Add the –л suffix with the appropriate ending to reflect the gender and number of the subject.

7. There is only one past tense in Russian.
8. The verb **быть** (to be).

Translation Exercises

1. Помогать Нине
2. Советовать другу
3. Предлагать план Елене
4. Покупать подарок моей маме
5. Рассказывать историю моей семье
6. Писать письмо Владимиру
7. Дать Мише тарелку
8. Помогать Вере
9. Мне нравится этот маленький дом.
10. Ей нравится красивая одежда.
11. Ему нравятся эти журналы и газеты.
12. Вам нравятся эти книги?
13. Им не нравится этот университет.
14. Хотеть подарок: я хочу подарок, ты хочешь подарок, он/она хочет подарок, мы хотим подарок, вы хотите подарок, они хотят подарок.
15. Готовить обед: я готовлю обед, ты готовишь обед, он/она готовит обед, мы готовим обед, вы готовите обед, они готовят обед.
16. Я не был / не была дома, но она там была.
17. Она готовила обед, а я была в университете.
18. Мы хотели писать письмо сенатору.
19. Они ждали учителей в классах.
20. Вы говорили Наташе правду.
21. I want to wish you a happy birthday. Я хотел(а) поздравить тебя с днём рождения!
22. He does not understand what you were telling him. Он не понимал, что ты ему говорил(а).
23. Pavel, did you think that this was a good book? Павел, вы думали, что это была хорошая книга?
24. Marina likes reading newspapers and magazines. Марина любила читать газеты и журналы.
25. Do you like the Russian language? Тебе нравится русский язык?

Listening Comprehension

1. Я помогаю маме. (I'm helping Mom.)

2. Он покупает подарок сыну. (He is buying a present for his son.)
3. Они готовят ужин. (They are making dinner.)
4. Мне нравится американское кино. (I like American movies.)
5. Я пишу письмо моему мужу. (I'm writing a letter to my husband.)
6. С днём рожденья! (Happy birthday!)

Chapter 12

Chapter Quiz

1. Two: the imperfective and perfective aspects.
2. To express whether the action is in process or completed.
3. No, only imperfective verbs can form present tense forms.
4. Many perfective verbs are formed by adding prefixes to imperfective verbs of similar lexical meaning.
5. Perfective
6. Imperfective
7. A word-formation strategy of adding prefixes and suffixes to the root.
8. Grammatical and lexical prefixes.
9. Either drop their prefix, or add an imperfective suffix and retain the prefix.
10. Perfective
11. Answers will vary, but may include any of these verbs: идти, гулять, ехать, ходить, ездить.

Translation Exercises

1. She has written/wrote a book.
2. Suddenly he screamed.
3. My sister draws well.
4. We spoke and drank tea for a long time.
5. Sometimes they went/used to go on a vacation to the countryside.
6. Он показал нам свою школу.
7. Обычно они завтракали дома.
8. Она уже это сделала.
9. Мой младший брат читает очень хорошо.
10. Ты уже написал письмо?

Reading Comprehension

1. Verbs of motion: идти, ехать, идти.
2. Imperfective verbs: идти, готовить, ехать, готовиться.
3. Perfective verbs: попросить, выучить, приготовиться, позвонить.
4. Conversational expressions: привет (hello), как дела (how are things?), спасибо (thank you), понятно (okay/understood), по-моему (in my opinion), молодец (well done!), ладно (okay), хорошо (good, well), пока (bye).

Translation Practice

1. Описывать
2. Переписывать
3. Дописывать
4. Записывать
5. The imperfective suffix -ыва
6. Independence – noun
7. Post-war – adjective
8. Антинаучный – adjective
9. Foreign – adjective
10. Safety – noun
11. Собеседник – noun
12. International – adjective
13. Where are you going? – To the post office.
14. Does this bus go to the center? – No, it goes toward the stadium.
15. Does Masha go to work by car or by bike? – Sometimes by car, and sometimes by bike.
16. Where is Olya? – She went to her brother.
17. Этот поезд идёт в Москву? – Нет, он идёт в Санкт-Петербург.
18. Вы ездите на работу на поезде или на автобусе? – На автобусе.
19. Обычно я хожу к маме обедать. – Каждый день? – Да.

Listening Comprehension

1. Вы хорошо говорите по-русски. (You speak Russian well.)

2. Вдруг он вздрогнул. (Suddenly he shuddered.)
3. На столе лежал словарь. (There was a dictionary on the table.)
4. Вчера мы долго играли в прятки. (Yesterday we played hide and seek for a long time.)
5. Ты прочитал эту книгу? (Have you read this book?)
6. Она быстро сделала уроки, а потом приготовила обед. (She quickly did her homework and then made lunch.)

Chapter 13
Chapter Quiz

1. Impersonal constructions
2. The dative case
3. No, it is not.
4. Formation and function/meaning.
5. At the end of the book.
6. There is no complete correspondence between Russian and English verbal forms.
7. There is no limit on the number of negative that are permitted in a Russian sentence.

Translation Practice

1. You are not allowed to eat chocolate.
2. He needs to go home.
3. Are you allowed to watch TV?
4. Where is it possible to buy/can one buy skates?
5. I need to complete reading this book.
6. Здесь можно курить? – Да.
7. Где можно купить хорошую машину? – Я не знаю.
8. Мне нужно идти на работу.
9. Им нужно написать письмо.
10. Тебе можно играть в парке?
11. She is feeling bad. Future: Ей будет плохо. Past: Ей было плохо.
12. Playing is not allowed here. Future: Здесь нельзя будет играть. Past: Здесь было нельзя играть.
13. I am allowed to ski. Future: Мне можно будет кататься на лыжах. Past: Мне можно было кататься на лыжах.
14. You need to go home. Future: Вам надо будет домой. Past: Вам надо было домой.

15. Today, it is cold outside. Future: **Завтра на улице будет холодно.** Past: **Вчера на улице было холодно.**

Conversational Practice

1. Answers will vary.
2. Answers will vary.
3. Answers will vary.
4. Answers will vary.
5. Answers will vary.

Chapter 14
Chapter Quiz

1. Reflexive verbs express actions that reflect back to the performer.
2. No, by definition reflexive verbs cannot be transitive.
3. Answers will vary, but may include the following roots: **крас-, здрав-, лекар-, боль-.**
4. Answers will vary, but may include learning commonly used roots and becoming aware of words with similar histories in English and Russian, such as borrowings and loan words.
5. To indicate the means, manner, or agent of the action.

Translation Practice

1. **Мой компьютер сломался. Как неприятно!**
2. **Мои ключи потерялись. Как неудобно!**
3. **Наша стиральная машина сломалась. Как неудобно!**
4. **Её новая сумка потерялась. Как жалко!**
5. **Что случилось?**
6. **У меня потерялся паспорт. / Мой паспорт потерялся.**
7. **Чем я могу помочь?**
8. **Мне нужно найти американское посольство.**
9. In confidence
10. And why not?
11. That can't be! or What are you saying!
12. My husband and I
13. Between heaven and earth: in suspension
14. We (all of us) and Marina, or Marina and I

Grammar and Vocabulary Drill

1. Answers will vary.
2. Answers will vary.
3. Answers will vary.

Listening Comprehension

1. **У меня сломалась машина.** (My car broke down.)
2. **Наши документы потерялись.** (Our documents got lost.)
3. **Он починил наш телевизор.** (He has repaired our TV set.)
4. **У меня сломался компьютер. Как неприятно!** (My computer broke. How unpleasant!)
5. **Мне нужно найти американское посольство.** (I need to find the American Embassy.)
6. **После института она долго работала инженером.** (After graduating from the institute, she worked for a long time as an engineer.)

Chapter 15
Chapter Quiz

1. To describe possession.
2. In constructions with the preposition "**у**", to modify a noun with another noun or noun phrase, and in negative constructions with "**нет**".
3. Adjectives and pronouns.
4. The consonant **г** in these is endings pronounced as the Russian consonant **в**.
5. Because sentences of this structure are naturally impersonal.

Translation Practice

1. **машина моей сестры**
2. **дом его брата**
3. **подарок их бабушки**
4. **тетрадь писателя**
5. **письмо твоей мамы**
6. **задание студентов**
7. **владелец ресторанов**

8. покупатель недвижимости
9. недостаток карандашей
10. недостаток школ
11. I have a brother and a sister.
12. The doctor has medicine.
13. I live at his house.
14. In my room there is a computer and a television set.
15. They don't have a cat, but they have a dog.
16. My sister has no degree.
17. He doesn't have a lecture today.
18. She didn't have a house.
19. Marina is not at home.
20. We will not have a test.

Vocabulary Practice

1. факультет международных отношений
2. преподаватель антропологии
3. лекция по искусству
4. клуб русского языка
5. занятие по географии
6. профессор физики
7. учебник математики
8. студент литературы
9. задание по химии

Comprehension Practice

1. владелец/владелица (дома)
2. олигархи
3. налоги на недвижимость
4. завещание
5. призыв

Listening Comprehension

1. Это квартира моего хорошего друга. (This is the apartment of my good friend.)
2. Он – владелец ресторанов и заводов по всей России. (He is an owner of restaurants and factories all over Russia.)
3. Это частная собственность. (This is private property.)
4. Вы смотрели балет Чайковского «Щелкунчик»? (Have you seen Tchaikovsky's ballet "The Nutcracker"?)
5. Вы читали роман Достоевского «Преступление и Наказание»? (Have you read Dostoevsky's novel "Crime and Punishment"?)
6. Моя мама – учительница английского языка в твоей школе. (My mother is an English teacher at your school.)
7. Его нет дома. (He is not at home.)

Chapter 16
Chapter Quiz

1. Simple, compound, and complex.
2. Compound sentences include coordinating conjunctions, whereas complex sentences have subordinating conjunctions.
3. Flexible word order and possible lack of a subject or a verb.
4. In many situations, it is not a priority.
5. To express the attitude of the speakers toward what they are saying.
6. Three: indicative, imperative, and conditional.
7. Commands, orders, permission, direct suggestions, warnings, and invitations.

Translation Practice

1. Не спеши!
2. Вера, иди домой!
3. Извините!
4. Володя, не говори глупости!
5. Не пей воду из-под крана!
6. Пусть дети играют.

Comprehension Exercise

1. What are their names? Виктор и Максим.
2. Who was late for the meeting? Максим.
3. Where are they going? На стадион.
4. Do they have time to get there? Да. / Да, если они поймают такси.

Chapter 17
Chapter Quiz

1. The indicative mood.
2. The conditional mood.
3. No, all tenses can be used.
4. The conditional mood is formed with the particle "бы" plus the verb in the past tense.
5. Russian conditional forms have no references to time.
6. Two types: conditional clauses and clauses that express a purpose or a goal.
7. In these sentences, tense is expressed exclusively through the verb in the main clause and the context.
8. Dreaming about doing things instead of actually doing them.
9. To get something not through work or merit, but because of one's connections.
10. Communal apartments in the Soviet Union where several families shared one apartment.

Translation Practice

1. Why are you at home? – Because today is a holiday.
2. Why are you late for work? – Because my car broke down.
3. Why are you screaming? – Because you don't understand me.
4. Why are you going home? – I am going home because I need to speak with my parents.
5. Why do you live in Moscow? – I live in Moscow to be close to my family.

Conversational Practice

Answers will vary.

Listening Comprehension

1 Я прочитаю эту книгу, чтобы найти ответ на этот вопрос. (I will read this book to find an answer to this question.)

2. Если бы у него были деньги, он бы купил ей подарок. (If he had money, he would buy her a present.)
3. Мне бы хотелось вам помочь, но я не могу. (I would like to help you, but I can't.)
4. Я иду домой потому, что мне надо делать уроки. (I'm going home because I need to do homework.)
5. Я хочу, чтобы ты написал мне письмо. (I want you to write me a letter.)

Chapter 18
Chapter Quiz

1. A word-formation strategy of adding prefixes and suffixes to the root.
2. Grammatical and lexical prefixes.
3. Either drop their prefix or add an imperfective suffix, while retaining the prefix.
4. Русь.
5. In 988.
6. Old Church Slavonic.

Cultural Exercise

1. A week-long spring celebration that has roots in pagan rituals.
2. A sacred painted image of a saint used for worship in a church or at home.
3. A simple folk print.
4. Russian Orthodoxy.

Russian-to-English Glossary

а and, but
август August
австрал**и**йский Australian
Австр**а**лия Australia
автобус bus
аг**е**нтство agency
акв**а**рель watercolor
акт**ё**р actor
актр**и**са actress
алгебра algebra
алког**о**льный alcohol (adj.)
алт**а**рь altar
америк**а**нец American male
америк**а**нка American female
америк**а**нский American (adj.)
америк**а**нский футб**о**л football
англ**и**йский English (adj.)
англич**а**нин Englishman
англич**а**нка Englishwoman
Англия England
антигуманит**а**рный inhumane
антина**у**чный unscientific
антропол**о**гия anthropology
апельс**и**н orange (noun)
аппар**а**т apparatus
аппар**а**тчик party functionary,
  official or bureaucrat
апр**е**ль April
апт**е**ка pharmacy
арт**и**ст performer, artist (male)
арт**и**стка performer, artist (female)
архитект**у**ра architecture
ат**а**ка attack
атом atom
аудит**о**рия lecture hall
аукци**о**н auction
аэроп**о**рт airport
б**а**бушка grandmother
бал**е**т ballet
банк bank
банкр**о**тство bankruptcy

б**а**ня Russian bathhouse
бар bar
баскетб**о**л basketball
б**а**сня fable
басс**е**йн swimming pool
беж**а**ть to run
б**е**жевый beige
безоп**а**сность safety
безоп**а**сный safe
бейсб**о**л baseball
б**е**лый white
Б**е**рингово м**о**ре the Bering Sea
бес**е**да conversation
библиогр**а**фия bibliography
библиот**е**ка library
б**и**знес business
биол**о**гия biology
благодар**и**ть to thank
благод**а**рность gratitude
бланк form
блат connections
бл**и**зко close
блин pancake
бл**у**зка blouse
бл**ю**до dish
бол**е**знь illness/sickness
бол**е**ть to be sick, to be ill
бол**о**то swamp
боль pain
больн**и**ца hospital
больн**о**й ill/sick person, patient
больш**о**й big
бор woods
борщ borsch (Russian beet soup)
бот**и**нки boots
Браз**и**лия Brazil
брат brother
брать/взять to take
бр**ю**ки pants
буд**и**льник alarm clock
бухг**а**лтер accountant

быт everyday life, daily routine
быть to be
в то вр**е**мя, как while
в**а**за vase
в**а**ленки wool boots
вал**ю**та currency
в**а**нная bathroom (usually
  separate from the toilet)
вар**е**нье jam
ваш your (pl., formal)
вдов**а** widow
вдов**е**ц widower
вдруг suddenly
вегетари**а**нский vegetarian
вел**и**кий great
велосип**е**д bicycle
в**е**ра faith
в**е**рить to believe
вес**ё**лый cheerful
весн**а** spring
весь all
ветерин**а**р veterinarian
в**е**чер evening
вечер**и**нка party
вещь thing
вздр**а**гивать/вздр**о**гнуть to shudder
в**и**деть/ув**и**деть to see
в**и**димость visibility
в**и**за visa
вин**о** wine
винов**а**тый guilty
в**и**рус virus
вк**у**сный delicious
влад**е**лец owner
вл**а**жный humid, damp
вл**а**сть power
влив**а**ть/влить to pour into
вм**е**сте together
внук grandson
вн**у**чка granddaughter
вод**а** water

водитель driver
военный military serviceman
возвращать/вернуть to return something
возить/привозить to bring something by vehicle
возможно possibly
возраст age
война war
вокзал train station
волейбол volleyball
волосы hair
вопрос question
вор thief
воробей sparrow
воскресенье Sunday
вписывать/вписать to write in
враг enemy
врач doctor
время time
время года season
все everybody
всё everything
всегда always
всего хорошего all the best
всласть to one's heart content
вспоминать/вспомнить to remember
вставать/встать to get up
встреча meeting
встречать/встретить to meet
вторник Tuesday
вход entrance
вчера yesterday
вы you
выгуливать/выгулять to walk the dog
выздоравливать/выздороветь to get better
вызывать/вызвать to summon, to send for
выигрывать/выиграть to win
выигрыш prize, winnings
вылетать/вылететь to fly out (of)
вылечивать/вылечить to cure
выносить/вынести to carry out
выписывать/выписать to write out
вырастать/вырасти To grow up
высший higher

выход exit
газета newspaper
галстук tie
гараж garage
где where
география geography
Германия Germany
гитара guitar
гладить to iron
глаз eye
глупость foolishness
говорить/сказать to say
говядина beef
голова head
голубой light blue
гора mountain
город city
горошек polka dots
горький bitter
горячий hot (to the touch)
господин mister
госпожа madam
гостиная living room
гостиница hotel
гость guest
государственный state
готовить/приготовить to prepare
готовиться/приготовиться to prepare oneself, to study
готовый ready
гражданин citizen
гражданство citizenship
граница border
Греция Greece
греческий Greek
гриб mushroom
громкий loud
грустный sad
груша pear
гуляние community celebration
гулять/погулять to walk, to stroll
гуманитарный humane
да yes
давать/дать to give
даже even
далеко far
дань tribute
даром free (at no cost)
дача country house (dacha)

дачник owner of a dacha
дверь door
двоюродная сестра cousin (female)
двоюродный брат cousin (male)
двухкомнатный two-room (adj.)
девочка girl
девушка young woman
дедушка grandfather
декабрь December
делать to do, to make
делать зарядку to do exercises
дело deed, business, affair (noun)
деловой business (adj.)
демократия democracy
демонстрация demonstration
день day
деньги money
деревня village
десерт dessert
десятилетие decade
дети children
дефицит deficit
дешёвый cheap
джинсы jeans
диван couch
диплом diploma
директор director
дискотека dance club, night club
дневник diary, journal
до свидания good-bye
до скорой встречи until our next meeting
добираться/добраться to get somewhere
доброе утро good morning
доброй ночи have a good night
добрый kind
добрый вечер good evening
добрый день good afternoon
доверять to trust
довоенный pre-war
доиграть to finish playing
доктор doctor
документ document
долг debt
долгий long
дом house
домашний domestic
доносить/донести to deliver to

дописывать/дописать to finish writing
дорога road, way
дорогой expensive
дочка daughter
дочь daughter
друг friend
другой different
дружить to be friends with
думать/подумать to think
душ shower
душный stuffy
дядя uncle
Египет Egypt
египетский Egyptian
еда food
ездить to go by vehicle
ёлка pine tree, Christmas tree
ель pine tree
ерунда nonsense
если if
есть/поесть to eat
ехать/приехать to go by vehicle/to come by vehicle
жалкий pitiful
жалоба complaint
жаркий hot
ждать to wait
желание wish, desire
жёлтый yellow
жена wife
жених groom, fiancé
женский women's
женщина woman
живот stomach
жительство residence
жить to live
житьё life
жук beetle
журнал journal, magazine
за behind, after
забегать/забежать to run in
заболевание illness
заболеть to fall ill
заварка strong tea
завещание will
зависимый dependent
завод factory, plant
завтра tomorrow

завтрак breakfast
завтракать/позавтракать to have breakfast
заговорить To start a conversation
заграница abroad (noun)
заграничный foreign
задание assignment
задерживаться/задержаться to be late
задержка delay
заём Loan
заждаться to get tired of waiting
зайти to drop in
заказывать/заказать to order
закрывать/закрыть to close
закуска appetizer
заложить to put, to pawn
замолчать to go silent, be quiet
занести to drop off
заниматься to study, to take interest in
занят busy
занятие class
запеть to start singing
записывать/записать to write down
заполнить to fill, to fill out
зарплата wage
засасывать to suck in
зашить to sew up
зашиться to be wiped out (colloquial)
заявление statement, application, announcement
звать/позвать to call
звонить to call on the phone
здание building
здесь here
здоровье health
здравие well-being
здравствовать to be well and healthy
здравствуйте hello
зелёный green
земля ground, earth, land
зеркало mirror
зима winter
злиться to get angry
знакомство acquaintance
знать to know

зуб tooth
зять son-in-law
и and
игра game
играть/поиграть to play
игрок player
игрушка toy
идея idea
идти/прийти to go/to come
известный famous
извините excuse me/I am sorry
извиняться/извиниться to apologize
из-за because of, from behind of
из-под from beneath of
икона icon
иконостас place where icons are put up
икра caviar
иметь to own
иммиграционная служба Immigration service
имя first name
инвалид disabled person
инженер engineer
иногда sometimes
институт institute
инструкция instruction manual
интересный interesting
Интернет the Internet
ирландский Irish
найти to find
искать to look for
искусство art
Испания Spain
испанский Spanish
исполнение fulfillment, performance
история history
Италия Italy
итальянский Italian
июль July
июнь June
к сожалению unfortunately
Кавказ the Caucasus
каждый each
как how
какой which, what
Канада Canada

канадец Canadian male
канадка Canadian female
канадский Canadian (adj.)
капуста cabbage
карандаш pencil
карта map
картина picture, film
картофель potatoes
касса checkout desk
кататься to ride
кафе coffee shop
кафедра university department
кафетерий cafeteria
каша kasha (a dish of cooked grain)
квартира apartment
квас kvass (a traditional
  Russian soft drink)
киевский Kievan
кино movie, movies
кинотеатр movie theater
Китай China
китайский Chinese
класс school grade
клетчатый checkered
клуб club
клубника strawberry
ключ key
книга book
книжный шкаф bookcase
княгиня wife of a prince, princess
княжество principality
княжна unmarried
  daughter of a prince
князь prince
ковёр carpet, rug
когда when
кожаный leather (adj.)
Кока-кола Coca-cola
коктейль milkshake
колбаса sausage
коммуналка communal apartment
комната room
компьютер computer
конечно of course
консенсус consensus
консул consul
консульство consulate
континент continent
контрольный control (adj.)

конфета candy
концерт concert
конь horse
коньки skates
коричневый brown
кормить to feed
костёр bonfire
костюм suit, costume
кот cat (male)
кофе coffee
кофеварка coffee machine
конфликт conflict
кофта sweater, sweatshirt
кран tap, faucet
краса beauty (dated)
красавец handsome man
красавица beautiful woman
красивый beautiful
краситься to put on makeup
красный red
красоваться to show off
красота beauty
кредит credit
кресло armchair
кричать to shout
кровать bed
кровотечение bleeding (noun)
ксерокс copy machine, Xerox copy
кто who
культура culture
купол dome
курить/закурить to smoke
курица chicken
курсовой course (adj.)
куртка jacket, coat
кухня kitchen, cuisine
ладно okay
лампа lamp
лежать to lie
лекарство medicine
лекарь doctor (dated)
лекция lecture
лес forest
лето summer
лётчик pilot
лечение treatment (medical)
лечить/вылечить to
  treat (medically)
лингвистика linguistics

лист leaf
литература literature
лицо face
лишний extra, superfluous
лодка boat
лубки folk pictures
лыжи skies
любимый favorite
любить to love
люди people
магазин shop, store
магнитофон stereo
май May
мак poppy seeds
макароны pasta
маленький small
мальчик boy
мама mom
маниловщина tendency to
  dream instead of acting
манить to tempt, pull toward
марка stamp
март March
Масленица Maslenitsa, Russia's
  pre-Lent pancake celebration
масло butter
математика mathematics
материал material
матч match (sports)
мать mother
машина car
мебель furniture
мёд honey
медицина medicine
между between
международный international
межпланетный interplanetary
Мексика Mexico
мексиканский Mexican
менеджер manager
меню menu
место place
месяц month
метро metro
меховой fur (adj.)
микроволновая
  печь microwave oven
милиция police
минута minute

мир   peace, world
младший   younger
много   many
мобильный телефон   cell phone
модель   model
модный   trendy
может быть   maybe
можно   allowed, permitted
мой   my
молодец   Well done! Good job! (literally, fine fellow)
молодой   young
молодой человек   young man, boyfriend
молоко   milk
молчать   to be quiet
море   sea
морковь   carrot
мороженое   ice cream
мороз   frost
мотоцикл   motorcycle
мочь   to be able
муж   husband
мужской   men's
мужчина   man
музей   museum
музыка   music
мы   we
мыть   to wash
мягкий знак   soft sign
мягкий   soft
мясо   meat
мяч   ball
надежда   hope (noun)
надеяться   to hope
надо   need
найти   to find
наконец   finally
налево   to the left
наличные   cash
налог   tax
нападать   to attack
напиток   drink
направо   to the right
народ   people
народный   folk
насмешить   to make (someone) laugh
наспех   in a hurry

настоящий   real, genuine
настроение   mood
наука   science
научный   scientific
находиться   to be located
национальность   nationality
начало   beginning
начинать   to begin
наш   our
Не за что.   Don't mention it.
небо   sky
небольшой   small
небоскрёб   skyscraper
невеста   bride
невестка   daughter-in-law
невкусный   not tasty
недвижимость   real estate
неделя   week
недешёвый   not cheap
недоверие   mistrust
недоделать   to do incompletely
недоесть   to not finish eating
недорогой   inexpensive
недоспать   to not get enough sleep
независимость   independence
независимый   independent
неинтересный   not interesting
некрасивый   homely, ugly
нельзя   not allowed, prohibited
немаленький   large (not small)
немедленно   at once, immediately
немецкий   German
неожиданный   unexpected
неосторожность   carelessness
неосторожный   careless
неплохой   not bad
неприятный   unpleasant
нервы   nerves
несвежий   not fresh
нестрашный   not scary
нет   no
неудобный   inconvenient, embarrassing
неуклюжий   clumsy
нехороший   bad
никак   by no means, in no way
никогда   never
никто   no one, nobody
ничего   nothing, it's alright

/ no big deal (colloquial)
но   but
новость   news (sing.)
новый   new
нож   knife
номер   number
номер рейса   flight number
нора   hole, burrow
ночь   night
ноябрь   November
нравиться   to like
нужно   need
обаятельный   charming
обед   lunch
обедать/пообедать   to have lunch
обида   offence
обидный   offensive
обкрадывать/обокрасть   to rob
обмен   exchange (noun)
образование   education
общежитие   dormitory
общественный   public
объезд   detour
объявление   announcement
объяснение   explanation
объяснять/объяснить   to explain
обычай   custom
обычно   usually
обязательно   by all means, necessarily
овощи   vegetables (plural)
огромный   huge
огурец   cucumber
одежда   clothes (sing.)
однокомнатный   one-room
озеро   lake
окно   window
октябрь   October
олигарх   oligarch
он   he
она   she
они   they
оно   it
опаздывать   to be late
опасный   dangerous
опера   opera
описывать/описать   to describe
опоздание   delay
оранжевый   orange

осень fall, autumn
осколок broken piece, shard
остановка stop
осторожно caution
осторожный careful
остров island
ответ answer
отвечать/ответить to answer
отдых rest
отдыхать/отдохнуть to rest, to be on vacation
отель hotel
отец father
открывать/открыть to open
отмывание денег money laundering
отнести to carry away/off
отношение attitude, relation
отойти to walk off
отчество patronymic
отчим stepfather
отъезд departure
офицер officer
официант waiter
официантка waitress
охота hunting
очень very
паб pub
падеж grammatical case
падчерица stepdaughter
пальто coat
папа dad
парк park
паспорт passport
пасынок stepson
певец singer (male)
певица singer (female)
педагогика pedagogy
пельмени Russian dumplings, pelmeni
пенсионер a retiree
первый first
перед in front of, before
передумать to change one's mind, rethink
перенести to carry over
переписывать/переписать to copy down (in writing)
перестать to stop
переход crosswalk

переходить to walk across
перец pepper
перо feather, quill
перчатки gloves
петь to sing
печальный sad
печка oven
печь to bake
пешком on foot
пианино piano
пивная beerhouse
пиджак jacket
пилот pilot
пирог pie
писатель writer (male)
писательница writer (female)
писать to write
письмо letter
пить to drink
плавать to swim
плакать/заплакать to cry
планета planet
платить/заплатить to pay
платок headscarf
платье dress
плач crying, weeping (noun)
племя tribe
племянник nephew
племянница niece
плита stove
плохой bad
площадь square, plaza
повар cook (male)
повариха cook (female)
повесть Short story
поворачивать to turn
повторить to repeat
поговорка proverb
погода weather
пограничник border guard
подарить to give as a present
подарок gift
подземелье underground (noun)
подземный underground (adj.)
поднимать to lift, to raise
подписывать/подписать to sign
подпись signature
подсказать to prompt
подъезд entrance to building

поезд train
поездка trip
пожалуйста please, you are welcome
пожар fire
позвать to call, to invite
позволять to allow
позвоночник spine
поздний late
поздравлять to congratulate
поймать to catch
пока bye, while, yet
показывать/показать to show
покупатель buyer
покупать/купить to buy
пол floor
полдник light meal between lunch and dinner
полка shelf
положить to put
полоска stripe
получать/получить to get, receive
получиться to work out
полчаса half-hour
полюбить to fall in love with, to develop a liking for
померить to try on
помидор tomato
помнить to remember
помогать/помочь to help
помощь help (noun)
понедельник Monday
понимать/понять to understand
попугай parrot
послать to send
после after
послевоенный post-war
пословица saying
посольство embassy
поспешить to hurry
Пост Lent
постоянный permanent
Строить/построить to build
посуда dishes (sing.)
потерять to lose
потолок ceiling
потом then, afterwards
потому, что because
почему why

починить   to fix
почта   post office
поэт   poet (male)
поэтесса   poet (female)
правда   truth
право   right, law
православие   Russian Orthodoxy
православный   Russian Orthodox
правый   right
праздник   holiday (noun)
праздничный   holiday (adj.)
прайс-лист   price list
предлагать   to offer, suggest
предмет   subject, discipline
президент   president
преподаватель   instructor (university/college)
пресный   fresh
привет   hello
приглашать   to invite
приглашение   invitation
придумать   to come up with
примерочная   fitting room
принести   to bring
принимать/ принять   to accept, to take
приписывать/приписать   to add in writing
прислоняться   to lean
приходить   to come
прихожая   hallway
пришить   to sew
Приятного аппетита!   Bon appetite!
проверять/проверить   to verify
провожать/проводить   to see off, accompany
прогноз   forecast
продавец   salesman
продавщица   saleswoman
продукт   product
продуктовый   grocery (adj.)
проиграть   to lose
проигрыш   loss
происходить   to happen
пройти   to walk through
просить/попросить   to ask for
Простите.   Excuse me. / I am sorry.
просьба   request

профессия   occupation
профессор   professor
проходить   to walk by
процентная ставка   interest rate
прощайте   farewell
прыгать/прыгнуть   to jump
прямо   straight
прятки   hide-and-seek
психология   psychology
публика   public
пусть   let it be, let (someone do something)
путешествие   travel, trip
путь   way
пылесос   vacuum cleaner
пьеса   play
пятница   Friday
работа   work
работать/поработать   to work
рабочая   manual worker (female)
рабочий   manual worker (male)
рад   glad
радио   radio
радость   joy
раз   time
разбить   to break
развитие   development
разговаривать   to talk, converse
размер   size
разорвать   to tear apart
разрешить   to allow
разрушить   to destroy
ранний   early
рассказ   story
рассказывать/рассказать   to tell
ребёнок   child
ребята   guys
революция   revolution
редко   rarely
рейс   flight
река   river
ремонт   repair works, renovation
ресторан   restaurant
рисовать   to draw
родственник   relative
рождение   birth
розовый   pink
роман   novel
Российская Федерация   Russian

Federation
Россия   Russia
россиянин   Russian citizen (male)
россиянка   Russian citizen (female)
рост   height
рот   mouth
рубашка   shirt
рубль   ruble
русский   Russian
ручка   pen
рыба   fish
рынок   market
рыть   to dig
рядом с   next to
сад   garden, orchard
садиться   To sit down
сажать   to plant
саксофон   saxophone
салат   salad
самовар   samovar
санаторий   spa resort
свежий   fresh
свёкр   father-in-law on husband's side
свекровь   mother-in-law on husband's side
светло   light (adj.)
свинина   pork
свистнуть   to whistle
свитер   sweater
свободный   free
свой   own (pronoun)
святой   saint
сглаз   evil eye
сегодня   today
сейчас   now
секрет   secret
сёмга   salmon
семья   family
сентябрь   September
серый   grey
сестра   sister
сидеть   to sit
симпатичный   good-looking
синий   navy blue
сирота   orphan
сказать   to say
сказка   fairy tale
сколько   how much, how many

скорая помощь   ambulance
скоро   soon
скрипка   violin
скучный   boring
сладкий   sweet
следующий   next
словарь   dictionary
слово   word
сломать   to break something
сломаться   to break
случиться   to happen
слушать/послушать   to listen
слышать   to hear
сметана   sour cream
смеяться   to laugh
смотреть   to watch
снег   snow
собака   dog
собеседник   conversation partner
собор   cathedral
собственность   property
советовать   to advise
совсем   thoroughly, at all
сок   juice
солдат   soldier
солёный   salty
солнце   sun
соль   salt
сотрудник   coworker
спальня   bedroom
спасибо   thank you
спектакль   performance
специи   spices
спешить   to hurry
список   list
Спокойной ночи!   Good
   night! (before bed)
спор   debate
спорт   sports
спортсмен   athlete
спрашивать/спросить   to ask
среда   Wednesday
ссора   argument
стадион   stadium
становиться/стать   to become
станция   station
старт   start
старый   old
статья   article

стена   wall
стиральная машина   washing
   machine
стихотворение   poem
стоить   to cost
стол   table
столовая   cafeteria, dining room
стоп   stop
страна   country
страница   page
страшный   terrifying
строитель   builder
студент   student (male)
студентка   student (female)
стул   chair
стюард   flight attendant (male)
стюардесса   flight attendant (female)
суббота   Saturday
субтитры   subtitles
сумасшедший   crazy
сумка   bag, purse
суп   soup
существовать   to exist
Счастливо!   All the best!
счастье   happiness
счёт   bill
считать   to count, to believe
съёмка   film shooting
сын   son
сыр   cheese
сырой   damp
так   so
такси   taxi
талантливый   talented
там   there
таможенная инспекция   customs
   inspection
таможня   customs
танцевать   to dance
тарелка   plate
твёрдый знак   hard sign
твёрдый   hard
твой   your (sing., informal)
театр   theater
текст   text
телевизор   TV set
телефон   telephone
тело   body
телохранитель   bodyguard

тема   theme
тёмный   dark
температура   temperature
теннис   tennis
тёплый   warm
территория   territory
тесть   Father-in-law on wife's side
тетрадь   notebook
тётя   aunt
тёща   mother-in-law on wife's side
тихий   quiet
товар   good, commodity, product
товарищ   comrade, friend
том   tome, volume
торт   cake
традиция   tradition
трамвай   tram
тратить   to spend
троллейбус   trolleybus
труд   work, labor
трудный   difficult
трудолюбивый   hardworking
туалет   bathroom
тумбочка   bed stand
турист   tourist (male)
туристка   tourist (female)
туфли   shoes
тухнуть   to rot
ты   you (sing., informal)
тяжёлый   heavy, difficult
тяжесть   weight, heaviness
Убирать   to tidy up
уверен   sure
удобный   comfortable
удовольствие   pleasure
ужасный   terrible
уже   already
ужин   dinner
ужинать/поужинать   to have dinner
улица   street
улыбка   smile
ультрамодный   ultra-trendy
ультраправый   ultra-right
ум   wit
уметь   to be capable of
умный   clever
универмаг   supermarket
универсальный   universal
университет   university

Ура! hooray!
Урал the Urals
урок class, lesson
успевать/успеть to be on time
утро morning
учебник textbook
учёный scientist
учитель teacher (male)
учительница teacher (female)
учить to teach
учиться/научиться to learn
ушанка fur hat with ear flaps
факультет college,
  university department
Фамилия last name
фармацевт, аптекарь pharmacist
февраль February
физика physics
Фонтан fountain
Фотоаппарат camera
Фотографировать/
  сфотографировать to photograph
Франция France
Французский French
Фрукты fruits (pl.)
футбол soccer
хвост tail
химия chemistry
хип-хоп hip-hop
хлеб bread
хлопоты worries
хлопчатобумажный cotton (adj.)
хобби hobby
ходить to go
ходьба walking
хоккей hockey
холодильник refrigerator
холодный cold
хороший good
хотеть to want
хотя although
хохот laughter, roar
христианство Christianity
хрустальный crystal
художник painter (male)
художница painter (female)
худой thin, bad
царевич son of a tsar
царевна daughter of a tsar

царица tsarina
царство country ruled by a tsar
царь Tsar
цвет color
цветок flower
целый whole
цель goal, purpose
центр center, downtown
центральный central
церковь church
цирк circus
чаевые tip
чаепитие Tea drinking
чай tea
частный private
часто often
чашка cup
человек human being, man, person
чемодан suitcase
Чёрное море The Black Sea
Чёрный black
четверг Thursday
число date, number, digit
чистить to clean
читать to read
читать лекцию to read a lecture
что what
чтобы in order to, so that
чужой alien (adj.), strange, other
чуть-чуть a little bit
шаль shawl
шапка hat
шарады charades
шарф scarf
шахматы chess
шёлковый silk (adj.)
шерстяной wool (adj.)
шкаф wardrobe
школа school
школьник pupil
шоколад chocolate (noun)
шоу show
шуба fur coat
шум noise
экзамен exam
экскурсия excursion, tour
электроника electronics
этимологический etymological
этот this

Эфиопия Ethiopia
эфиопский Ethiopian
Юбка skirt
юриспруденция jurisprudence
юрист lawyer
я I
яблоко apple
язык language
язычество paganism
январь January
Япония Japan
японский Japanese
яркий bright
ясли nursery
ясный clear
яхта yacht

English-to-Russian Glossary

a little bit   чуть-чуть
abroad (noun)   заграница
accept   принимать/принять
accountant   бухгалтер
acquaintance   знакомство
   (concept) знакомый (person)
actor   актёр
actress   актриса
add in writing   приписывать/
   приписать
advise   советовать
after   за, после
afterwards   потом
age   возраст
agency   агентство
airport   аэропорт
alarm clock   будильник
algebra   алгебра
all   весь
All the best!   Всего хорошего!
allow   позволять, разрешить
allowed   можно
already   уже
altar   алтарь
although   хотя
always   всегда
ambulance   скорая помощь
American (noun)   американец
   (male)/ американка (female)
American (adj.)   американский
and   и, а
answer (noun)   ответ
answer (verb)   отвечать/ответить
anthropology   антропология
apartment   квартира
apologize   извиняться/извиниться
appetizer   закуска
apple   яблоко
application   заявление
April   апрель
architecture   архитектура

armchair   кресло
art   искусство
article   статья
ask   спрашивать/спросить
ask for   просить/попросить
assignment   задание
at once   немедленно
athlete   спортсмен
atom   атом
attack (noun)   атака
attack (verb)   нападать
attitude   отношение
attract   привлечь, манить
auction   аукцион
August   август
aunt   тётя
Australia   Австралия
Australian   австралийский
bad   плохой, нехороший
bag   сумка
bake   печь
ball   мяч
ballet   балет
bank (noun)   банк
bankruptcy   банкротство
bar   бар
baseball   бейсбол
basketball   баскетбол
bathroom   туалет (public)/
   ванная (private)
be   быть
be able   мочь
be friends with   дружить
be ill   болеть
be late   задерживаться/
   задержаться
be late   опаздывать
be located   находиться
be on time   успевать/успеть
be sick   болеть
be silent   молчать

be well and healthy   здравствовать
be wiped out   зашиться (colloquial)
beautiful   красивый
beautiful woman   красавица
beauty   красота, Краса (dated)
because   потому, что
because of   из-за
become   становиться/стать
bed   кровать
bed stand   тумбочка
bedroom   спальня
beef   говядина
beerhouse   пивная
beetle   жук
before   перед
begin   начинать
beginning   начало
behind   за
beige   бежевый
believe   верить
Bering Sea   Берингово море
between   между
bibliography   библиография
bicycle   велосипед
big   большой
bill (noun)   счёт
biology   биология
birth   рождение
bitter   горький
black   чёрный
Black Sea   Чёрное море
bleeding   кровотечение
blouse   блузка
blue   голубой (light)/синий (dark)
boat   Лодка
body   тело
bodyguard   телохранитель
Bon appetite!   Приятного аппетита!
bonfire   костёр
book   книга
bookcase   книжный шкаф

boots ботинки
border граница
border guard пограничник
boring скучный
borsch (Russian beet soup) борщ
boy мальчик
boyfriend молодой человек, друг
Brazil Бразилия
bread хлеб
break (verb) разбить, сломаться
break something сломать
breakfast завтрак
bride невеста, fiancée
bright яркий
bring принести
bring something by
   vehicle возить/привозить
brother брат
brown коричневый
brush (verb) чистить
build (verb) строить/построить
builder строитель
building здание
burrow нора
bus автобус
business (adj.) деловой
business (noun) бизнес, дело
busy занят
but но, а
butter масло
buy (verb) покупать/купить
buyer покупатель
by no means никак
bye пока
cab такси
cabbage капуста
cafeteria кафетерий
cake торт
call Звать/позвать
call on the phone Звонить
camera Фотоаппарат
Canada Канада
Canadian (adj.) Канадский
Canadian female Канадка
Canadian male канадец
candy конфета
car машина
careful осторожный
careless неосторожный

carelessness неосторожность
carpet ковёр
carrot морковь
carry away отнести
carry out (verb) выносить/вынести
carry over перенести
case (in grammar) падеж
cash наличные
cat (male) кот
catch (verb) поймать
cathedral собор
Caucasus, the Кавказ
caution осторожно
caviar икра
ceiling потолок
celebration гуляние
cell phone мобильный телефон
central центральный
chair стул
change one's mind передумать
charades шарады
charming обаятельный
cheap дешёвый
checkered клетчатый
checkout desk касса
cheerful весёлый
cheese сыр
chemistry химия
chess шахматы
chicken (noun) курица
child ребёнок
children дети
China Китай
Chinese китайский
chocolate (noun) шоколад
Christianity христианство
church (noun) церковь
circus цирк
citizen гражданин
city город
class занятие, урок
clear ясный
clever умный
close близко
close (verb) закрывать/закрыть
clothes одежда (sing.)
club клуб
clumsy неуклюжий
coat пальто

Coca-cola Кока-кола
coffee кофе
coffee shop кафе
coffee machine кофеварка
cold (adj.) холодный
color цвет
come приходить/прийти
come by vehicle приехать
come up with придумать
comfortable удобный
complaint жалоба
computer компьютер
comrade товарищ
concert концерт
conflict конфликт
congratulate поздравлять
connections блат
consensus консенсус
consul консул
consulate консульство
continent континент
control (adj.) контрольный
conversation беседа
conversation partner собеседник
cook повар (male)/
   повариха (female)
copy down (verb) переписывать/
   переписать
copy machine ксерокс
cost (verb) стоить
cotton (adj.) хлопчатобумажный
couch диван
count (verb) считать
country страна
course (adj.) курсовой
cousin двоюродный брат (male)/
   двоюродная сестра (female)
coworker сотрудник
crazy сумасшедший
credit кредит
crosswalk переход
crying (noun) плач
cry (verb) плакать/заплакать
crystal хрустальный
cucumber огурец
cuisine кухня
culture культура
cup чашка
cure (verb) вылечивать/вылечить

currency валюта
custom обычай
customs таможенная инспекция, таможня
dacha дача
dad папа
dance club (noun) ночной клуб, дискотека (dated)
dance (verb) танцевать
dangerous опасный
dark тёмный
date (noun) число, дата
daughter дочка, дочь
daughter-in-law невестка
day день
debate спор
debt долг
decade десятилетие
December декабрь
deed дело
deficit дефицит
delay задержка, опоздание
delicious вкусный
deliver доносить/донести
democracy демократия
demonstration демонстрация
department (at a university) Факультет
departure отъезд
dependent зависимый
describe описывать/описать
dessert десерт
destroy разрушить
detour объезд
development развитие
diary дневник
dictionary словарь
different другой
difficult Трудный
dig (verb) рыть
dining room столовая
Dinner ужин
diploma диплом
director директор
disabled person инвалид
discipline (noun) предмет
dish блюдо
dishes посуда (sing.)
disinterested неинтересный

do делать
do incompletely недоделать
doctor врач, доктор, лекарь (dated)
document документ
dog собака
dome купол
domestic домашний
Don't mention it. Не за что.
door дверь
dormitory общежитие
downtown центр
draw (verb) рисовать
dress (noun) платье
drink (noun) напиток
drink (verb) пить
driver водитель
drop in зайти
drop off занести
dumplings пельмени
each каждый
early ранний
eat есть/поесть
education образование
Egypt Египет
Egyptian египетский
electronics электроника
embassy посольство
enemy враг
engineer инженер
england Англия
English (adj.) английский
Englishman англичанин
Englishwoman англичанка
entrance вход
Ethiopia Эфиопия
Ethiopian эфиопский
etymological этимологический
even даже
evening вечер
everybody все
everyday life быт
everything всё
evil eye сглаз
exam экзамен
exchange (noun) обмен
excursion экскурсия
Excuse me. Извините!, Простите!
exercize делать зарядку
exist существовать

exit выход
expensive дорогой
expensive недешёвый
explain объяснять/объяснить
explanation объяснение
extra лишний
eye глаз
fable басня
face лицо
fairy tale сказка
faith вера
fall (noun) осень
fall ill заболеть
fall in love with something полюбить
family семья
famous известный
far далеко
farewell прощайте
father отец
father-in-law on husband's side свёкр
father-in-law on wife's side тесть
faucet кран
favorite любимый
feather перо
february февраль
feed (verb) кормить
fiancé жених
fill out заполнить
film shooting съёмка
finally наконец
find (verb) найти
finish playing доиграть
finish writing дописывать/дописать
fire пожар
first первый
first name имя
fish рыба
fitting room примерочная
fix (verb) починить
flight рейс
flight attendant стюард (male)/ стюардесса (female)
floor пол
flower цветок
fly out вылетать/вылететь
folk (adj.) народный
folk pictures Лубки

food еда
foolishness глупость
football американский футбол
forecast прогноз
foreign заграничный
forest лес
form бланк
fountain фонтан
France Франция
free свободный, даром (at no cost)
French французский
fresh свежий
fresh (water) пресный
Friday пятница
friend друг
from behind из-за
from beneath из-под
frost мороз
fruit фрукты (pl.)
fulfillment исполнение
fur (adj.) меховой
fur coat шуба
fur hat ушанка
furniture мебель
game игра
garage гараж
garden сад
geography география
German немецкий
Germany Германия
get angry злиться
get better (in health)
выздоравливать/выздороветь
get silent замолчать
get somewhere добираться/
   добраться
get tired of waiting for заждаться
get up вставать/встать
gift подарок
girl девочка, девушка
give (verb) давать/дать
give as a present дарить/подарить
glad рад
gloves перчатки
go идти, ходить
go by vehicle ехать, ездить
goal цель
good (adj.) хороший, неплохой
Good afternoon! Добрый день!

Good evening! Добрый вечер!
Good morning! Доброе утро!
Good night! Доброй ночи!,
   Спокойной ночи! (before bed)
Good-bye! До свидания!
good-looking симпатичный
goods товар (sing.)
grade (in school) класс
granddaughter внучка
grandfather дедушка
grandmother бабушка
grandson внук
gratitude благодарность
great великий
Greece Греция
Greek греческий
green зелёный
grey серый
grocery (adj.) продуктовый
groom жених
ground земля
grow up вырастать/вырасти
guest гость
guilty виноватый
guitar гитара
guys ребята
hair волосы (pl.)
half-hour полчаса
hallway прихожая
handsome man красавец
happen происходить, случиться
happiness счастье
hard твёрдый, трудный
hard sign твёрдый знак
hardworking трудолюбивый
hat шапка
have breakfast завтракать/
   позавтракать
have lunch обедать/пообедать
have dinner ужинать/поужинать
he он
head (noun) голова
headscarf платок
health здоровье
hear слышать
heaviness тяжесть
heavy тяжёлый
height рост
hello здравствуйте

help (noun) помощь
help (verb) помогать/помочь
here здесь
hi привет
hide-and-seek прятки
higher высший
hip-hop хип-хоп
history история
hobby хобби
hockey хоккей
holiday (adj.) праздничный
holiday (noun) праздник
homely некрасивый
honey мёд
hooray ура
hope (noun) надежда
hope (verb) надеяться
horse конь
hospital больница
hot горячий (to the touch),
   жаркий (outside), острый (spicy)
hotel отель, гостиница
house дом
how как
how many сколько
how much сколько
huge огромный
human being человек
humane гуманитарный
hunting охота
hurry (verb) спешить/поспешить
husband муж
I я
I am sorry. Извините!, Простите!
ice cream мороженое
icon икона
idea идея
if если
illness болезнь, заболевание
immigration
   service иммиграционная служба
in a hurry наспех
in front of перед
in order to чтобы
inconvenient неудобный
independence независимость
independent независимый
inexpensive недорогой
inhumane антигуманитарный

write in вписывать/вписать
institute институт
instruction manual инструкция
instructor (at university/
    college) преподаватель
interest rate процентная ставка
interesting интересный
international международный
Internet Интернет
interplanetary межпланетный
invitation приглашение
invite (verb) приглашать, позвать
Irish ирландский
iron (verb) гладить
island остров
it оно
Italian итальянский
Italy Италия
jacket пиджак
jacket (knitted) куртка
jam (noun) варенье
January Январь
Japan Япония
Japanese японский
jeans джинсы
joy радость
juice сок
July июль
jump (verb) прыгать/прыгнуть
June июнь
jurisprudence юриспруденция
kasha каша
key ключ
Kievan киевский
kind (adj.) добрый
kitchen кухня
knife нож
know знать
know how (to do something) уметь
kvas квас
lake озеро
lamp лампа
land земля
language язык
large большой, немаленький
last name фамилия
late поздний
laugh (verb) смеяться
laughter хохот

law закон, право
lawyer юрист
leaf лист
lean (verb) прислоняться
learn учиться/научиться
leather (adj.) кожаный
lecture лекция
lecture hall аудитория
lecture in a non-educational
    setting читать нотации
Lent Великий Пост
letter письмо
library библиотека
lie (verb) лежать
life жизнь, житьё
lift (verb) поднимать
light (adj.) светлый
like (verb) нравиться
linguistics лингвистика
list список
listen слушать/послушать
literature литература
live жить
living room гостиная
loan заём
long долгий (time), длинный
    (measurable, i.e. 'long list')
look смотреть
look for искать
lose (verb) потерять, проиграть
loss проигрыш
loud громкий
love (verb) любить
lunch обед
madam госпожа
magazine журнал
make (verb) делать
make laugh насмешить
man мужчина
manager менеджер
manual worker рабочий
many много
map карта
March март
market рынок
Maslenitsa Масленица
match (sports, noun) матч
material материал
mathematics математика

May (noun) май
maybe может быть
meat мясо
medicine лекарство, медицина
meet (verb) встречать/встретить
meeting встреча
men's мужской
menu меню
metro метро
Mexican мексиканский
Mexico Мексика
microwave oven микроволновая
    печь
milk молоко
milkshake коктейль
military serviceman военный
minute минута
mirror зеркало
mister господин
mistrust недоверие
model модель
mom мама
Monday понедельник
money деньги
money laundering отмывание денег
month месяц
mood настроение
morning утро
mother мать
mother-in-law on husband's
    side свекровь
mother-in-law on wife's side тёща
motorcycle мотоцикл
mountain гора
mouth рот
movie кино
movie theater кинотеатр
museum музей
mushroom гриб
music музыка
my мой
nationality национальность
necessarily обязательно
need надо, нужно
nephew племянник
nerves нервы
never никогда
new новый
news новость

newspaper газета
next (adj.) следующий
next to рядом с
niece племянница
night ночь
night club ночной клуб
no нет
no one никто
nobody никто
noise шум
nonsense ерунда
normally обычно
not finish eating недоесть
not get enough sleep недоспать
notebook тетрадь
nothing ничего
novel роман
short story повесть
November ноябрь
now сейчас
number номер
nursery ясли
occupation профессия
October октябрь
of course конечно
offence обида
offensive обидный
offer (verb) предлагать
officer офицер
often часто
okay ладно
old старый
oligarch олигарх
on foot пешком
one-room однокомнатный
open (verb) открывать/открыть
opera опера
orange (adj.) оранжевый
orange (noun) апельсин
order (verb) заказывать/заказать
orphan сирота
our наш
oven печка
own (pronoun) свой
own (verb) иметь
owner владелец
paganism язычество
page страница
pain боль

painter художник
pancake блин
pants брюки
paper бумага
park (noun) парк
parrot попугай
party вечеринка; партия (political)
party functionary
   (Soviet) аппаратчик
passport паспорт
pasta макароны
patient (noun) больной
patronymic отчество
pawn (verb) заложить
pay (verb) платить/заплатить
peace мир
pear груша
pedagogy педагогика
pen ручка
pencil карандаш
people люди, народ
pepper перец
performance спектакль
performer артист (male)/
   артистка (female)
permanent постоянный
pharmacist фармацевт, аптекарь
pharmacy аптека
physics физика
piano пианино
picture картина
pie пирог
pilot лётчик, пилот
pine tree ёлка, ель
pink розовый
pitiful жалкий
place место
planet планета
plant (noun) завод
plant (verb) сажать
plate тарелка
play (noun) пьеса
play (verb) играть/поиграть
player игрок
plaza площадь
please пожалуйста
pleasure удовольствие
poem стихотворение
poet поэт

police милиция
polka dots горошек
pool бассейн
poppy seed мак
pork свинина
possibly возможно
post office почта
post-war послевоенный
potatoes картофель
pour into вливать/влить
power власть
prepare готовить/приготовить
prepare oneself готовиться/
   приготовиться
president президент
pre-war довоенный
price list прайс-лист
prince князь
private частный
prize выигрыш
product продукт
professor профессор
prohibited нельзя
prompt (verb) подсказать
property собственность
proverb поговорка
psychology психология
pub паб
public (adj.) общественный
public (noun) публика
pupil школьник
put положить
put on makeup краситься
quarrel (noun) ссора
question вопрос
quiet тихий
radio радио
raise (verb) поднимать
rarely редко
read (verb) читать
ready готовый
real настоящий
real estate недвижимость
receive получать/получить
red красный
refrigerator холодильник
relative родственник
remember помнить
repairs ремонт

repeat (verb) повторить
request просьба
residence жительство
rest (noun) отдых
rest (verb) отдыхать/отдохнуть
restaurant ресторан
retiree пенсионер
return something возвращать/
  вернуть
revolution революция
ride (verb) кататься
right (adj.) правый
right (noun) право
river река
road дорога
rob обкрадывать/обокрасть
room комната
rot тухнуть
routine быт
ruble рубль
run (verb) бежать
run in забегать/забежать
Russia Россия
Russian русский
Russian bathhouse баня
Russian citizen россиянин
  (male)/ россиянка (female)
Russian Federation Российская
  Федерация
Russian Orthodox православный
Russian Orthodoxy православие
sad грустный, печальный
safe безопасный
safety безопасность
saint святой
salad салат
salesman продавец
saleswoman продавщица
salmon сёмга
salt соль
salty солёный
samovar самовар
Saturday суббота
sausage колбаса
saxophone саксофон
say (verb) говорить/сказать
saying пословица
scarf шарф
school школа

science наука
scientific научный
scientist учёный
sea море
season время года
secret (noun) секрет
see видеть/увидеть
see off провожать/проводить
send послать
send for вызывать/вызвать
September сентябрь
shared apartment коммуналка
shawl шаль
she она
shelf (noun) полка
shirt рубашка
shoes туфли
shop магазин
shout (verb) кричать
show (noun) шоу
show (verb) показывать/показать
show off (verb)
  красоваться
shower душ
shudder вздрагивать/вздрогнуть
sickness болезнь
sign (verb) подписывать/подписать
signature подпись
silk (adj.) шёлковый
sing петь
singer певец (male)/
  певица (female)
sister сестра
sit сидеть
sit down садиться
size (noun) размер
skates коньки
skis лыжи
skirt юбка
sky небо
skyscraper небоскрёб
small маленький, небольшой
smile улыбка
smoke (verb) курить/закурить
snow (noun) снег
so так
soccer Футбол
soft мягкий
soft sign мягкий знак

soldier солдат
sometimes иногда
son сын
son-in-law зять
soon скоро
soup суп
sour cream сметана
sew (verb) пришить
sew up зашить
spa resort санаторий
Spain Испания
Spanish испанский
sparrow воробей
spend (verb) тратить
spices специи
spine позвоночник
sports спорт
sports coat куртка
spring (noun) весна
square площадь
stadium стадион
stamp марка
start (noun) старт
start a conversation заговорить
start singing запеть
state (adj.) государственный
station станция
stepdaughter падчерица
stepfather отчим
stepson пасынок
stereo магнитофон
stomach живот
stop (noun) остановка, стоп
stop (verb) перестать
store story рассказ
  магазин
stove плита
straight прямо
strange чужой
strawberry клубника
street улица
stripe полоска
stroll (verb) гулять/погулять
student студент (male)/
  студентка (female)
study (verb) готовиться/
  приготовиться, заниматься
stuffy душный
subtitles субтитры

suck in   засасывать
suddenly   вдруг
suit   костюм
suitcase   чемодан
summer   лето
summon (verb)   вызывать/вызвать
sun   солнце
Sunday   воскресенье
supermarket   универмаг
sure   уверен
swamp   болото
sweater   свитер, кофта
sweet   сладкий
swim (verb)   плавать
table   стол
tail   хвост
take (verb)   брать/взять
take a photograph   фотографи
   ровать/сфотографировать
talented   талантливый
talk (verb)   разговаривать
tax   налог
tea   чай
tea drinking   чаепитие
teach   учить
teacher   учитель
tear apart   разорвать
telephone   телефон
tell   рассказывать/рассказать
temperature   температура
tennis   теннис
terrible   ужасный
terrifying   страшный
territory   территория
text   текст
textbook   учебник
thank (verb)   благодарить
thank you   спасибо
theater   театр
theme   тема
then   потом
there   там
they   они
thief   вор
thin   худой
thing   вещь
think   думать/подумать
this   этот
thoroughly   совсем

Thursday   четверг
tidy up   убирать
tie   галстук
time   время, раз
tip   чаевые
to the left   налево
to the right   направо
today   сегодня
together   вместе
tomato   помидор
tome   том
tomorrow   завтра
tooth   зуб
tour   экскурсия
tourist   турист
toy   игрушка
tradition   традиция
train (noun)   поезд
train station   вокзал
tram   трамвай
travel (noun)   путешествие
treat (medically) (verb)   лечить/
   вылечить
treatment (medical)   лечение
trendy   модный
tribe   племя
tribute   дань
trip   поездка
trolleybus   троллейбус
trust (verb)   доверять
truth   правда
try on   померить
tsar   царь
Tuesday   вторник
turn (verb)   поворачивать
TV set   телевизор
two-room (adj.)   двухкомнатный
ultra-trendy   ультрамодный
ultra-right   ультраправый
uncle   дядя
underground (adj.)   подземный
underground (noun)   подземелье
understand   понимать/понять
unexpected   неожиданный
unfortunately   к сожалению
universal   универсальный
university   университет
university department   кафедра
unpleasant   неприятный

unscientific   антинаучный
Urals   Урал
vacuum cleaner   пылесос
vase   ваза
vegetables   овощи (plural)
vegetarian (adj.)   вегетарианский
verify   проверять/проверить
very   очень
veterinarian (noun)   ветеринар
village   деревня
violin   скрипка
virus   вирус
visa   виза
visibility   видимость
volleyball   волейбол
wage   зарплата
wait (verb)   ждать
waiter   официант
waitress   официантка
walk (verb)   гулять/погулять
walk across (verb)   переходить
walk by   проходить
walk off   отойти
walk the dog   выгуливать/выгулять
walk through   пройти
walking   ходьба
wall   стена
want (verb)   хотеть
war   война
wardrobe   шкаф
warm   тёплый
wash (verb)   мыть
washing machine   стиральная
   машина
watch (verb)   смотреть
water   вода
watercolor   акварель
way   путь
we   мы
weather   погода
Wednesday   среда
week   неделя
well-being   здравие
wet   мокрый
what   какой, что
when   когда
where   где
which   какой
while   в то время, как; пока

whistle (verb) свистнуть
white белый
who кто
whole целый
why почему
widow вдова
widower вдовец
wife жена
will (noun) завещание
win (verb) выигрывать/выиграть
window окно
wine вино
winter зима
wish (noun) желание
wit ум

woman женщина
women's женский
wonderful прекрасный
woods бор
wool (adj.) шерстяной
word (noun) слово
work (noun) работа, труд
work (verb) работать/поработать
work out (verb) получиться
world мир
worries хлопоты
write писать
write down записывать/записать
write out (verb) выписывать/
  выписать

writer писатель (male)/
  писательница (female)
xerox copy ксерокс
yacht яхта
yellow жёлтый
yes да
yesterday вчера
yet пока
you ты (sing., informal)/
  вы (pl., formal)
you are welcome пожалуйста
young молодой
younger младший
your твой (sing., informal)/
  ваш (pl., formal)

Index

The EVERYTHING Series!

BUSINESS & PERSONAL FINANCE

Everything® Accounting Book
Everything® Budgeting Book
Everything® Business Planning Book
Everything® Coaching and Mentoring Book, 2nd Ed.
Everything® Fundraising Book
Everything® Get Out of Debt Book
Everything® Grant Writing Book
Everything® Guide to Foreclosures
Everything® Guide to Personal Finance for Single Mothers
Everything® Home-Based Business Book, 2nd Ed.
Everything® Homebuying Book, 2nd Ed.
Everything® Homeselling Book, 2nd Ed.
Everything® Improve Your Credit Book
Everything® Investing Book, 2nd Ed.
Everything® Landlording Book
Everything® Leadership Book
Everything® Managing People Book, 2nd Ed.
Everything® Negotiating Book
Everything® Online Auctions Book
Everything® Online Business Book
Everything® Personal Finance Book
Everything® Personal Finance in Your 20s and 30s Book
Everything® Project Management Book
Everything® Real Estate Investing Book
Everything® Retirement Planning Book
Everything® Robert's Rules Book, $7.95
Everything® Selling Book
Everything® Start Your Own Business Book, 2nd Ed.
Everything® Wills & Estate Planning Book

COOKING

Everything® Barbecue Cookbook
Everything® Bartender's Book, 2nd Ed., $9.95
Everything® Calorie Counting Cookbook
Everything® Cheese Book
Everything® Chinese Cookbook
Everything® Classic Recipes Book
Everything® Cocktail Parties & Drinks Book
Everything® College Cookbook
Everything® Cooking for Baby and Toddler Book
Everything® Cooking for Two Cookbook
Everything® Diabetes Cookbook
Everything® Easy Gourmet Cookbook
Everything® Fondue Cookbook
Everything® Fondue Party Book
Everything® Gluten-Free Cookbook
Everything® Glycemic Index Cookbook
Everything® Grilling Cookbook
Everything® Healthy Meals in Minutes Cookbook
Everything® Holiday Cookbook

Everything® Indian Cookbook
Everything® Italian Cookbook
Everything® Low-Carb Cookbook
Everything® Low-Cholesterol Cookbook
Everything® Low-Fat High-Flavor Cookbook
Everything® Low-Salt Cookbook
Everything® Meals for a Month Cookbook
Everything® Mediterranean Cookbook
Everything® Mexican Cookbook
Everything® No Trans Fat Cookbook
Everything® One-Pot Cookbook
Everything® Pizza Cookbook
Everything® Quick and Easy 30-Minute,
   5-Ingredient Cookbook
Everything® Quick Meals Cookbook
Everything® Slow Cooker Cookbook
Everything® Slow Cooking for a Crowd Cookbook
Everything® Soup Cookbook
Everything® Stir-Fry Cookbook
Everything® Sugar-Free Cookbook
Everything® Tapas and Small Plates Cookbook
Everything® Tex-Mex Cookbook
Everything® Thai Cookbook
Everything® Vegetarian Cookbook
Everything® Wild Game Cookbook
Everything® Wine Book, 2nd Ed.

GAMES

Everything® 15-Minute Sudoku Book, $9.95
Everything® 30-Minute Sudoku Book, $9.95
Everything® Bible Crosswords Book, $9.95
Everything® Blackjack Strategy Book
Everything® Brain Strain Book, $9.95
Everything® Bridge Book
Everything® Card Games Book
Everything® Card Tricks Book, $9.95
Everything® Casino Gambling Book, 2nd Ed.
Everything® Chess Basics Book
Everything® Craps Strategy Book
Everything® Crossword and Puzzle Book
Everything® Crossword Challenge Book
Everything® Crosswords for the Beach Book, $9.95
Everything® Cryptic Crosswords Book, $9.95
Everything® Cryptograms Book, $9.95
Everything® Easy Crosswords Book
Everything® Easy Kakuro Book, $9.95
Everything® Easy Large-Print Crosswords Book
Everything® Games Book, 2nd Ed.
Everything® Giant Sudoku Book, $9.95
Everything® Kakuro Challenge Book, $9.95
Everything® Large-Print Crossword Challenge Book
Everything® Large-Print Crosswords Book
Everything® Lateral Thinking Puzzles Book, $9.95

Everything® Literary Crosswords Book, $9.95
Everything® Mazes Book
Everything® Memory Booster Puzzles Book, $9.95
Everything® Movie Crosswords Book, $9.95
Everything® Music Crosswords Book, $9.95
Everything® Online Poker Book, $12.95
Everything® Pencil Puzzles Book, $9.95
Everything® Poker Strategy Book
Everything® Pool & Billiards Book
Everything® Puzzles for Commuters Book, $9.95
Everything® Sports Crosswords Book, $9.95
Everything® Test Your IQ Book, $9.95
Everything® Texas Hold 'Em Book, $9.95
Everything® Travel Crosswords Book, $9.95
Everything® TV Crosswords Book, $9.95
Everything® Word Games Challenge Book
Everything® Word Scramble Book
Everything® Word Search Book

HEALTH

Everything® Alzheimer's Book
Everything® Diabetes Book
Everything® Health Guide to Adult Bipolar Disorder
Everything® Health Guide to Arthritis
Everything® Health Guide to Controlling Anxiety
Everything® Health Guide to Fibromyalgia
Everything® Health Guide to Menopause
Everything® Health Guide to OCD
Everything® Health Guide to PMS
Everything® Health Guide to Postpartum Care
Everything® Health Guide to Thyroid Disease
Everything® Hypnosis Book
Everything® Low Cholesterol Book
Everything® Nutrition Book
Everything® Reflexology Book
Everything® Stress Management Book

HISTORY

Everything® American Government Book
Everything® American History Book, 2nd Ed.
Everything® Civil War Book
Everything® Freemasons Book
Everything® Irish History & Heritage Book
Everything® Middle East Book
Everything® World War II Book, 2nd Ed.

HOBBIES

Everything® Candlemaking Book
Everything® Cartooning Book
Everything® Coin Collecting Book
Everything® Drawing Book

Everything® Family Tree Book, 2nd Ed.
Everything® Knitting Book
Everything® Knots Book
Everything® Photography Book
Everything® Quilting Book
Everything® Sewing Book
Everything® Soapmaking Book, 2nd Ed.
Everything® Woodworking Book

HOME IMPROVEMENT

Everything® Feng Shui Book
Everything® Feng Shui Decluttering Book, $9.95
Everything® Fix-It Book
Everything® Green Living Book
Everything® Home Decorating Book
Everything® Home Storage Solutions Book
Everything® Homebuilding Book
Everything® Organize Your Home Book, 2nd Ed.

KIDS' BOOKS

All titles are $7.95

Everything® Kids' Animal Puzzle & Activity Book
Everything® Kids' Baseball Book, 4th Ed.
Everything® Kids' Bible Trivia Book
Everything® Kids' Bugs Book
Everything® Kids' Cars and Trucks Puzzle and Activity Book
Everything® Kids' Christmas Puzzle & Activity Book
Everything® Kids' Cookbook
Everything® Kids' Crazy Puzzles Book
Everything® Kids' Dinosaurs Book
Everything® Kids' Environment Book
Everything® Kids' Fairies Puzzle and Activity Book
Everything® Kids' First Spanish Puzzle and Activity Book
Everything® Kids' Gross Cookbook
Everything® Kids' Gross Hidden Pictures Book
Everything® Kids' Gross Jokes Book
Everything® Kids' Gross Mazes Book
Everything® Kids' Gross Puzzle & Activity Book
Everything® Kids' Halloween Puzzle & Activity Book
Everything® Kids' Hidden Pictures Book
Everything® Kids' Horses Book
Everything® Kids' Joke Book
Everything® Kids' Knock Knock Book
Everything® Kids' Learning Spanish Book
Everything® Kids' Magical Science Experiments Book
Everything® Kids' Math Puzzles Book
Everything® Kids' Mazes Book
Everything® Kids' Money Book
Everything® Kids' Nature Book
Everything® Kids' Pirates Puzzle and Activity Book
Everything® Kids' Presidents Book
Everything® Kids' Princess Puzzle and Activity Book
Everything® Kids' Puzzle Book
Everything® Kids' Racecars Puzzle and Activity Book
Everything® Kids' Riddles & Brain Teasers Book
Everything® Kids' Science Experiments Book
Everything® Kids' Sharks Book

Everything® Kids' Soccer Book
Everything® Kids' Spies Puzzle and Activity Book
Everything® Kids' States Book
Everything® Kids' Travel Activity Book

KIDS' STORY BOOKS

Everything® Fairy Tales Book

LANGUAGE

Everything® Conversational Japanese Book with CD, $19.95
Everything® French Grammar Book
Everything® French Phrase Book, $9.95
Everything® French Verb Book, $9.95
Everything® German Practice Book with CD, $19.95
Everything® Inglés Book
Everything® Intermediate Spanish Book with CD, $19.95
Everything® Italian Practice Book with CD, $19.95
Everything® Learning Brazilian Portuguese Book with CD, $19.95
Everything® Learning French Book with CD, 2nd Ed., $19.95
Everything® Learning German Book
Everything® Learning Italian Book
Everything® Learning Latin Book
Everything® Learning Russian Book with CD, $19.95
Everything® Learning Spanish Book with CD, 2nd Ed., $19.95
Everything® Russian Practice Book with CD, $19.95
Everything® Sign Language Book
Everything® Spanish Grammar Book
Everything® Spanish Phrase Book, $9.95
Everything® Spanish Practice Book with CD, $19.95
Everything® Spanish Verb Book, $9.95
Everything® Speaking Mandarin Chinese Book with CD, $19.95

MUSIC

Everything® Drums Book with CD, $19.95
Everything® Guitar Book with CD, 2nd Ed., $19.95
Everything® Guitar Chords Book with CD, $19.95
Everything® Home Recording Book
Everything® Music Theory Book with CD, $19.95
Everything® Reading Music Book with CD, $19.95
Everything® Rock & Blues Guitar Book with CD, $19.95
Everything® Rock and Blues Piano Book with CD, $19.95
Everything® Songwriting Book

NEW AGE

Everything® Astrology Book, 2nd Ed.
Everything® Birthday Personology Book
Everything® Dreams Book, 2nd Ed.
Everything® Love Signs Book, $9.95
Everything® Love Spells Book, $9.95
Everything® Numerology Book
Everything® Paganism Book
Everything® Palmistry Book
Everything® Psychic Book
Everything® Reiki Book
Everything® Sex Signs Book, $9.95

Everything® Spells & Charms Book, 2nd Ed.
Everything® Tarot Book, 2nd Ed.
Everything® Toltec Wisdom Book
Everything® Wicca and Witchcraft Book

PARENTING

Everything® Baby Names Book, 2nd Ed.
Everything® Baby Shower Book, 2nd Ed.
Everything® Baby's First Year Book
Everything® Birthing Book
Everything® Breastfeeding Book
Everything® Father-to-Be Book
Everything® Father's First Year Book
Everything® Get Ready for Baby Book, 2nd Ed.
Everything® Get Your Baby to Sleep Book, $9.95
Everything® Getting Pregnant Book
Everything® Guide to Pregnancy Over 35
Everything® Guide to Raising a One-Year-Old
Everything® Guide to Raising a Two-Year-Old
Everything® Guide to Raising Adolescent Boys
Everything® Guide to Raising Adolescent Girls
Everything® Homeschooling Book
Everything® Mother's First Year Book
Everything® Parent's Guide to Childhood Illnesses
Everything® Parent's Guide to Children and Divorce
Everything® Parent's Guide to Children with ADD/ADHD
Everything® Parent's Guide to Children with Asperger's Syndrome
Everything® Parent's Guide to Children with Autism
Everything® Parent's Guide to Children with Bipolar Disorder
Everything® Parent's Guide to Children with Depression
Everything® Parent's Guide to Children with Dyslexia
Everything® Parent's Guide to Children with Juvenile Diabetes
Everything® Parent's Guide to Positive Discipline
Everything® Parent's Guide to Raising a Successful Child
Everything® Parent's Guide to Raising Boys
Everything® Parent's Guide to Raising Girls
Everything® Parent's Guide to Raising Siblings
Everything® Parent's Guide to Sensory Integration Disorder
Everything® Parent's Guide to Tantrums
Everything® Parent's Guide to the Strong-Willed Child
Everything® Parenting a Teenager Book
Everything® Potty Training Book, $9.95
Everything® Pregnancy Book, 3rd Ed.
Everything® Pregnancy Fitness Book
Everything® Pregnancy Nutrition Book
Everything® Pregnancy Organizer, 2nd Ed., $16.95
Everything® Toddler Activities Book
Everything® Toddler Book
Everything® Tween Book
Everything® Twins, Triplets, and More Book

PETS

Everything® Aquarium Book
Everything® Boxer Book
Everything® Cat Book, 2nd Ed.
Everything® Chihuahua Book

Everything® Cooking for Dogs Book
Everything® Dachshund Book
Everything® Dog Book
Everything® Dog Health Book
Everything® Dog Obedience Book
Everything® Dog Owner's Organizer, $16.95
Everything® Dog Training and Tricks Book
Everything® German Shepherd Book
Everything® Golden Retriever Book
Everything® Horse Book
Everything® Horse Care Book
Everything® Horseback Riding Book
Everything® Labrador Retriever Book
Everything® Poodle Book
Everything® Pug Book
Everything® Puppy Book
Everything® Rottweiler Book
Everything® Small Dogs Book
Everything® Tropical Fish Book
Everything® Yorkshire Terrier Book

REFERENCE

Everything® American Presidents Book
Everything® Blogging Book
Everything® Build Your Vocabulary Book
Everything® Car Care Book
Everything® Classical Mythology Book
Everything® Da Vinci Book
Everything® Divorce Book
Everything® Einstein Book
Everything® Enneagram Book
Everything® Etiquette Book, 2nd Ed.
Everything® Guide to Edgar Allan Poe
Everything® Inventions and Patents Book
Everything® Mafia Book
Everything® Martin Luther King Jr. Book
Everything® Philosophy Book
Everything® Pirates Book
Everything® Psychology Book

RELIGION

Everything® Angels Book
Everything® Bible Book
Everything® Bible Study Book with CD, $19.95
Everything® Buddhism Book
Everything® Catholicism Book
Everything® Christianity Book
Everything® Gnostic Gospels Book
Everything® History of the Bible Book
Everything® Jesus Book
Everything® Jewish History & Heritage Book
Everything® Judaism Book
Everything® Kabbalah Book
Everything® Koran Book

Everything® Mary Book
Everything® Mary Magdalene Book
Everything® Prayer Book
Everything® Saints Book, 2nd Ed.
Everything® Torah Book
Everything® Understanding Islam Book
Everything® Women of the Bible Book
Everything® World's Religions Book
Everything® Zen Book

SCHOOL & CAREERS

Everything® Alternative Careers Book
Everything® Career Tests Book
Everything® College Major Test Book
Everything® College Survival Book, 2nd Ed.
Everything® Cover Letter Book, 2nd Ed.
Everything® Filmmaking Book
Everything® Get-a-Job Book, 2nd Ed.
Everything® Guide to Being a Paralegal
Everything® Guide to Being a Personal Trainer
Everything® Guide to Being a Real Estate Agent
Everything® Guide to Being a Sales Rep
Everything® Guide to Being an Event Planner
Everything® Guide to Careers in Health Care
Everything® Guide to Careers in Law Enforcement
Everything® Guide to Government Jobs
Everything® Guide to Starting and Running a Catering Business
Everything® Guide to Starting and Running a Restaurant
Everything® Job Interview Book
Everything® New Nurse Book
Everything® New Teacher Book
Everything® Paying for College Book
Everything® Practice Interview Book
Everything® Resume Book, 2nd Ed.
Everything® Study Book

SELF-HELP

Everything® Body Language Book
Everything® Dating Book, 2nd Ed.
Everything® Great Sex Book
Everything® Self-Esteem Book
Everything® Tantric Sex Book

SPORTS & FITNESS

Everything® Easy Fitness Book
Everything® Krav Maga for Fitness Book
Everything® Running Book

TRAVEL

Everything® Family Guide to Coastal Florida
Everything® Family Guide to Cruise Vacations
Everything® Family Guide to Hawaii
Everything® Family Guide to Las Vegas, 2nd Ed.
Everything® Family Guide to Mexico
Everything® Family Guide to New York City, 2nd Ed.
Everything® Family Guide to RV Travel & Campgrounds
Everything® Family Guide to the Caribbean
Everything® Family Guide to the Disneyland® Resort, California Adventure®, Universal Studios®, and the Anaheim Area, 2nd Ed.
Everything® Family Guide to the Walt Disney World Resort®, Universal Studios®, and Greater Orlando, 5th Ed.
Everything® Family Guide to Timeshares
Everything® Family Guide to Washington D.C., 2nd Ed.

WEDDINGS

Everything® Bachelorette Party Book, $9.95
Everything® Bridesmaid Book, $9.95
Everything® Destination Wedding Book
Everything® Elopement Book, $9.95
Everything® Father of the Bride Book, $9.95
Everything® Groom Book, $9.95
Everything® Mother of the Bride Book, $9.95
Everything® Outdoor Wedding Book
Everything® Wedding Book, 3rd Ed.
Everything® Wedding Checklist, $9.95
Everything® Wedding Etiquette Book, $9.95
Everything® Wedding Organizer, 2nd Ed., $16.95
Everything® Wedding Shower Book, $9.95
Everything® Wedding Vows Book, $9.95
Everything® Wedding Workout Book
Everything® Weddings on a Budget Book, 2nd Ed., $9.95

WRITING

Everything® Creative Writing Book
Everything® Get Published Book, 2nd Ed.
Everything® Grammar and Style Book
Everything® Guide to Magazine Writing
Everything® Guide to Writing a Book Proposal
Everything® Guide to Writing a Novel
Everything® Guide to Writing Children's Books
Everything® Guide to Writing Copy
Everything® Guide to Writing Graphic Novels
Everything® Guide to Writing Research Papers
Everything® Screenwriting Book
Everything® Writing Poetry Book
Everything® Writing Well Book